HV 6439 .U7 L788 2002
Vigil, James Diego, 1938–
A rainbow of gangs

P9-CJD-158

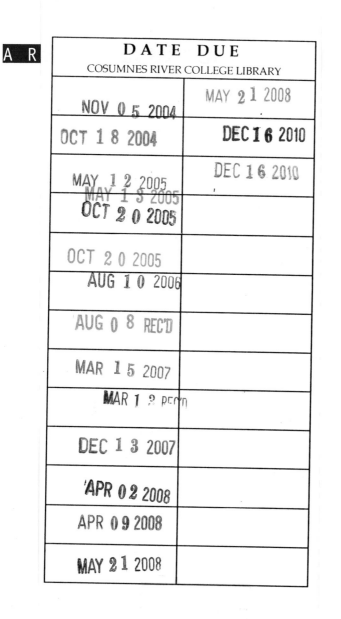

A R

DATE DUE

COSUMNES RIVER COLLEGE LIBRARY

NOV 0 5 2004	MAY 2 1 2008
OCT 1 8 2004	DEC 16 2010
MAY 1 2 2005 MAY 1 3 2005 OCT 2 0 2005	DEC 16 2010
OCT 2 0 2005 AUG 1 0 2006	
AUG 0 8 REC'D	
MAR 1 5 2007 MAR 1 2 REC'D	
DEC 1 3 2007	
APR 0 2 2008	
APR 0 9 2008	
MAY 2 1 2008	

COSUMNES RIVER COLLEGE
LEARNING RESOURCE CENTER
8401 Center Parkway
Sacramento, California 95823

A Rainbow of Gangs

STREET CULTURES IN THE MEGA-CITY

James Diego Vigil

Foreword by Joan W. Moore

University of Texas Press
Austin

Copyright © 2002 by the University of Texas Press

All rights reserved
Printed in the United States of America
Second printing, 2003

Requests for permission to reproduce material from this work should be sent to Permissions, University of Texas Press, Box 7819, Austin, TX 78713-7819.

♾ The paper used in this book meets the minimum requirements of ANSI/NISO Z39.48-1992 (R1997) (Permanence of Paper).

Library of Congress Cataloging-in-Publication Data

Vigil, James Diego, 1938–
    A rainbow of gangs : street cultures in the mega-city / James Diego Vigil.
        p.   cm.
Includes bibliographical references and index.
    ISBN 0-292-78748-0 (cloth : alk. paper) — ISBN 0-292-78749-9 (pbk. : alk. paper)
    1. Gangs—California—Los Angeles.   I. Title: Street cultures in the mega-city.   II. Title.
    HV6439.U7   L788   2002
    364.1'06'60979494—dc21

                                                                        2002001063

Contents

*To the families, teachers, and police officers who can
shape a new future for troubled urban youth*

Foreword

Joan W. Moore

DIEGO VIGIL'S CAREER has been bound up with youths. He has taught them, studied them, and been an eloquent advocate for adolescent youngsters, and it has been my pleasure to work with him over the course of many years. Until now, he has focused primarily on Chicano youths, especially those having difficulties in school or on the streets. In his book *Barrio Gangs* (1988) he looked closely at the background of Chicano gang formation in Los Angeles. He emphasized the economic and ecological marginality of Mexican immigrants, analyzing the ways in which Mexican families and neighborhood have become less and less effective in socializing their children. In his book *Personas Mexicanas* (1997) he looked at successful as well as faltering students and at the ways in which school and family factors interact to produce these varying outcomes.

In this book, Vigil expands his focus—first to describe the ways in which the institutions of four ethnic communities have been systematically vitiated, and second to link the life histories of individual gang members to those community histories. These biographies are vivid, and the links between individual problems and community strains are painfully obvious. Of course, most young men in these Los Angeles communities do not wind up in gangs and are rarely seriously involved with the criminal justice system. But for these four individuals, the stresses within their families and the mixed signals from teachers and fellow students at school seem to drive them to the institutions (or quasi institutions) of the streets.

It is all too easy for middle-class people to discount street institutions.

Our lives, and those of our children, are largely spent in conventional institutionalized settings—home, work, school, formal organizations. The street world is one that we pass through without paying very much attention. Even in poor communities, "successful" adolescents, it has been found, are those whose lives are immersed in conventional groups—at home, at school, and in formal extracurricular activities and youth clubs that are under conventional adult supervision.[1] Youths who turn to street-oriented peers are likely to get into trouble.

Vigil's book emphasizes what he calls "street socialization." He argues that when fellow adolescents become the principal agents of socialization for preteenagers, the street culture that emerges is surprisingly similar across ethnic groups—even those that have sharply dissimilar histories. This is an innovative finding, and looking further at the implications of street socialization might help us to understand why this happens. In his focus on street socialization, Vigil inherits a venerable tradition. It goes all the way back to William Foote Whyte's classic 1949 study of an Italian community in the 1940s. His book was, significantly, titled *Street Corner Society*. Whyte commented that "the younger generation has built up its own society relatively independent of the influence of its elders."[2] The "society" that these second-generation Italians created was based on what Vigil would call street socialization, with its own values and norms. A few years later, researchers noted with concern that it was not only the children of immigrants who were creating their own society. In fact, all U.S. adolescents—even those following conventional lifestyles and living largely in adult-controlled settings—were, paradoxically, structurally isolated from adult influences. James Coleman, in his book *The Adolescent Society*, expressed the concern that "adolescents are looking to each other rather than to the adult community for their social rewards." Clearly he felt that this pattern posed serious threats to society.[3]

Today, however, we take it for granted that peer socialization exists and is important to almost all U.S. adolescents. In fact, the many and diverse forms of what we now call youth subcultures have become a feature of virtually every developed society—especially those in which there is rapid social change. Youth cultures have had political as well as cultural impacts, and have become a significant focus for academic research (as well as a topic for endless exploitation by the media). These youth cultures range from those that are fully supportive of mainstream goals and norms to those that overtly reject or violate conventional expectations. Some rebellious youth subcultures seem to encompass transitory stylistic fads, of no general long-range consequence to either youth or to society as a whole—though they do attract TV talk-show hosts. Street subcultures and street socialization, on the other hand, refer to a more enduring and troubling issue: In marginalized communities a rebellious youth culture can become institutionalized in gangs. This is most apparent in the case of Chicano gangs in Los Angeles, which in some neighborhoods have been in continuous existence since the 1930s.[4] Thus, although peer socialization plays an important role for all adolescents, its street variant is particularly vital in the growth and development of gang youth. I will discuss three aspects of street socialization that seem particularly relevant to Vigil's concerns.

First, ironically, one of the most tantalizing issues in the analysis of off-beat youth cultures has been how, despite their trappings of rebellion, defiance, and deviance, those subcultures tend to perpetuate the status quo. An anecdote may help to make the point. In one of our research projects, a forty-something former gang member, who was fiercely proud of his gang, had been interviewing fellow members for almost a year. One day he came up to me with a very worried look on his face. "Joan, I'm beginning to think that the gang is mostly a mechanism for sending people to prison." His painfully acquired revelation is, of course, a cliché in the middle class, and I am sure that many teachers, probation officers, and employers had told him something similar about his own gang membership. His dramatic epiphany sounds laughable and naive to most conventional people. But this insight is alien to the culture of the streets into which this man had been socialized. Research in England during the 1970s made a similar point: The rowdy, insubordinate (but not delinquent) "counter-school" culture of working-class boys actually presocializes them to the attitudes and behaviors that suit them for working-class jobs.[5] But street socialization goes further. It not only reproduces the status quo in the sense that it drives members toward the criminal justice system and its devastating career consequences, but it also reproduces the gang itself. Without street socialization, the Chicano gangs of East Los Angeles would have disappeared generations ago. This is partly because peer socialization deals with deep issues of identity.

By this, I refer to a second aspect of peer socialization that is important for all youth. This concerns adult activities that are legally and morally debarred to adolescents. Young people are not supposed to have sex, or to drink, or to use drugs, or to fight—and the adults around them rarely do an effective job of socializing their youngsters in dealing with these issues. Sex education, for example, is notoriously inadequate; anger management is usually discussed only among a small group of school social workers, and, though consultant firms make enormous profits by selling drug-abuse prevention programs to schools, it is obvious to all concerned that it is the peer group, not the school, that defines appropriate behavior.

Fine (1987) argues that learning how to manage these activities is an "imperative of development," and that this learning happens largely within the peer group.[6] He explains why young people flirt with deviance when they act out these developmental imperatives. This happens even in groups he studies, like the Little League, that are overtly conventional and controlled by adults. Each group establishes its own norms for appropriate behavior in each of these areas. A boy may go "too far" or "not far enough," and both types of boys are disparaged within the peer group. However, the young people are convinced that adults will be shocked at their behavior, and they keep it secret. This secrecy and the protection of members become part of the group's culture. It is what Fine calls "normal deviance."

These are exactly the processes that go on within the gangs. The internal dynamics are the same. (Of course, what a Little Leaguer defines as "going too far" might well be defined as normal or "not going far enough" on the street; what is normal in a gang is deviant in a "nicer" group.) However, there is an additional factor in the gang that makes street socialization particularly powerful. Actual delinquency—breaking the law—gives gang members an additional reason to keep their activities secret. Each gang cohort develops a deep commitment to secrecy and to the protection of its members from all adults, not just the police, and from outsiders in general. A sense of loyalty becomes a paramount value. Almost all young gang members in this book talk about the gang as family. This implies that the gang commands a much heavier commitment on the part of its members than does the ordinary clique of adolescent friends. Street socialization, then, is probably more intense than is peer socialization in less all-encompassing groups. But the basic point is that the gang, like other adolescent peer groups, is a special group within which normal developmental needs are met. Vigil's case histories make this connection glaringly obvious.

Finally, these developmental imperatives are intimately involved in what it means to be a man or woman. This is the third aspect of street socialization, and one that assumes lifelong importance. In a broad sense, youth gangs are all about intensely gender-conscious peer group socialization of male adolescents. As R.W. Connell noted in his book *Gender and Power*, the street is a "zone of occupation by men"[7] (133). In this book Vigil also provides a few teasing glimpses of how females deal with this world, and this is an area where more research clearly needs to be done.[8] Girls who join gangs may be violating norms in two spheres. First, in most of the ethnic groups dealt with in this book, women are clearly relegated to the domestic sphere, and they violate the norms of their group by venturing into the world of gangs. But they also violate the norms of the street, and are continuously reminded of that fact. In many ways the streets are far more dangerous, both physically and psychologically, for adolescent females than they are for adolescent males. We know very little about what street socialization actually means for females, and especially about its meaning in terms of female gender roles.

Vigil makes it crystal clear that existing approaches to controlling gangs are not working. And his analysis of the communities and of the gangs makes it crystal clear why they are not working. By putting a human face on four individual and very different gang members, and by placing them in the context of their own communities, Vigil has opened the door for many readers to gain insight into this deeply troubling and shockingly long-lasting phenomenon. His book is in a long tradition of social research that humanizes those aspects of urban life that make us fearful and lead us to increasingly harsh and costly but ineffectual correctives. In so doing, he permits the reader to gain the kind of understanding of what is crudely called "gang life" that can demystify the phenomenon. The value of Vigil's comparative approach cannot be overestimated: it is essential to any serious effort to change the way we think—and, more important, the way we act toward gangs.

Preface

GANGS HAVE REMAINED in the headlines for over twenty years. They have been researched and debated in legislative bodies; have helped spur government programs and forced special policing and legal measures; and have been fictionalized in novels and cinema and reported on in print journalism. More viscerally, however, gangs have caused a lot of public anxiety, stirring fears of an inner-city rabble poised for revolution. Always hidden in the swirl of coverage and debate on gangs are proposed solutions, some practical and others political: build more prisons, reform our urban schools, offer more social and recreational programs, strengthen the family, get rid of welfare, and a host of other remedies. With the exception of more prisons, very few of the proposed remedies have been seriously and consistently attempted.

What has been noticeably missing from the dialogue is a solid consensus on what causes gangs. If we understood what causes them, could we come up with better remedies than we have now? Further, in knowing the complexities of the causes, might we come up with a multilevel strategy of solutions that showed coordination and cooperation? Looking at the group and personal histories of four ethnic populations in Los Angeles in which gangs exist, as I have done in this book, is a measured step in the direction of identifying the causes of gangs and generating more balanced, inclusive strategies for combating them.

The writer who engages in cross-cultural analyses like those presented here had better have a firm command of the ethnographic evidence. Growing up in the South Central Los Angeles area in the mid-1950s, I witnessed firsthand the lives and experiences of street children from various ethnic groups. Chicanos had street gangs by the 1940s, and I hung around with members of the 32nd and 39th Street gangs in the 1950s; blacks were just beginning to assume a street gang presence then. By the time of the Great Society in the 1960s, when I was a youth worker at the Teen Post and attended many community events throughout Los Angeles, the city had a full-fledged gang problem. My work with youth stimulated my interest in gang life and activities, which was buttressed by my stint as a public school teacher in the 1960s. Through graduate school, my interest in street gangs continued and, when I eventually undertook formal investigations, led to my producing several publications on Chicano gangs.

Once I realized that there was a dearth of information on the gangs of other ethnic groups, I launched a long-term study which, after several years of research, has resulted in this book. First, I reacquainted myself with the black community through contacts I had nurtured when I was director of Ethnic Studies at the University of Southern California, an administrative and teaching post that extended and sharpened my interest in comparative ethnicity. By the 1980s, black gangs were in full swing and had become a major street force. Bloods and Crips attracted not only the attention of law enforcement personnel, but soon that of the media as well.

In the summer of 1989, with the help of Al Villanueva at the Nelles School for Boys in Whittier, California, some of my students (Steve Casanova, Chris Vasquez, and Steve Yun at the University of Wisconsin, Madison, and Rosa Franco from the University of California, Berkeley), and a special undergraduate fellowship from the Social Science Research Council, I undertook a cross-cultural investigation with a questionnaire-guided survey of 150 out of 820 incarcerated youths at the Nelles School, sampling blacks, Chicanos, Salvadorans, and Vietnamese in the wards. We gathered life histories for fifty of the individuals surveyed, then, throughout the 1990s, augmented this baseline information with ethnographic research in the various ethnic communities, including a three-year project at a public housing development in East Los Angeles from 1992 to 1995 funded by a grant from the U.S. Department of Health and Human Services (Grant #90-CL-1105, 1992–1995). Father Gregory J. Boyle helped launch this effort. Two community researchers, Norma Tovar and Breavon McDuffie, were largely responsible for the success of the investigation and deserve special mention. Intensive fieldwork in the Vietnamese immigrant community in Southern California was largely conducted by Dr. Steve C. Yun, my able assistant and some-time co-author, as part of a broader Social Science Research Council initiative under the Committee on the Ecology of Crimes and Drugs in the Inner City. Dr. Yun finished his medical residency at the University of California, Los Angeles, in June 2000 and is now a practicing physician in Orange County. He also was responsible for early drafts of the chapter on the Vietnamese, as well as some of the photos, and to him I owe a great debt. The other photos of the Vietnamese were graciously provided by Tina Nguyen.

The next step was establishing a research base in the Pico-Union neighborhood of Los Angeles, home of Central American gangs, particularly Salvadorans. Later, during a trip to El Salvador, I met and got to know the founders of Homies Unidos, a group of Salvadoran youths who had been deported from the United States and who previously had been active in either the 18th Street or Mara Salvatruchas gangs in Los Angeles. On this trip I became acquainted with Donna DeCesare, a noted photojournalist, and she agreed to provide photos to strengthen the message of this book. Moreover, students from a number of my classes at both USC and UCLA aided by conducting fieldwork and gathering data in the Pico-Union neighborhood. They also carried out investigations in South Central Los Angeles and East Los Angeles. Eric Taylor, in particular, took on the task of conducting preliminary research on the African American and Salvadoran populations, initially as my student at USC and later when we met again at UCLA.

Space is not available to give credit to all of the people who aided me in this quest. Some of the more noteworthy are Jesse Cheng, Melissa Sawyer, Juma Crawford, and Matilde Soriano at Harvard University; Walker Flores, Jeanette Villanueva, Robert Nico, Ariade Della Dea, Rena Wong, Bong Vergara, Tiffany Simmons, Danielle Devereaux, Dimitri Nichols, Wendy Estevez, Cecile Monterrosa, Hirad Dadgostar, Nazanin Lahejrani, Jenny Banh, Janette Kawachi, Beth Caldwell, Sonia Shah, Jennifer Ybarra, Wendy Lin, and Alfonso Gonzalez at UCLA as part of their undergraduate training at the Center for the Study of Urban Poverty; Dan Koenig, Michael Moore, and Steve Senna of the Los Angeles Police Department; Bill Howell, Tony Argott, Gil Jurado, Rufus Tamayo, and Robert Lawrence of the Los Angeles Sheriff's Department (Robert Lawrence also provided the photos from his work in South Central Los

Angeles); Bill Johnson of the Garden Grove Police; Fred Martel from the Board of Prison Terms; Mike Jaurequi from the California Youth Authority; and Henry "Topper" Toscano from the Association of Community-Based Gang Intervention Workers.

For assistance from the University of Texas Press, special thanks to editors Theresa May, Lois Rankin, Allison Faust, Lynne Chapman, and Letitia Blalock, as well as to the many others involved in the production process. Professor Robert Garfias of the University of California, Irvine, was especially helpful with the graphics. John M. Long helped with many phases of the project, acting first as the supervisor of the student fellows in the 1989 investigation and later helping with the final editing of the manuscript. His assistance over the decades has been invaluable in the many research ventures that we have collaborated on. Both of us are indebted to Joan W. Moore—I especially for her guidance, first on the Chicano Pinto Research Project and later on other work we carried out. Joan also graciously agreed to write the foreword, a special honor for me since her work has always been an inspiration. Finally, my children helped with different tasks and duties, and to them a loving embrace: Nick "Little King" Vigil, Joan Vigil-Rakhshani, Matthew P. Vigil, and Viviana R. Vigil. My wife Polly, as always, helped in all phases of the work and deserves special thanks for making sure that female gang members' experiences were integrated where appropriate.

To control for such an extended time span, I have attempted to keep the discussion, especially the life histories, in the ethnographic present, around the middle 1990s. Even with this effort to provide depth and balance to a cross-cultural assessment, I realize that some of the information and accounts are uneven. Nevertheless, I believe that the analysis presented here, at the very least, illuminates the dynamics of social control as they relate to youth gang activity in the Los Angeles community.

Gaining this comparative understanding of how gangs and gang members emerge as a result of broader and deeper forces affecting family life, schooling paths, and police-community relations can help us formulate better solutions to the gang problem. Knowing that the process starts early in a youth's life challenges us to begin thinking of prevention and intervention strategies to team with the already highly developed and well-financed tactics of law enforcement, which have probably reached their limits of effectiveness.

A RAINBOW OF GANGS

1

Introduction

IN THE SECOND HALF of the nineteenth century, young immigrant men of Irish, Italian, German, and Polish origin gathered on the street corners of their respective neighborhoods to confront together the rigors of their new life in the industrialized cities of the eastern United States. They were often given colorful names by their society— one early Irish group was known as the Plug Uglies. What were these early gangs like, and how do they compare to today's gangs?

> For the most part, they were Irish, joining together in the face of
> poverty, squalid conditions, and great prejudice. In general they
> were older than the gang members of today, although a considerable
> number were in their late teens. The products of unhealthy slums
> and malnutrition, . . . [the gangs] were considerably larger than
> those of today, numbering in the hundreds; one gang claimed 1,200
> members. . . . The weapons the gangs used were deadly and imagi-
> native. Some were fortunate enough to own pistols and muskets, but
> the usual weapons were knives and brickbats and bludgeons. For
> close work, there were brass knuckles, ice picks, pikes and other
> interesting paraphernalia.[1]

Today, at the beginning of a new century, the names of gangs are still colorful, though self-chosen—Nip 14, Crips, Maravilla, the Business-men. Today, too, the processes young immigrants go through in dealing with life in a new country are essentially the same as in the past, and gangs continue to be a byproduct of migration, though migrants today come from more places throughout the world into more areas of this

country. Unfortunately, one way the gang scene has changed, dangerously, is in the greater use of drugs and guns during the second half of the
twentieth century.[2]

The fact is that throughout the twentieth century the outcome of the
acculturation process proved to be a negative one for many individuals,
and thus also negative for U.S. society at large. In the early decades of the
century, writers and researchers looked at the problems involved in the
process of adapting to U.S. culture and produced compelling portraits of
those who were struggling through it.[3] Not much recent research, however, has taken another look at the lives of those who fall out of the system. This book seeks to do so by providing an in-depth, multicultural
portrait of the contemporary gangs that dominate the street corners of
Los Angeles, a city that has seen an extraordinary influx of peoples from
all over the world. They have had to find their way in a local society
that itself is undergoing great change, which makes them an especially
rich source of information on the problems of acculturation at this point
in time.

Los Angeles is a model of urban diversity, a growing megalopolis
stretching in all directions from the city center. It is a place full of different languages and cultural traditions, but also one filled with ethnic and
racial tensions that threaten to erupt at any time, as they did during the
1992 Rodney King riots. Relatively new as major cities go, in the first
half of the twentieth century Los Angeles experienced rapid economic
growth which led to expansion into suburban areas. When civil unrest
threatened white working- and middle-class families in the 1960s, that
expansion accelerated as many of them moved into the suburbs. At the
same time the city was undergoing these demographic shifts, it also was
experiencing changes in its labor market and structure.[4] Both internal
migration (from small towns and various regions of the country) and
large-scale immigration from foreign countries increased exponentially.
Los Angeles was no longer primarily a white working- and middle-class
American city but a new global metropolis.

These dramatic social transformations strained the city's infrastructure and institutional support system. Housing became a problem for
many, especially in older neighborhoods like Pico-Union, where Central
Americans made their home. Up to a dozen persons crammed into apartment units meant for two or three, so that as many as one hundred people might be living in a single four-story building. Schools built for seven

hundred students were expected to hold twice that number, and the needs of the large and growing number of non-English-speaking students could not be quickly and smoothly accommodated; bilingual programs were in place but greatly underfunded and overwhelmed. Long gone were the days when the Los Angeles Police Department, the city's "finest," enjoyed the wholehearted support and admiration inspired by *Dragnet*, the popular television police drama set in Los Angeles. For decades black and Chicano leaders had been railing against unfair and disrespectful treatment of the people in the mostly low-income communities they represented.[5] As more and more new people, including thousands of political refugees, flooded into the city, police-community relations worsened, despite an increase in the number of minority and female officers in the department.

Los Angeles is more than a model of the mega-city; it is the prototypical mega-city with problems, problems that to some degree are also afflicting other urban centers worldwide. These cities have generated or are in the process of generating mega-gangs, mostly within their poor communities. This subcultural process unfolds in like manner from place to place, although as it does the unique history and culture of each place leaves its stamp.

It is unavoidably clear that gangs constitute one of the most important urban youth issues in the United States today.[6] Recent estimates place the number of gangs nationwide at 30,533 and the number of gang members at 815,896.[7] The Los Angeles area tops the list with close to 1,000 gangs and 200,000 gang members.[8] These figures are for males only; female gang members are many fewer in number (from 4 to 10 percent of all Los Angeles gang members),[9] but their significance is considerable, for studies show that nationwide a high percentage of all incarcerated females belong to gangs.[10] Furthermore, the arrest rates of young women recently have increased at a faster pace than for nongang males,[11] and the types of offenses committed by them are becoming more serious and violent.

Since the early 1980s, drug trafficking and abuse, gang violence (often tied to drugs), and all sorts of other criminal activities have increased markedly across the United States.[12] In Los Angeles County, gang homicides have recently gone down, but in the 1982–1991 period they climbed from 205 to 700,[13] and by the middle of the 1990s they nearly topped 1,000. As U.S. society attempted to keep up with the crime problem during that period, the prison population tripled.[14] In Los Angeles, the use of gang injunctions, battering rams, specialized gang law-enforcement units, and harsher penalties such as "three strikes" attest to a pervasive law and order preoccupation in dealing with youth in minority areas.

Street gangs do emerge primarily in low-income ethnic minority neighborhoods. Some of the Los Angeles gangs can be traced as far back as the 1930s. Initially no more than small bands of wayward children in East Los Angeles Chicano communities, these "boy gangs" metamorphosed over the decades into a deeply rooted gang subculture characterized by a collection of gangs fashioned within the communities of various ethnic groups.[15] Social neglect, ostracism, economic marginalization, and cultural repression were largely responsible for the endurance of the subculture. When the economic structure of the city changed and large-scale immigration swept into the city from the 1960s forward, gang formation accelerated. No ethnic community has been immune to the problem, although the Chicano, African American, Vietnamese, and Central American communities have been especially affected.

Looking at these four ethnic groups comparatively, as I do here, is important for a number of reasons.[16] Besides revealing obvious differences between groups—their time of arrival in the city, their destination within it, types of intragroup variations, and so forth—the comparative approach can tell us a great deal about gang dynamics and street life. Ethnicity plays an important role when cultural groups live in close contact and their physical or cultural characteristics are used to create social boundaries.[17] In Los Angeles, as elsewhere in the United States, ethnic minorities whose physical characteristics most clearly distinguish them from the white majority are most readily subjected to prejudice and discrimination.

As we shall see, the gang experience is shaped by the way in which the particular history and culture of each ethnic group and family interact with the overriding economic and psychological forces in the larger society.[18] Time, place, and gender are central to this dynamic. For example, on the one hand, criminal justice practices are less gender-biased today: females who engage in deviant gang behavior are no longer perceived as immoral or mentally disturbed but delinquent.[19] On the other hand, traditional mores of an immigrant culture can come into conflict with those of the host society: expectations concerning the role of the female can be quite different within the home than they are outside it.

Basically, the street gang is an outcome of marginalization, that is, the relegation of certain persons or groups to the fringes of society, where social and economic conditions result in powerlessness. This process occurs on multiple levels as a product of pressures and forces in play over a long period of time. The phrase "multiple marginality" reflects the complexities and persistence of these forces.[20] Macrohistorical and macrostructural forces—those that occur at the broader levels of society—lead to economic insecurity and lack of opportunity, fragmented institutions of social control, poverty, and psychological and emotional barriers among large segments of the ethnic minority communities in Los Angeles. These are communities whose members face inadequate living conditions, stressful personal and family changes, and racism and cultural repression in schools.

Again, consider the pressures and strains in the lives of females, which are especially pronounced. They must contend with major forces from without and from within their own ethnic group and social class that deepen their experiencing of marginalization: exacerbated sexism (such as male dominance and exploitation), family friction related to the conflict between traditional cultural attitudes toward females and those of the general society, barriers to achieving economic well-being, and childbearing and childcare burdens. For them the marginalization processes are doubly compounded, since the protection and supervision traditionally afforded girls in a family's country of origin is lessened and they frequently become vulnerable to physical and sexual abuse and exploitation, often within their own families.[21]

Daily strains from many directions take their toll and strip minority peoples of their coping skills. Being left out of mainstream society in so many ways and in so many places relegates these urban youths to the margins of society in practically every sense. This positioning leaves them with few options or resources to better their lives. Often, they seek a place where they are not marginalized—and find it in the streets. Thus, a result of multiple marginalization has been the emergence of street gangs and the generation of gang members. The same kinds of pressures and forces that push male youth into gangs also apply to females.[22]

Society and the criminal justice system have so far not fashioned adequate responses to curtail gang growth. Families, schools, and law enforcement merit special scrutiny in this regard for two main reasons.

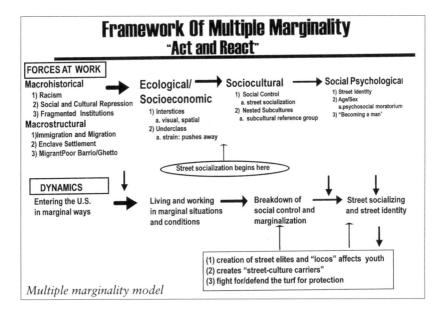

Multiple marginality model

First, they are the primary agents of social control in society. Second, they are uniquely adaptive and responsive to the concerns of society. Although each of these institutions has made its separate contribution to the gang problem, it is their joint actions (or inactions) that make the problem worse. It is in the vacuum of their collective failure that street socialization has taken over and rooted the quasi institution of the street gang.

Families

Family life and parenting practices play the initial role in the socialization of a child. It is within the family that individuals form their first significant relationships, and family training first guides and directs them onto a conventional path of participation in society. In short, parents are the primary caretakers who introduce the child to the world. They gradually expand the child's social space (i.e., from the cradle to the bedroom to the home to the neighborhood) to include other, non-kin influences. Disruptions in family life place stress on parenting practices and duties. In poverty-ridden, ethnic minority communities, these disruptions often result in abbreviated or curtailed supervision and direction of household children.[23] Female gang members are often twice affected, since they generally become single parents—"stroller queens," in the words of one flippant observer. Despite the alarming statistics, however, it must be noted that some of these women successfully navigate a life of poverty, mature out of gangs, and become strong and committed mothers.

Schools

Clearly, educational institutions serve as society's primary arena for turning out citizens and trained members of the workforce. In the United States, schools are next in importance to the family in providing structure and meaning to children's lives and acting as an agency for social control. As a child grows up, schools eventually assume the responsibilities of the family for the bulk of each child's daytime activities.

The members of the ethnic groups included here have come mostly from an immigrant background, and so the U.S. system of formal education is new to them.[24] The shift in care and supervision of a child from family to school, into the hands of non-kin, can be particularly troublesome for those who have migrated to Los Angeles from small communities where they enjoyed extensive kinship networks (which serve to provide what has been called social capital). If stressed parents, now without these networks, are already crippled in socializing their children, then sending them to school under the charge of schoolteachers compounds the problem.

Low-income and ethnic minorities have historically suffered negative, damaging experiences in the educational system. Research shows that standard school policies such as tracking by ability group and the use of standardized tests as the ultimate measure of educational performance and ability have worked against minority students. These students often attend segregated, underfunded, inferior schools, where they encounter cultural insensitivity and an ethnocentric curriculum.[25]

The motivation and strategies for seeking a higher status begin in the family but are formally forged in the educational system and process. In complex societies, schools serve as the mechanism for youths to translate their aspirations into conventional, constructive goals. In terms of reaching for a higher status, many low-income children exhibit a gap between aspirations and expectations. Even though they might have high hopes, they are led (often unaware) to see their goals as outside of their world, exceeding their grasp. Being pragmatic, they assume they won't realize their dreams.[26]

Law Enforcement

The acceptance of the "rightness" of the central social value system is pivotal to social control and citizenship, for individuals are obviously more likely to break the rules if they do not believe in the rules and regulations. Social order depends on the personal internalization of the values of society (the "ought-tos") and of patterned behavior that adheres to the norms of society (the blueprints for action). The latter are first and primarily inculcated by parents, followed by schools, and reinforced early on by peers, especially during the passage from childhood to adulthood.

Youths who are weakly (or not at all) tethered to home and school have weakened ties to society's conventional institutions and values. Because of this deficit, members of law enforcement—the street social-control specialists—often step in as the controlling authority of last resort for our youth. Law enforcement and the criminal justice apparatus serve as the sanctioning source for individuals who consistently fail to conform. When they enter the picture, it is clear that society has not only failed to properly integrate its low-income members but additionally, as we will shortly note, is making it easier for them to become street-socialized.

Street Socialization

Multiple forces working jointly lead to children spending more time on the streets, under the purview and guidance of a multiple-aged peer group.[27] In various Los Angeles ethnic communities, this group often takes the form of the street gang. For girls as well as boys, the street becomes a haven and gang life is romanticized, even though it often ultimately brings them trouble and, for girls, additional victimization.[28] What established gangs in the neighborhood have to offer is nurture, protection, friendship, emotional support, and other ministrations for unattended, unchaperoned resident youth. In other words, street socialization fills the voids left by inadequate parenting and schooling, especially inadequate familial care and supervision. This street-based process molds the youth to conform to the ways of the street. On the streets, the person acquires the models and means for new norms, values, and attitudes.

Macrostructural forces have all too often warped or blocked the educational trajectories of minority children, especially the most marginalized gang youth segments of the population.[29] Dropout rates for ethnic minorities, especially for Latinos and African Americans, are notoriously

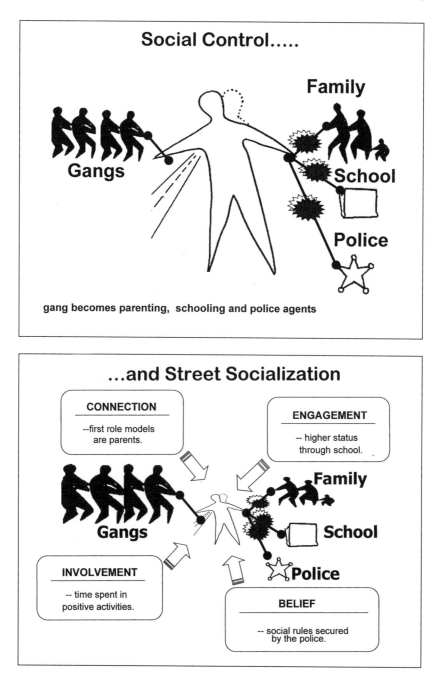

high, and the children most affected are the street-based ones[30]: In some South Central Los Angeles high schools, the rates are as high as 79 percent.[31] Once out of school, the students drop into gangs and commit to the gang's values and norms.

Street socialization alienates youths from what is learned in the schools, while societal discrimination and economic injustice further erode allegiance to conventional commitments. Boys and girls from these backgrounds are regularly truant from school and organize "ditching parties," a practice that reinforces "we-ness" among street peers.[32] (Ditching parties are get-togethers, often to share drinks or drugs, by adolescents who are "ditching," i.e., illicitly not attending school.) With such a weak educational foundation, coupled with family voids, it is no wonder that a conventional path to a higher status escapes the purview of most gang members. Generally poor job prospects exacerbate the situation for minority youth who already have family and school difficulties.

Through the marginalization and street socialization of urban youth and the creation of a street gang subculture, with values and norms of its own, the street gang becomes a subsociety. Once this subsociety has been created to meet the needs of its creators, it persists and becomes an urban fixture in certain neighborhoods, compelling future generations of youth to join it or otherwise come to terms with it. In these ways, at home and in schools, urban youth acquire a gang-oriented set of rules and regulations.

Gang norms perpetuate a state of male dominance, and females, with few exceptions, largely follow these rules and regulations. Once a member of a gang, a girl or young woman gains status recognition mostly from other homegirls and only occasionally from homeboys. Generally speaking, female street gangs are auxiliaries to the male set. The few autonomous or mixed gangs that exist do not last as long as the auxiliaries, even though the female members continue their street life and associations in another context. Of the few examples cited in the literature, one black female gang in San Francisco was reported to have separated from the males when they discovered that as drug traffickers they could keep all the profits for themselves.[33]

To complicate matters, most of the experiences gang youth have with law enforcement are hostile and antagonistic. For example, special gang units sometimes fan the flames of conflict between rival gangs, police seek and arrest undocumented youths and turn them over to immigration authorities for deportation, and prison guards single out incarcerated gang members for special treatment. Overall, ethnic minority youths, gang or non-gang, resent the "dissing" (disrespect) meted out by patrol officers. These experiences further undermine the recognition and acceptance of the dominant value system, for once youths have begun to reject the law and its underlying values, they often develop a resistance orientation and take a defiant and destructive stance.[34]

Toward a More Complete Understanding of Gangs

Although family, schools, and law enforcement are the key elements of social control in any industrialized, urban society and largely responsible for street socialization developments, they are also accessible and open to human intervention and alteration. Throughout the last half century or more, our society has attempted to aid and assist struggling families, introduced innovative schooling programs intended to spark learning among the less fortunate, and sought to correct and improve law enforcement strategies and techniques designed to increase conformity. Our leaders and policymakers who think they are heeding the concerns of the citizenry initiate many of these formulas for change and improvement in each institution. However, political leaders and policymakers typically miss the point in assessing the issue of urban gangs, failing to recognize the importance of formulating strategies based on the characteristics of a low-income population of long-term duration.[35]

Adaptation and integration into the city for many racially distinct and culturally different newcomers usually entails starting off on the bottom rung of the ladder. However, some groups have had the rungs above them sawed off, in effect. Most of them are therefore unable to move up as quickly or smoothly as, say, white ethnics of the nineteenth-century. Some particularly talented or assertive individuals manage to stretch past gaps in the rungs to make their way up the metaphorical ladder, but others cannot escape the conditions they find themselves in. The persistent pattern of inferior living situations and substandard working conditions that they confront results in major family stresses and strains, deep-rooted schooling barriers and difficulties, and hostile and negative relations and interactions with law enforcement personnel. From this context the street culture and subsociety has emerged.

Structural causes must therefore be at the forefront of any serious discussions on what causes gangs and creates gang members, which is why the multiple marginality framework begins with ecological and economic factors that are at the root of the breakdown of social control.[36] Those who set policy have lapsed into facile answers, thus allowing ideological arguments (e.g., moral evaluations) to cloud the debate on how to guide our approach to this problem. Often, perspectives and decisions on policy make for a triangulation approach that gives equal weight to every or any side. To help guide our thinking on policy, it is imperative that we examine more closely the multiple factors that affect the youths from various ethnic backgrounds who join gangs.

A cross-cultural, comparative look will sharpen our understanding of the similarities and differences among gang youths in various ethnic groups. We will learn more about how ethnic customs and habits play out when other forces begin to dominate the socialization routines of each group, especially during adolescence. When street socialization takes over, a remarkably similar street orientation and culture emerges for each group, irrespective of ethnic traditions, and, with only slightly greater variation, regardless of gender. Moreover, a comparative examination will afford us a broad, historical approach to how and why social control was disrupted, when and where groups and individuals became social outcasts, and what political forces overshadowed the process. By looking at different groups and isolating the key issues that collectively shape gang behavior and attitudes, we might better generate strategies and approaches to help alleviate and resolve the worst effects of gang life. If nothing else, we can begin to put to rest the contemporary politically tainted dialogue that interferes with a balanced consideration of the problem. Society needs objective investigations and evidence, not "moral panic"[37]—in short, facts, not fears.

Ideally, the solution to the gang problem is linked to resolving all problems arising directly or indirectly from the tremendous social and economic inequalities in our society. Clearly, causes built into the social system are crucial to understanding gangs and gang members, even though not all poverty-stricken children join gangs.[38] But poverty areas generate most gang members, and the poorest of the poor are often more marginalized and thus more subject to street socialization and joining gangs, an indication that even within poverty populations there is internal variation.[39]

As the economic and social system prevalent in the United States increasingly becomes dominant around the globe, gangs likewise are becoming a worldwide phenomena, typically linked to the migration of large numbers of people to cities.[40] The adaptation to cities by already poor people, sometimes made poorer in the transition, too often results in marginalization processes. Studies worldwide indicate that the migration of former peasants and rural workers often carries with it a series of living and working disruptions that strongly undermine traditional social control institutions,[41] as it has for the youths focused on in this comparative study. Thus, many children in these situations are forced to grow up on the streets. To eliminate this marginalization process and the resultant street socialization would require massive changes in our way of life at the macrostructural level.

However, if we focus on the intermediate (meso and micro) levels of social control, such as families, schools, and law enforcement, we can do something for the proximate future. To pull off even this will require a great engagement and involvement and a retooling of the connections among these agents. Put another way, if we are powerless to address changes at the macro level, then we certainly can and must muster the resources to work at them at the intermediary or micro level. Though there are many worldwide similarities in the breakdown of social control resulting from unpredictable social and economic changes, this account examines only the situation in the United States and particularly in its gang capital, Los Angeles.

To begin with, ethnohistorical nuances and contours will be an important consideration when we look at the ways in which gangs unfolded within each ethnic population. This is because every ethnic group's history (as well as every nation's) differs in such important aspects as time, place, and people—that is, when and where the people settled, how their communities formed, and what distinguished them from other people in the city. Paying attention to time factors allows us to appreciate the specific conditions in Los Angeles that greeted members of each group when they arrived and to understand how those conditions affected the way they settled.

Two of the communities examined have been present in Los Angeles since its inception in 1781. Chicanos, descendants of the original inhabitants, were repressed and overwhelmed by Anglo newcomers in the nineteenth century as an aftermath of the Mexican American War, then rediscovered as newcomers throughout different ebbs and flows of immigration in the twentieth century.[42] As immigration augmented the original plaza settlement, the focal area of the Mexican population moved eastward into barrios (neighborhoods). These barrios were often located in ecologically inferior spaces (low areas subject to periodic flooding or hills that could only be reached by poor, winding roads).[43]

African Americans also have a long history in Los Angeles. Blacks and mestizos of partly African origin were an important part of the Mexican population from its beginnings, but U.S. blacks did not migrate to Los Angeles in large numbers until after World War I and again after World War II, seeking to benefit from a somewhat booming economy and a tight labor market in each time period. Racism and prejudice in those decades segregated and isolated most blacks in a narrow belt along the Central Avenue district, and the migrants underwent a marginalization process that is still playing out today. The struggles to change those conditions grew during and after the 1960s with an acceleration of civil rights strivings and inroads.[44]

In contrast to the above ethnic groups, the Salvadoran and Vietnamese populations share a more recent migratory background, in both cases from homelands wracked by civil war. Most of the Vietnamese immigrants and a large proportion of those from El Salvador arrived in the United States as political refugees. The unraveling of social control actually began for both groups in their home countries, where the United States played a prominent role in volatile military situations. Thus, geopolitical considerations are paramount for both groups.

The Salvadoran—and other Central American—populations in Los Angeles are relatively new. These groups had to find their way to the United States during a time of economic instability and an intense anti-immigrant social and political climate. The Salvadorans carry the burden of having had to leave their homeland in the midst of a highly charged civil war, with death threats propelling hundreds of thousands out of the country.

Along similar lines, the Vietnamese are best examined within the context of a war-torn homeland and an especially strife-ridden journey to the United States. Most found their way to the United States as members of a second wave of refugees known as the "boat people."

As we move across history and across different groups in Los Angeles that have produced gangs, we will find some obvious differences. What is remarkable is the similarities that underscore how multiple marginality acts and reacts within populations to drive children into the streets and how immigration or migration adaptation is a central part of this process.[45] As children undergo street socialization they form a street sub-culture, namely a gang. Some of the street groups have formed gangs to protect themselves from the "street elites,"[46] while others have shaped gangs over several decades.[47] What is important is that as we develop a better understanding of gangs we learn a better way to address the problems that generate gangs and gang youth.

Looking at Gangs
Cross-Culturally

THE FORMATION and evolution of Los Angeles street gangs is an issue that has many dimensions. The cross-cultural approach adopted here is useful because it helps account for historical, political, and ethnic differences among the marginalized populations from which gang members come. An appreciation of each group's experiences, as that group understands them, illuminates the forces, events, and circumstances that have pushed gangs to the forefront among contemporary Los Angeles issues. Comparing the groups' experiences can add breadth and depth to an appraisal of gangs, especially when their differences are examined from a variety of perspectives. Looking across groups in this way can help identify trends and tendencies, advancing our knowledge base and sharpening our theoretical perspective without leading us into a morally charged ideological debate over what to do about gangs. For example, clarifying the distinguishing features of the new Asian (particularly Vietnamese) and Central American (particularly Salvadoran) gangs connects Los Angeles events to previous events in Central America and Southeast Asia and at the same time provides insights that we can apply in reconsidering the older, more established African American and Chicano populations.

In comparing groups, this book interprets each community in terms of the historical processes that characterize the street gang experience—racism, socioeconomic segregation, education problems, gender distinctions, and so on. The four communities examined are obviously racially distinct and, being physically distinguishable from dominant whites, all have faced race-based discrimination, though the impact of race and racism on each group is not always the same. Furthermore, each immigrant group comes to the city with unique cultural traditions that collide with the attitudes and practices of the dominant group (an example is the more restrictive gender expectations parents place on young females, which are at odds with gender roles in this country). The effects of neighborhood and community processes are different for each arriving group, and economic conditions and shifts at the time of arrival and afterward clearly affect the rate and direction of a group's integration. The boom/bust economic cycle so common to a free-market system carries with it changes in social attitudes and practices, even policies. In other words, economic ebb and flow strongly colors the dominant group's treatment of newcomers. Competition between the dominant group and ethnic minorities for economic and social rights and resources often determines where a group of newcomers settles. Poverty, of course, dictates that the poorest neighborhoods, with the least expensive housing, will be the newcomers' most likely place of residence. Social rejection and ostracism further assure that poor, racially and culturally different people will decide to settle apart from the dominant population.

While it is clear that breakdowns of social control create and perpetuate street gangs throughout Los Angeles, we need to know how these disruptions occurred and how each ethnic group experienced the pattern. It is equally important to unravel the degree to which individual responses and outcomes contrast within an ethnic group and across ethnic groups. In short, we must collect and examine evidence on social control issues in such key areas as family life, schools, and law enforcement and then analyze it within a wider context.

A holistic, integrative assessment and interpretation of street gangs must recognize the many strands and sources of gang delinquency.[1] A discussion of the marginality experienced by those who must adapt to a new culture and place is a move in that direction, for immigration affects family structure and stability, schooling readiness in the context of language and cultural differences, and level of involvement with police and the criminal justice system. As a theory-building framework, multiple marginality addresses ecological, economic, sociocultural, and psychological factors.[2] Most researchers agree that major macrohistorical and macrostructural forces form the backdrop to street gangs, but the debate over causes becomes contentious and heated when the focus is on the intermediate and micro levels of analysis. A systematic examination of the major agents of socialization—families, schools, and law enforcement—can enlarge our understanding of gangs and gang members and of how the gang subculture emerged. Set against a broad canvas and analyzed cross-culturally, such an investigation can add immensely to our insights on these street subcultures.

It is when social forces and influences do not function as they should that street subcultures arise to fill the void. Society through its social control institutions "always . . . seeks to ensure that people behave in acceptable ways, and defines the proper action to take when they don't." As anthropologists have long noted, social control is an important function of all cultures, one in which the family universally plays a key role.[3] The structure and form of the family and other institutions of social control vary from society to society, and in the case of immigrant families the disruptions and marginalization they face in moving from one society to another greatly affect how successfully the family can function as an agent of social control. Blacks have also experienced the upheavals associated with immigration and adaptation as migrants from the rural South, a quite different region which contrasts sharply with their northern or western destination.

Some social controls are internalized (i.e., within the individual), others are externalized mechanisms (i.e., from the outside), and there are also various sanctions, formal and informal, that encourage conformity.[4] Thus, families, schooling, and law enforcement are particularly important in examining how people learn to adjust and conform in the context of the broader and deeper forces of a modern, urban society. By focusing on these socialization experiences, we can gather facts, describe transformations, and offer interpretations of where family life and its structures unravel, how schools fail, why law enforcement remains disconnected from low-income communities, and when a multiple-aged peer group and street socialization begin to dominate the life of a youth. Only when we have command of this information can new prevention, intervention, and suppression strategies be formulated and applied. It is a micro framework (analysis of social control) within a macro framework (multiple marginality) that is parsimonious and focused and lends itself to cross-cultural analysis and policy formation.

In order to apply social control theory to the street gangs of Southern

California, however, the theory needs to be modified somewhat in order to take into account certain elements in the full gang equation that are vital to understanding gangs.[5] Social control theory "as integrated into ecological and other perspectives [i.e., multiple marginality] appears to be fundamental to understanding the formation and illegal behavior of juvenile gangs."[6] Accordingly, the social control framework used here is heavily influenced by an eclectic mix of concepts and theories, including (besides multiple marginality) theories of social ecology, opportunity, and strain.[7]

To begin with, perhaps we should take the question most researchers ask and turn it upside down. Instead of wanting to know why youth deviate from the values and norms of society, we should rather inquire, Why do youth *conform* to the values and norms of society? This question recognizes that humans are born unsocialized and must learn to relinquish their natural inclinations and conform to society.[8] The answer to the question is found in the socialization processes, which are defined as the bonds an individual forms as a result of different influences operating at various levels of society.[9] Where these societal bonds are weak, the individual is more likely to deviate.

The social bonds that encourage and facilitate conformity can be viewed as going through a formation process that has four stages: connection, engagement, involvement, and belief. The process of socialization, in my view, can be measured by evaluating the extent to which an individual develops, through these stages, full acceptance of a society's values and norms. In the case of marginalized, street-socialized urban youth who are seeking other sources of influence, conformity to their subculture or subsociety differs greatly in form and content from the patterns found more generally in society. How does this alternate conformity happen?

An individual's connections, or social bonds, with significant others ordinarily begin with the family and gradually extend to others outside kinship networks. However, the breakdown of family life and schooling routines is a major outcome of multiple marginalization. This can result in a generally untethered existence for a youth, which leads to more time spent on the streets. Outside the purview and supervision of adult caretakers (in the home and school specifically), the youth undergoes a socialization influenced and guided by a street-based peer group—the resident gang.[10]

When street socialization replaces socialization by conventional care-takers, it becomes a key factor in developing not only different social bonds but different aspirations for achievement, levels and intensities of participation, and belief patterns. Whom you associate with, what you strive for, how you spend your time, and why you embrace a belief system are strongly connected to the street subculture. However, macrohistorical and macrostructural forces also often undermine the normal attachment processes of many youths who end up in gangs, and these forces can even generate shocks that detach family members from each other.[11] Socioeconomic factors such as poverty, economic dislocation, divorce, single-parent households, and racism place severe stresses on many families, so that home life is regularly unstable. Unable to provide adequate sustenance to their children, many parents lose their coping skills entirely and fail to supervise and guide their offspring as they develop social bonds. When this unstable situation persists for years, an attitude of resignation and defeat gradually develops. Mother-centered households are especially vulnerable, and many gang youths suffer the additional consequences of an absent father.

His mother liked to go dancing and have a good time. She felt she owed it to herself from working all week cleaning houses with no time for herself. One time one of her boyfriends took her and the children (two brothers and a sister; he was the oldest at age five) to the cantina dance hall down the street. At first the boy thought they were going to go in with the adults and sit down someplace, so he felt reassured that he would be with his mother, although he thought it was strange that she dressed them all in pajamas. When they arrived in the boyfriend's car in front of the place, the boyfriend looked for a parking spot as close to the entrance as he could find. The boyfriend carefully rolled up the window on his side and exited and walked around the front of the two-door car to politely open the door for the boy's mother. Meanwhile, the boy and his siblings were sitting in the back seat of the car, waiting for him to push the passenger seat forward for them to exit, too. He didn't. The mother told them to go to sleep and she would be right back, as she was just a few feet away, and for them not to worry. The boyfriend rolled up the window and locked the car, and he and the boy's mother walked into the cantina that was rocking with Latin country music. Then the cacophony began. All of the children started to cry, each with a distinct, plaintive voice, and by the time the evening was over the curbside back window was smeared with tears and mocos (snot). The boy felt so close yet so far from his mother. He consoled the others and they eventually fell asleep, but he stayed up and whimpered throughout the night, even though his mother would look out the cantina doorway every now and then, just to make sure they were still okay.

Based on a conversation with Luis Rodriguez about an incident described in his book The Concrete River

Even when families are intact, stresses may be so great that neither parent is very attentive to child-rearing responsibilities. But for a male youth from a female-centered family who is without a father, the irony is that he must learn to contend with male-dominated street life when he is subjected to street socialization. In the absence of a positive male role model, many such untethered youths grow up on the streets with a hypermasculine predisposition, feeling constrained to "act like a man." This conflicting gender clarification process, which is part of the adolescent psychosocial moratorium,[12] often fosters wild and unpredictable personal habits, behavior that defies conventional authority and prosocial behavior but works well on the streets, where wild and unpredictable pressures and expectations are imposed daily.

For female gang members, the conflict in gender identification and the need to act out aggressively is considerably more complex. Females are especially hard hit in the street socialization process, for like males they must struggle with the same forces that generated their street experience but in addition must contend with their own homeboys, who devalue them. In essence, as gender roles continue to change generally, the role of females in gangs will be transformed. The recent increases in violence among female gang members clearly indicates that these changes are underway.[13] Moreover, of the 94 percent of gang females who will have a child in their life, 84 percent will themselves become a single parent.[14]

From childhood on, many female youths are vulnerable to negative forces already noted: culture conflict and devaluation, stricter child-rearing experiences, tension-filled gender role expectations, and problems with self-esteem stemming from all these forces. Their sexual abuse and exploitation experiences can lead to pent-up rage, which some young females channel into holding their own in the violence of the street gang world. Often, such sexual traumas start with male relatives and later involve male street peers. With a constant cultural tug-of-war raging, and with molestation and sexual exploitation in their seemingly safe households as a backdrop, young women may encounter a street-socialization experience that further victimizes them. The end result in such instances is a decidedly convoluted mindset.[15] It is not unusual for some females to take on the persona of a crazy person, as for instance the Chicanas who embrace the nickname Loca and live up to it. Male gang members generally walk more gingerly around such homegirls—there is crazy, then there is crazier!

A cultural or generational strain often exists between parents and children, especially during adolescence, when many children rebel against their parents and seek other socialization experiences. In the context of immigration and adaptation, the situation is more complicated, for language, cultural habits, and ethnic loyalties interfere with normal socialization routines and rhythms. During this adolescent passage, peers assume an inordinate influence over what a person thinks and does. Indeed, the gang is a source of attraction for both males and females, because it provides many family-like functions and new cultural customs that signify membership in something. It is a source of familial compensation and a reservoir of connections when all others have failed. Within it, friendship and mutual trust are reinforced by sharing the dangers of the street, which also provides a certain amount of adolescent adventure. Learning to back each other up during times of trouble cements the bonds between youths in a gang, creating a type of fictive kinship network. The development of this emotion-charged network is a core aspect of gang life. The gang begins as an alternative control system but over time becomes rooted as a competing, sometimes dominant, socialization institution.

The second stage of socialization is engagement, and is an expression of well-defined goals and the striving for higher status. Our schools are intended to reinforce constructive goals and aspirations inculcated initially within the family. Low-income children often exhibit a gap between aspirations and expectations, as they often realize that what they might wish for is beyond their means of attaining. Conventional engagements, such as wanting a high-paying job, are usually related to an aspiration for higher status, but they can also be a reflection of the simple desire just to be somebody. This desire can overlap with connections such as role models, in that the individual, because of strong social bonds, seeks the approval of significant others or wants to demonstrate the motivation to pursue laudable goals. Stressed parents might short circuit the connections and thus the engagement processes of children under their care. In the same way, overburdened, understaffed schools generally miss the mark in engaging students to strive for higher aspirations, especially those students whose language difficulties marginalize them.

> Going to school became tough after a while, because he never learned to read correctly, even though his family tried to help him by lying about his age so that he would be put in the fourth grade, although he was actually three years older than his classmates. It was exhausting coming to America after the war and the communist takeover and unrest, and then arriving in the Midwest and moving on to the West Coast. Learning what these different places and people expected from you was bad enough. But learning the English language when you were from Vietnam and only a small minority of students from that background were at school with you and other students often made fun of you made the classroom situation almost impossible. The teacher would try to help, but the groups she put him in were made up of other students like him—foreigners and immigrants with a language and learning problem. What he learned from the other children in those learning groups was how to make life miserable for the teacher. There was no one at home to help him, no books in his language to get him started, no teachers and aides who could communicate with him, and no school officials who could talk to his parents, who understood only Vietnamese. In school he began hanging around with other similarly disaffected youths, and eventually skipping school became the order of the day. Just "kickin' it" with friends took over.

Because ethnic minorities have historically encountered insensitive (or outright racist) policies and personnel in the public school system, minority children, especially the most marginalized gang-youth segments of the population, often leave school at an early age and commit themselves to the gang's values and norms. Their alienation from conventional values, reinforced by ongoing street socialization, intensifies the discrimination that minority group members so often face. These problems with societal engagement engendered by family and school difficulties are exacerbated by the generally poor job prospects for minority youth.

In recent decades, affirmative action programs have led efforts to improve opportunities in some large businesses and government agencies. Most new jobs, however, are created by small businesses, which these programs do not reach. Moreover, such businesses, which tend to hire nearby residents, are largely absent from the rundown areas where most marginalized youths live. Consequently, these youths have little realistic chance of obtaining jobs that would improve their status. Studies that examine the social and cultural strains of the lower-income, impoverished U.S. population have underscored the importance played by inequalities in access to desired roles and goals—for example, attaining a high-status job.[16] Alienated youths whose lack of education and occupational opportunities preclude their entering the respectable status system face severe problems in establishing a social identity for themselves.[17] This disjunction between goals and the avenues to achieve them serves as a catalyst for an alternate opportunity structure, one which leads to crime and delinquency. In this substitute system, the gang directs the youth toward activities by which the youth can attain a respectable status in the streets. For example, getting arrested in a failed attempt to commit a crime, fighting a rival gang member, or periodically acting *loco* elevates a youth's social status and enhances his street reputation.

Most youths participate in conventional activities, such as homework, that lead to socially acceptable forms of success. Ideally, appropriate and vigilant role models direct the youth toward activities at home, in school, and elsewhere that enhance a commitment to socially acceptable goals. Examples of prosocial activities, in addition to schoolwork, include chores, part-time jobs, volunteer services, and recreational sports. Marginalized youths, however, typically lack exposure to such activities. Their attenuated connections to parents, teachers, and coaches provide few opportunities for such activities. Gang youths also lack the necessary engagement to strive in a disciplined way to complete tasks, either for monetary or personal reasons. Moreover, the low-income areas where they are apt to reside typically have less recreational space and limited social and recreational programs, to say nothing of fewer job opportunities.[18] Several years ago, for example, when the Los Angeles Unified School District (LAUSD) had to trim its budget, it cut many of the extracurricular programs—music, sports, clubs—that kept children occupied. Unfortunately, some students had very little else going for them besides those activities.

Lacking involvement in conventional activities, youths spend an inordinate amount of time on the streets with their peers. Some of their experiences and activities there are actually quite benign; others are clearly dangerous and antisocial. Contacts and interactions with the police, sometimes leading to incarceration, begin to play a role in their lives. Over time, seemingly petty activity can lead to gang involvement that is more dangerous, especially if police and detention facilities are unable to deter street youths early on. This tilt toward a destructive, nonproductive path serves to warn us of the need for suitable recreation facilities in the city. Providing such facilities and activities would at least occupy the youths' free time. Involvement in productive activities helps them avoid the attractions of the street and encourages them to pursue more conventional goals.

A crucial element in establishing social control is achieving acceptance of the rightness of the central social value system—that is, as noted in Chapter 1, personal internalization of the values of society (the "ought-tos") and patterned behavior which adheres to the norms of society (the blueprints for action). Individuals are obviously more likely to break the rules if they do not believe in the rules and regulations. When the development of connections, engagements, and involvement is stunted, youths have weakened ties to the conventional values of society. Clearly, this sequence ends with little or no adherence to its belief system or even any real understanding of it.

Beliefs are primarily inculcated by parents, followed by schools and, especially during the passage from childhood to adulthood, by peers. It is law enforcement and the criminal justice apparatus that serve as the sources of sanctions for individuals who consistently fail to conform. The marginalization and street socialization of urban youth create a street gang subculture with values and norms of its own, which become the belief system of the street gang subsociety. Born of need, this subsociety persists and becomes a neighborhood fixture, certain to turn out future gang members. (Some families, in fact, have produced several generations of members of the same gang.) When marginalized children are at a young age, schools place them in groups to remediate academic weaknesses, with the result that any weak links in their street bonding are strengthened by their association with marginalized peers at school.[19] In these ways, at home and in school, urban youths acquire a gang-oriented set of beliefs. Complicating matters, most of the experiences they have with law enforcement are hostile and antagonistic. This further undermines the recognition and acceptance of the dominant value system and generates a defiant resistance orientation. Sometimes not even the very young are spared frightening encounters with law enforcement.

Law enforcement has often shown a dark, stern, unfeeling side to low-income communities. One youth from South Central Los Angeles recalls with hurt and bewilderment how, when he was five years old, police officers from the Los Angeles Police Department broke down the bedroom door in his parent's house. Sweeping into the room looking for drugs, guns, or whatever (he does not know to this day what they were after), they turned everything upside down as they ransacked the room. He was in the upper bunk bed looking out at them, clearly visible to them and crying with fear at the abrupt shift from quiet sleep to the sudden noise of crashing furniture and heavy-footed movement. As his parents were being strong-armed and handcuffed, one of the officers pulled the top mattress out from under the young child's body and he came crashing down to the floor. Bleeding from where his mouth was cut by his teeth when he hit from the floor, he cried even louder, filled with terror as he lay there.

When family and schooling fail to provide adequate social and psychological sustenance, the youth turns to the street to fulfill the basic human needs of friendship and emotional support, obtaining thereby a fictive sense of family. The street gang also emphasizes beliefs that can help ensure the survival of a person under duress. Street life, with its crime, drugs, and predators of all kinds, necessitates that one acquire protection against dangerous situations and people. Thus, much of the camaraderie and homeboy and homegirl bonding involves a practical consideration—help when one's life is at stake or potential risks are at hand. The brotherhood or sisterhood that is forged involves the approval of one's peers, and by following the rules and regulations of the gang, respect and status are gained and maintained, especially among females, who more often look to each other for status recognition. Oftentimes, daring and crazy actions are conducted to show peers that one is with them, and these instances underscore how the influence of street peers has outweighed the primary social control agents of family, school, and law enforcement.

In the chapters that follow, the context for looking at social control dynamics is an examination of how four ethnic groups (Chicanos, African Americans, Vietnamese, and Salvadorans) have adapted to Los Angeles, detailing first what their neighborhoods are like and how they became a part of the city. Analysis of macro forces sets the stage for evidence showing why and how a life of poverty and instability, and the associated struggles linked to want and insecurity, can fracture and marginalize a people and especially affect children and youth. Embedded in this macrostructural arrangement are the inequities and injustices stemming from racism, job discrimination, educational hindrances, and institutional isolation. Moving from this broad backdrop to a look at the micro events in the life of an individual gang member will show how connections, engagements, involvements, and beliefs unfold. Family organization, schooling experiences, and interactions with law enforcement institutions will surface as sources of problems, as they are in the lives of many marginalized youths. In assessing the different ethnic gangs along the four social control dimensions—connections, engagements, involvements, and beliefs—a common theme emerges: The weakening of these bonds "frees" the adolescent from the paths of conformity and, with street socialization and the acquisition of a street subculture, ensures that unconventional behavior is likely among, with some variations, both males and females.

What follows, then, are macro to micro accounts of each ethnic group, starting with a chapter assessing the group's history in Los Angeles and followed by a chapter featuring a case study of a gang member from that group—four ethnic groups, eight chapters in all that combine history and ethnobiography. The case studies are not intended to be typical, but each of the life histories captures the marginalization dynamics of the community and some aspects of the historical background of the group. Indeed, the forces that interact to produce gang involvement are too manifold for all to be exemplified in any individual's experience. Instead, the individuals selected for the close-up studies represent the gang experience specifically within their own communities. It is intended that, in the manner in which anthropologists Margaret Mead and Robert Redfield long ago represented cultures as variously embedded in and acted out by individual humans, their stories together will enlarge our understanding of the gang culture.

Mexican Americans in the Barrios of Los Angeles

CHICANO GANGS have existed in the Los Angeles area since the 1940s.[1] When Emory Bogardus first studied Chicano street youth in the 1920s, he remarked that the "boy gang" problem could be quickly remedied,[2] but city officials ignored his recommendations, as they have the advice of many youth workers over the years. The result is a Chicano gang problem that has only worsened with time. The longevity of gangs is such that some include second- and third-generation family members, and the gang subculture is so much a fixture of the streets that immigrant youths must contend with it in one way or another.

The remarkable persistence of gangs in Los Angeles has been due in large part to continuous immigration of Mexicans into Southern California and the problems these immigrants face in adjusting to urban society, especially their marginalization within it, which often also affects later generations.[3] The first wave of immigrants into the United States came in the 1920s, when the arrival of nearly two million Mexicans virtually doubled the resident Mexican American population. From 1940 through 1964, another four million settled in the country, and in the 1970s an additional six to twelve million arrived. This dynamic upward trend has continued unabated to the present[4]—and not to be forgotten are the untold millions of Mexicans who entered the country without legal documents. The Los Angeles area has been host to the largest number of immigrants; by 1990 the number of native Mexican Americans and immigrant Mexicans in Los Angeles County exceeded three million.[5]

The ongoing arrival of masses of newcomers has provided a steady stream of potential gang members.[6] Earlier ethnic gangs, such as the late-nineteenth-century Irish gangs in Boston and New York described earlier, dissipated as immigration diminished and the immigrants already in the country were assimilated into mainstream society. The Chicano gangs of Southern California are a different matter.

> [They are a] long-lasting, not transitory phenomen[on]. . . . With
> few exceptions, the Chicano communities have never been invaded
> by another ethnic group, nor has another ethnic group succeeded
> them, nor has there been total cultural disintegration. Instead, there
> has been more or less continuous immigration of yet more Mexi-
> cans, with a reinforcement of some of the traditional culture.[7]

Although research on Chicano gangs has expanded in recent years[8] and has included autobiographical accounts that offer new, in-depth information,[9] the fresh perspectives have not altered the commonly voiced response to gangs: "Just get rid of them!" The favored approach to accomplishing this has been to emphasize a criminal justice solution.[10] (As an example, witness the recent passage of Proposition 21 in California, which lowered the age at which children may be tried as adults.) This law-based strategy became a welfare system of sorts for employees in law enforcement agencies, courts, and law offices. Yet, despite the billions of dollars spent, crime rates continued to rise and the prison population increased dramatically.

It is fairly clear by now that a problem as complex as gangs has multiple sources, as the multiple marginality model suggests. To cope with the problem, there must be a broader-based strategy that embraces prevention, intervention, and suppression approaches. In this chapter we look at the Chicano case to determine whether the seeds of the solutions to gangs can be found in root causes. The analysis begins with a group history that focuses on the macro forces which laid the foundation of the Chicano gang experience.

Los Angeles in the middle of the nineteenth century was a Mexican pueblo (town) of roughly ten thousand people, mostly native Mexicans.[11] The urbanization process did not begin until Anglos flooded into the area late in the century. By 1900 the city had grown to over 100,000 residents, with Anglo Americans now in the majority. During the Anglo influx, the Mexican section of town, the old pueblo near modern-day

Old housing stock is common.

Olvera Street, was avoided; Anglos built and developed to the south and west. By doing so, they changed the pueblo into a barrio (literally, "neighborhood," but often understood in this country as a Mexican enclave). The move toward a segregated city was underway. Later, Mexican immigrants, much poorer than California's Mexicans, were enticed to Los Angeles as workers but felt unwelcome once there. Considered socially unacceptable, they settled away from the rest of the city in barrios along the eastern margin of the town center,[12] across the Los Angeles River in an area now known as Greater East Los Angeles. Usually they selected a neighborhood near a work site, where rents were low—or even nonexistent if they could find empty space in which to set up their ramshackle shacks made of cardboard and corrugated tin. Often the makeshift residences were built on undesirable land, the ravines, hollows, and low hills that were easily flooded or inaccessible and therefore had been bypassed by urban developers.

The White Fence and El Hoyo Soto barrios near the town center were set in hollows that were close to light industry and textile jobs. Barrio Simon was a brickyard, and the workers and their families resided on the land next to it almost as in a company town, with Okies and Arkies joining Mexicans to create one of the first biracial barrios. In the greater Los Angeles community, literally dozens of such barrios began as residential sites determined by work sites (for agriculture, railroads, textiles, and so on).[13]

Being in the socially marginal space of the city, the barrios were segregated and overcrowded and lacked many of the amenities found in the Anglo sections of town. Pushed into the ecologically inferior interstices of the city,[14] away from commercial and business zones, the isolated populations established barrio-based churches, self-help groups known as *mutualistas*, and mom-and-pop stores. The barrio dwellers thus were located apart from higher-income Anglos in defined spaces that were visually distinct from the more prosperous sections of town. Substandard—even dangerous—housing facilities prevailed, for homes were older, smaller, and poorly constructed and many had no sewer facilities. One such barrio was El Hoyo Maravilla ("El Hoyo" translates literally as "The Hole"). Established in the 1930s, it has been described as a place where "lots in the tract were very cheap; its most conspicuous feature was its unsuitability for houses. . . . El Hoyo became a barrio inside an area of barrios. There was no water service, no sewer, no pavement, and no gas main."[15]

Government programs under President Roosevelt and the New Deal administration attempted to ameliorate housing problems by providing public housing for low-income citizens. Because of these efforts, many people's lives improved. Within East Los Angeles, there are now five such housing projects. But even though the intention of public housing was to help poor people combat crime and other social problems, a Methodist minister prophesied "sociological decline" for one being built in the 1940s.[16] Shortly after construction was completed, gangs began to emerge.

In short, in the early decades of Mexican immigration and adjustment, the settlement pattern resulted in isolated, insulated, urban villages. Residents, arriving poor and being racially distinct, were made to feel inferior and different. The barrios in rural areas near early twentieth-century Los Angeles, such as Cucamonga, Los Nietos, Canta Ranas (Singing Frogs), and Pacoima, remained isolated much longer, but in the end many of them were engulfed by suburban sprawl.

The early type of neighborhood just described comprises what I term a classic barrio, and some have persisted as such to the present. More recently, however, the immigrant settlement pattern has been different, especially since the 1970s. Almost all the open spaces have been filled up, and building and safety restrictions prevent the establishment of squatter-like settlements. Job sites still largely determine living sites, but service occupations now dominate the job market. Today work as custodians, gardeners, waiters, and dishwashers, as well as in the garment-related industries, attracts and keeps immigrants in Los Angeles. These newcomers and their families take up residence in older, rundown neighborhoods that earlier residents have left to resettle elsewhere in the city. What once was housing for Anglos in south and southeast Los Angeles, and for blacks in the south central area, has now been inundated by Mexicans and Central Americans. Neighborhoods like South Gate and Huntington Park, for example, have become predominantly Mexican and Mexican American, with home ownership reflecting a much higher income status than earlier generations of immigrants could have hoped for. Even white, middle-class strongholds on the west side, like Venice and Santa Monica, now have a sizable Mexican population. Thus, the service job sector that attracts Mexicans is fostering an immigrant population more dispersed throughout the city, as job sites beget living sites.

In many instances, changes in particular areas of the city have created new types of barrios. For example, a relatively recent set of barrios has been established in the Pico-Union area just west of downtown Los Angeles, which once housed lower-level Anglo salesclerks and clerical workers (see Chapter 9). In the 1970s immigrant Mexicans began to gradually displace the Anglos, a process that accelerated when Central American refugees flooded the neighborhood (it is now home mostly to them). Several barrio names, and gangs associated with those names, presently dot the densely populated landscape. One of the gangs, 18th Street, is recognized as the largest and perhaps most threatening in the area, with an alleged membership of twenty thousand.[17]

These barrios are unlike the classic barrio described above in that their residents settled in already built-up areas, but the areas nonetheless are spatially distanced from whites, rundown in appearance, and subject to the usual marginalization experiences that generate street gangs. Such barrios are more diffuse and loosely connected than early ones, and consequently gangs like 18th Street are less defined by territorial boundaries and more dispersed socially, with cliques and gang affiliates radiating in all directions from the gang's place of origin, Pico-Union. The influence of the many street gangs in areas surrounding a barrio spurs the creation of new gangs within the barrio.

Besides needing proximity to their work site, Mexicans, like immigrants of other ethnicities, initially chose to live in the barrios because they wanted to live in communities that soften culture shock by providing a sense of ethnic security. Shared language, religion, values, customs, and habits make for a more comforting environment. However, they were there also because of compelling pressure to stay: Houses were prohibitively expensive elsewhere, and even when they could afford them Anglos would refuse to sell or rent residences in Anglo neighborhoods to Mexicans.[18] In recent years, this type of restrictiveness has been relaxed, largely due to civil rights laws and regulations enacted in the last three decades. Nevertheless, stories related by Mexican homeowners in Huntington Park and South Gate suggest that Anglo residents there attempted to exclude them from the area well into the 1970s and 1980s.

Living in inferior ecological niches has undermined the ability of large numbers of Mexicans to integrate successfully into the fabric of the United States. The social segregation and discrimination barriers of the twentieth century strongly affected and reshaped acculturation, assimilation, and other social and cultural changes. Large-scale immigration to the present has also tended to harden attitudes and practices toward Mexican newcomers. In any case, the presence of a large critical mass of Mexicans, combined with a high proportion of youth in this population, eventually ensured that a certain percentage of the youth would become street-socialized and available for gang recruitment.

Along with an inferior and spatially distinct environment, the Mexican population has had to contend with a life of poverty and the lack of status that comes with a low income. Historically, Mexicans have been used as a source of cheap labor, and discrimination has barred them from educational opportunities and higher-income employment.[19] With the passage of decades, each generation nonetheless has generally improved its situation over that of the previous one. As matters have improved, many have moved out of the barrios and into the middle class. Yet the poverty rate among Mexicans in Los Angeles remains high and overall average income levels remain low, for the constant infusion of new immigrants dilutes the gains that have been made by earlier newcomers.

The social reality of want and limited opportunities that begins when a people set foot in a new land has consequences beyond the generation

A fork in the road going nowhere

that experiences them. As early as 1912, researchers noted that the loss of a job or income instability triggers repercussions that affect home and family life.[20] Once a family's footing becomes shaky, it is hard for the family to return to a firmer base. Although most families who have had such destabilizing experiences regain their balance, the severe, widespread social and economic problems experienced by the Mexican population have caused a significant percentage to fall victim to a cycle of persistent and concentrated poverty. A life of poverty and underclass status creates a whole new set of problems.

To begin with, poverty multiplies the effects of the ecological conditions, having an incredibly insidious impact on the psychological well-being of barrio dwellers, particularly the youth. Knowing they live on the other side of the tracks (or freeway, river, hill, highway, or other boundary marker) gives them a sense of being social outcasts, pariahs. Venturing out of the barrio to see what others have and compare it to their material level makes them feel unwanted and restricted in what they can reach for. A psychological state of bitterness and resentment often becomes another burden that weighs them down.

As might be expected, most gang members come from the more impoverished families, which are often mother-centered and have either no father figure or one whose attachment to the family is tenuous.[21] A recent study on a public housing project in East Los Angeles affirmed that the poorest families are more likely to have children in gangs and, further, that these families have a higher incidence of single parent households.[22] Single parents must cope with the emotional and psychological problems of going it alone, not only because they are the only parent present, but because they typically lack readily available social capital, that is, people living nearby to whom they can turn in a crisis (relatives, for example).

These facts of barrio life stand in stark contrast to typical Mexican family life. The Mexican family, including the extended family, has a strong tradition of being a close-knit, strong, and cohesive unit of social control. Youths are taught to respect their elders and are quickly and sternly disciplined if they misbehave. However, the effects of poverty, social discrimination, and culture conflict have undermined this tradition and appear to have affected the overall well-being of Mexican immigrants' offspring especially. Mexicans themselves fare better on a number of health and well-being indicators than do second-generation Mexicans or subsequent generations.[23] What this indicates is that the longer a Mexican family lives in poverty in the United States, the longer marginalization of all sorts takes its toll and the more the family's well-being declines. Part of this downturn means that street life begins to dominate and gang subcultures start to take hold of youths.

One key factor in the breakdown of poverty families is the absence of the father, which I observed in many of the life histories of gang members that I interviewed. The father is traditionally the head in the Mexican family, and his stable presence brings a great deal of social control and security to the family. Thus, when the father is absent for whatever reason, the results can be traumatic. Because of the persistence of poverty and a gang subculture, fathers are sometimes themselves former gang members or are involved in criminal activity (commonly drug dealing), or both. Absent and unable to provide the ongoing direction and supervision his children need, such a father's life and behavior nevertheless influence his offspring by providing a symbolic source of antisocial identification for them to emulate.

Lack of a father figure may be particularly detrimental during a male youth's adolescent period, as he begins to form his sexual identity. Gang members from mother-centered households have to adjust to a male-dominated street gang and may experience some role confusion as they try to mediate their self-identity. Some youths might attempt to resolve this conflict by overemphasizing their male qualities, acting aggressively, and modeling themselves after "street warrior" role models.[24]

With the breakdown of the family, traditionally the strongest source of social control in the Mexican community, the burden of providing goals, direction, and sanctions has shifted to the schools and law enforcement. However, for a variety of reasons, both of these institutions have also failed to exert a mitigating influence on youth impelled toward gang membership.

Again, historical analysis lends us valuable insight into the problem. Initially, Mexican immigrants and even their children were too busy in the fields to pursue education, and children who did attend school obtained a spotty and inconsistent education, since they left and came back to school as their parents moved in and out of the migratory stream. What passed for education usually took place in a poorly financed "little red schoolhouse" (the "Mexican school"), with one teacher half-heartedly going through the motions of what was more training for citizenship than sound, basic education. It was known as Americanization.[25]

When eventually Mexicans were included in the regular education system, their first experience at a public institution added new wrinkles to the realities of barrio life: alienation, isolation, and exclusion.[26] In urban and rural schools, Mexicans were subjected to the prejudice of their teachers and to programs such as ability tracking, which placed Mexican students in inferior educational courses of study.[27] Similar problems persist to the present time, including academic tracking that places Mexican students into remedial classes, biased counseling and testing practices that steer Mexican students into vocational training and lower-income career paths, and the hiring of teachers who are unable or unwilling to handle the minority student's culture conflicts and needs.[28] Language in particular has been a problem between teachers and students. The older generation of barrio dwellers have numerous stories of teachers punishing students for speaking Spanish. Later, up to the 1970s in some areas, children who spoke Spanish were tested in English and the test scores were used to place them in EMR (educably mentally retarded) classes. Even today, despite the educational successes of bilingual and ESL (English as a second language) programs, split-language predominance (Spanish at home, English at school) can cause significant problems.

Prejudice in the school is a common theme among barrio Chicanos. Mexican American students face pressure, not only from their teachers and Anglo peers, but also from their gang peers. A common student reaction to blatant discrimination and the concomitant sense of alienation he or she feels is to resist authority figures by deciding not to do well, not to become a schoolboy or schoolgirl. Resistance is shown by sitting in the back of the classroom, not carrying books, ditching school to show disrespect, and joining with other similarly harassed Chicanos or Chicanas for fall "race riots" (at Anglo majority schools). Dropping out is the ultimate act of defiance, nurtured by school officials' practice of kicking or pushing students out.

Many parents of school-defiant children, particularly those whose own problems have already contributed to their children's susceptibility to gang involvement, encourage dropping out— sometimes consciously, sometimes without awareness. It might be because of the parent's unfamiliarity with schools or their own negative experiences there; they may need an additional household member to work and contribute financially; or they may be just plain ignorant of their children's needs and neglectful of their future.[29]

Gang members have particular difficulty in adjusting to school, and by age 16 most have dropped out of the educational system.[30] Among the reasons typically cited for their turning off from school are language problems, cultural and ethnic identity conflict, general malaise, and discrimination. What is important to note is that school problems generally precede and contribute to involvement in the gang. Thus, if only we could find effective ways to turn students on to the benefits and values of an education, the educational system could be a powerful factor in preventing students from joining gangs. Unfortunately, California society has not been moving in this direction. Rather than trying to turn students on to education by training bilingual, culturally sensitive teachers and making more spaces available for students at universities, we have cut bilingual education and removed affirmative action from universities.

The last part of the social control triad is law enforcement, which includes the whole criminal justice apparatus. Again, like the family and the schools, law enforcement has failed to exert social control over the growing gang problem. Historically, community-police relations have been poor, marked more by hostility and conflict than by respect and cooperation. This pattern of strain and antagonism began with the Mexican War of 1846 and continued in its aftermath. Lynchings, gun battles, range wars, kangaroo courts, and the Wild West lawlessness of that era have been replaced by more balanced legal machinations in the modern period, but even so disputes and irregularities are common in community-police relations.

As immigration increased and affected the nature of the Chicano population, the Anglo authorities' negative attitude toward Mexicans sharpened into an anti-foreign, anti–illegal-alien stance, particularly during and after the Great Depression of the 1930s. Besides regular run-ins with police—large group encounters and protests, as well as personal frays—there was now harassment of newcomers. La Migra (immigration officials) mounted one offensive after another to rid neighborhoods of Mexicans, sparking many incidents that attracted public attention.

Thus, from the beginning and over time barrio residents were made to feel that they were seen as deviant and criminal, and came to resent the extra police attention they received just because they lived in a barrio.[31] Given the seething friction, violent eruptions and police-community

Graffiti upon graffiti dominate in some barrios.

confrontations became commonplace. The most recent, as well as the most costly and widespread, was the Rodney King rioting of 1992, which followed the acquittal of police officers who a citizen had videotaped brutally beating a nonresisting African American during an arrest. The outbreak initially involved only blacks, but Chicanos and other Latinos living in the same and adjacent neighborhoods soon joined in. Numerous smaller outbreaks mark the latter half of the twentieth century, with different barrios having their own history of aggressive and violent interactions with law enforcement.[32] One of the most celebrated early incidents was known as the Zoot Suit Riots of 1943, which involved hundreds of Anglo servicemen and citizens. Over several days, participants took it upon themselves to attack Mexicans, as well as other ethnic minorities, that were dressed as zoot-suiters or pachucos (more on this cultural style below).[33] The resistance of the youths attacked and the community protests against the white establishment generated public awareness that Mexicans were a force to be reckoned with.

In this history of poor relationships and mostly insensitivity to how barrio life and poverty take a toll, the societal response usually has been punishment and suppression, especially since the 1970s. Aggressive police behavior is often useful but can be counterproductive in terms of social control if the expected results do not materialize. When some of the antigang programs and suppression strategies were initiated by different sectors of the criminal justice apparatus, the gang problem was expected to disappear. That did not happen. What we have instead are more gangs, more gang members, and more prisons and prisoners, most of whom are former gang members. Street youths in general have a shockingly intense hatred of the police and complain often about receiving disrespectful treatment, being detained for no reason, and getting hit without provocation. For example, residents of one public housing project, both adults and youths, widely believe that the Los Angeles Police Department regularly and without provocation takes gang members to nearby vacant industrial buildings to beat them. Generally, this belief and the insistence with which it is verbalized reflect barrio dwellers' paranoia and suspicion of law enforcement, but such beatings have occurred often enough to reinforce the widely repeated stories. The ongoing Ramparts police station scandal, involving planted guns and drugs, shooting gang members without provocation, and lying in court testimony, also lends support to the contention that police often plan and provoke incidents to control people—especially those, in certain neighborhoods, they believe to be gang members or drug traffickers.

As neighborhood ecological effects and intense poverty altered the Mexican immigrants' social control networks, gradually changing them for the worse, other social and cultural mechanisms developed which also affected their adaptation (or maladaptation!) to U.S. life. Two main transformations have been street socialization and choloization.[34]

Street socialization results when home and school socialization are nonexistent or have failed. In the 1930s and 1940s, when the paths of immigrants were particularly troublesome and social control networks disrupted, the many street-raised youths that congregated together began to form gangs. The first gangs were the pachucos of the zoot suit generation, a sharply dressed group of Americanized Mexicans who favored a Spanish/English slang and flamboyant presentation of themselves. Gangs filled the voids other caretakers had left and became substitutes for parenting (providing friendship, emotional support, and protection), schooling (providing a model for dress, speech, and behavior styles), and policing (providing rules and regulations and sanctions for breaking them). In sum, what began as a boy gang problem in the 1920s became a full-blown gang problem in the 1940s and 1950s. Today the gang subculture has a life and existence all its own, with street elites at the ready to recruit and guide youths who have little recourse except to spend time in the streets.[35] The fact that community outlets for social and recreational events are limited in areas like East Los Angeles ensures that street life is the only game in town.

The cultural attribute choloization, or cultural marginalization, goes hand in hand with street pressures and influences. Rapid culture change and uneven acculturation, like that experienced by the children of immigrants, often is a haphazard affair that generates a sense of cultural marginality and ambiguous ethnic identity.[36] The term *cholo* dates from the Spanish colonial period when it meant "mestizo." Today in the United States, it tends to mean "on the margins," betwixt and between cultures. Modern-day Chicano gang members have adapted "cholo" to express cultural identification tied to street identity, and through diffusion the street label has spread to the border area in Mexico.[37] Its popular usage became commonplace during the pachuco generation, especially after World War II.

Like the pachuco lifestyle, the cholo lifestyle has been fueled by culture conflict and psycho-socioeconomic conditions in the barrios. Indeed, the conditions in the barrios are so marginalizing that the Chicano gang problem has become progressively more severe, although gang homicide rates in Los Angeles, which rose to a high level in the mid-1990s, have since dropped considerably.[38] The gang problem, nevertheless, is particularly severe in Los Angeles County, where at least half of all Chicano gangs are located.

Because choloization is a syncretic process—that is, a mixing and blending of cultures to create a new culture or subculture, sometimes in an erratic way—it has resulted in a variety of characteristics that reflect the Chicano gang subculture in terms of organization, structure, values and norms, and social and cultural habits. Both choloization and street socialization apply to Chicana gang members, but a double domination compounds the processes for cholas, who have to contend with oppression from the dominant society and additionally from the males in their subsociety. The tension and stress associated with culture conflict is magnified when gender attitudes and practices are part of the mix. Female youths face the difficult task of coping with a traditional culture that

Cholos in mural convey a cool image.

adheres to a rigid definition of female roles and expectations while they are aware of the less restrictive gender roles of the Anglo world. Furthermore, chola self-identification strivings often are strongly colored by individual experiences females might have had in their living environment (e.g., sexual exploitation, sometimes even molestation) and in the context of the street gang (e.g., male domination, being treated as a sexual object, and having to conform to gang rules and expectations in order to gain acceptance).

The customs and activities that characterize the gang subculture are both formal and informal; some stem from Anglo/Mexican cultural mixing, while others reflect the street realities and adaptations found in most modern U.S. cities.[39] There are different types of barrios—urban, rural, suburban, classic, modern—and each barrio has its own name: White Fence, El Hoyo Maravilla, 18th Street, and so on. Gang members differ in the intensity and duration of their involvement, depending on the variation in neighborhood histories and influences and on personal proclivities. Homegirls join together with other homegirls their age mostly as auxiliaries of male cliques. Size and structure of the traditional gangs vary, from as few as 8 or 10 to as many as 80 or 100. (Some of the more recently established urban gangs, lacking the territorial boundaries of earlier barrios, have grown to immensely greater sizes with much more complex internal structures.) Some barrio gangs have been around since the 1940s and have had as many as thirteen cliques, grouped by age (e.g., ages 9–12, 13–15, 16–19, and so on) and each with its own name.[40] Short-lived barrio gangs are also common, either due to a lack of available recruits to renew membership or to being absorbed by a nearby bigger and stronger barrio neighborhood group.

Where street socialization and choloization have occurred, with the concomitant breakdown in social control, a youth might join a gang by the preteen years. Many have been pregang-socialized by older brothers or sisters or other relatives who were gang members. For females the onset of puberty is often the catalyst for pregang involvement. Since gang membership occurs during the "psychosocial moratorium" when age/sex role clarification is important,[41] most barrios have an initiation rite called "courting-in" or "jumping-in," which involves a beating at the hands of three or more regular gang members. For male recruits, the ritual affirms the initiate's gang identity and commitment and emphasizes the super-masculine role he takes on.[42]

The role for female gang members, born of the streets, also requires being tough and acting out aggressively when necessary. While the initiation ceremony for females sometimes is the same as for males, gangs instead might require the initiate to have sex with one or several of the male gang members. The latter practice, of course, is a reflection of how male domination sets the tone for gender relations: females must be submissive.

It must be underscored that early sexual activity among females and early motherhood often involve very complicated and seemingly contradictory feelings as well as consequences. Young women (some still girls, in fact) often feel particularly powerless but, ironically, to them pregnancy often represents an opportunity for control over some aspect of their lives. It guarantees that they will have someone to love and care for and they will know that at least one person loves them unconditionally. Empowered by this experience, they temporarily enjoy the benefits of parenting but soon learn how challenging it is. Some teen mothers succeed, but many more, sadly, add their children to the poverty cycle reflected in the street conditions that create gangs.

The 1970s cholo style

The gang serves different needs, among them protection, camaraderie (they call each other "homeboy" or "carnal"—blood brother), friendship, and, most important, a fictive family/kin role. Once gang affiliation is confirmed, tattoos are placed on the body, showing that a person belongs to the barrio (the person's gang nickname and the barrio name form a type of private graffiti).[43] The same moniker and affiliation are also scrawled throughout the neighborhood and area as public graffiti.

In the gang subculture, many other symbolic features—movements, sounds, and images—are used to characterize the street and cultural identity of gang members. The dress, walk, talk, and body language are distinct and assert a streetwise sense of control and command of life's challenges and threats. Particularly fascinating in this regard is the dress and style of female gang members. For example, exaggerated makeup, tattoos, and hairstyle can send messages to onlookers and provide a means to show power or a way to mask the former identity of the person who is now a gang member.[44] Some females adopt the dress style of khakis and gang garb, but those who wish to flaunt their sexuality or indicate that they accept being a sex object dress in very skimpy clothing. The same girl may alternate between these dress styles, depending on the occasion.

Cholo/chola orientation is also apparent in the way gang members party with alcohol and drugs and how they fix their cars up—as lowriders, slung low to the ground and driven slowly, with the driver acting accordingly and his equally cool chola beside him. However, most of the attention gangs and gang members attract is from the mayhem and violence associated with gang conflicts and homicides. An inordinate amount of media and public attention focuses on these unconventional, destructive activities, although gangs engage in them only a small percentage of the time. However, alcohol and drugs check the rational processes, guns accelerate acts of aggression, and cars make it easier to effect a getaway.

By way of summary, Mexican immigrants historically have been pushed into the ecological, socioeconomic, and cultural margins of city life. Over time, nevertheless, many of these immigrants have been able to overcome the obstacles of poverty and discrimination and achieve relative prosperity. They have adopted a bilingual and bicultural lifestyle.[45] However, a small but significant portion of barrio dwellers have been unable to cope successfully with the pressures of modern urban life. These marginalized families are overwhelmed by larger-than-life pressures, externally imposed community forces that override individual characteristics in influencing family life. Little wonder, then, we see increasing levels of unconventional and deviant lifestyles in the families.

When a family breaks down as a form of social control, more problems begin. Many times an alienated youth escapes family life by joining the street culture, whose values teach the youth to defy and ignore other forms of social control, namely, the schools and law enforcement. Lost on the margins of society, both socioeconomically and culturally, the youth blindly searches for ways to reaffirm identity. The gang provides a readily accessible lifestyle that offers familial bonding, peer acceptance, freedom, and excitement. Given the stresses of barrio life, it is remarkable, not that there are gangs, but that only a small minority of barrio youths join them (about 4 to 14 percent). Nonetheless, regardless of how few or how many youths are actually involved, gangs are a serious problem that merits concentrated, in-depth attention, not just media special reports or law enforcement bulletins and statistics.

The answer to stopping gang behavior will lie, first, in understanding the breakdown in social control and, second, in reestablishing positive social controls, starting with families (i.e., connections) and schools (i.e., engagements and involvements). The life history that follows shows how a barrio group's social and historical experience is played out in the personal experiences of Puppet, one of a small but growing number of intergenerational gang members. In his case, extreme poverty and family disorganization dominated his choices so thoroughly that no matter what neighborhood he moved to (and he moved a lot as a foster child), he joined the street gangs and so underwent continuous socialization under their purview. Essentially state-raised, he exemplifies the social reverberations that lead a youth to the street gang and brushes with the law, although in his case the story ends on an upbeat note, as he is trying to go straight.

4

"I Just Wanted to Act *Loco*"

Puppet's Story

HE WAKES UP, looks to his side, and sees that his brother is fast asleep. This seems to happen every night. He doesn't feel bad if someone else is awake, because then they have each other. But when he's the only one awake and his mother is still out with whomever, wherever, he gets scared. Scared of the night, scared of the loneliness, scared that his mother may never come back. That happened one night, and the neighbors came over to quiet the boys down in the early morning. He and his brothers had awakened to a home without a mother, no cereal on the table, no caring hands to help them dress, so all they could think of doing was to cry. It was more like screams and yelling: "Mama! Mama!"

The little boy is now 22 years old and goes by the nickname Puppet. He has the kind of face that recalls the features he must have had as a baby. His cheeks are full and his nose is rounded. His skin is a coarse, light brown. Standing with his hands in his pockets, the five-foot four-inch muscular young man looks down as he tries to give more details. His head is covered with short, prickly hair. Despite his dispassionate tone, he seems willing to go on talking, willing to dig for more memories of a time that he treasures.

Puppet was born in 1973 at Los Angeles County's General Hospital in East Los Angeles. His parents were young, former gang members who struggled with drug addiction. Puppet is the youngest of four children—all boys. His oldest brother is only five years older than he is. During his early childhood, the family lived in a dilapidated home in East Los Angeles. The toilet and the bathtub were often broken and the heater never worked. The other homes in the neighborhood were not much better; actually, they were all shabby. There were no shopping malls or major chain stores nearby. The only businesses, in fact, were small mom and pop grocery stores, *tienditas*.

The children had to get their exercise playing at school or on the street because there were no parks or recreation facilities nearby; the front porch and sidewalk were their playgrounds. Since his home was so small, they sometimes visited their aunt's home, where they played with cousins. It was really fun, he said, when all the cousins showed up with all his aunts; sometimes one of the uncles married to an aunt showed up and played ball with all the boy cousins. But it was crazy, too. There was yelling, fighting, crying all the time when they all played together. When they would go outside without permission, the playing and fighting would spill out into the streets and neighbors' sidewalks and front yards.

> They [our parents] would just lose track of us and we stayed out till real late, unless someone got real hurt. Like one time I fell off a roof and split my forehead. It took nine stitches.

But Puppet said that there was always a lot of fun doing this—the family getting together and eating good Mexican food, beans and tortillas, forgetting who hurt whom and starting all over again. But, he remembered, "When my aunt's husband went to jail, then this all stopped—when she had to move further away and later found another guy to marry." He missed the big family affairs, but they all seemed to have their own problems and he was too little to understand.

Puppet's father spent a lot of time with his mistress and even more time in jail on drug-related charges. When he was at home he did spend some time telling stories to his sons, stories of his days as a gang member.

> He would tell us about his days with Varrio Nuevo Estrada. He remembered all kinds of shit about everyone, what each of his brothers in the gang were like, what their mother cooked, how crazy they all were. He didn't want me to join but, with his stories—you know how a boy will think. I thought maybe my father was more of a man in the old days. At least he stood up for something then. I don't like to admit it, but those stories made me respect him more than what I saw when I was a kid. I mean, shit, the last time I saw

him he was being handcuffed and a judge was going off on him. My mom took me to the court that day to see him, and that's what I saw. I haven't even talked to him since then. I don't even know where he is anyway.

Varrio Nuevo Estrada, the inspiration for these stories, was not really new (*nuevo*) as its name implies. The Varrio Nuevo gang had actually began in the Boyle Heights area in the 1940s. The government relocated many families from that area to the Estrada Courts Housing Project, near Olympic and Soto, about two to three miles from Boyle Heights. By the late 1950s, scores of low-income Chicanos dominated the Estrada projects. The new gang emerged out of this group of relocated colonists from Boyle Heights. Varrio Nuevo Estrada is still one of the largest Chicano gangs in East Los Angeles. But as large as the organization is, no one made any provisions for Puppet and his brothers when they lost their father or, more precisely, when their father lost his sons.

Puppet's mother tried to support her boys. Lacking a high-school diploma, she had limited job options. Most often she worked as a maid, occasionally at a plastic or other small manufacturing plant. The work was always for just a short time, and there was barely enough money to pay the rent and buy food. When she lost her job, she would get help from her sister until she found another one. Because she was tired all the time, the family would eat out at McDonald's or she would buy pizza, and every now and then she brought chicken home. Her jobs often required her to be away in the evening.

The bleakness of the family situation depressed Puppet's mother tremendously. In addition to never having enough money, she (and the boys) lost her family support network. Mainly, it was her sister they lost, who cut ties when she decided to get away from the lifestyle of her former husband. That meant she also had to get away from Puppet's father, who, like her husband, was in and out of prison.

Puppet's mother escaped from her situation by indulging in marijuana and cocaine—even heroin when she could get it. When her husband was in jail, she sometimes found boyfriends who could help her get it. Her periods of escape would often escalate into binges, and she would miss work. During these binges, Puppet, then a preschooler, and his brothers were free to roam the streets—running in front of moving cars to hear the brakes screech when the driver tried to avoid them, throwing rocks at cars and then hiding, getting into dirt clod fights with the kids down the block, and just generally getting into mischief (*haciendo travesuras*) by following the example of some of the older kids in the neighborhood. This intermittent lack of supervision and pregang street socialization continued for several years.

Without an adult to control them, Puppet and his brothers wandered around. His older brother would try to watch over him, but it was tough because "he was a kid too." Sometimes they would walk to the other side of the freeway, looking for bikes to steal. They soon began shoplifting candy and other goods as well. Puppet recalls an incident that happened when he was seven.

> Me and my brothers all got caught stealing candy. They took us to the police station. One of my brothers was crying all night long. I didn't cry because I knew my ma is going to come and get us. She did, but she had to walk a long way because we didn't have a car, so we were in there pretty long. Maybe now I don't think it was that long, but it was long for us then. She didn't say much—just took us home.

Despite the lack of supervision and attention during his childhood, Puppet maintains that he was fairly happy during those years.

> I could see that my mom was having a bad time, but still I was kinda happy as a little kid. As bad as it sounds, I guess what happened later was worse. Little kids don't know what worse things there are out there or what better things there are, so you are just happy.

Puppet's mother was declared an unfit mother by the authorities sometime between Puppet's seventh and eighth birthdays, after the police had picked him and his brothers up many times. The last time had been when his older brother reached his arm through a grated fence and took a cardboard tube from an upholstery shop just as an unmarked police car was passing by. They were all piled into the car and taken to the station. It was just a tube without leather or material on it, but the police called it burglary.

The brothers were separated and each placed in a foster home except for Puppet, who because he was younger got to stay with relatives. For the rest of his life, Puppet would have no significant extended contact with either his brothers or his mother. His hopes of finding a permanent home among his extended family were soon dashed.

> I was really hoping one of my relatives, maybe my aunt [who used to care for them] would let us stay with them. But she had married a guy who didn't like us. He tolerated us. I asked at the first place we stayed if they could come get me and they said no. I didn't know why, but now I know that no one offered. I realize now that they didn't give a damn.

Puppet spent the rest of his childhood in fourteen different homes, sometimes with reluctant relatives but mostly with foster parents. The very first family he lived with made an effort to treat him well.

> They made me feel like I was really part of the family. They tried to help me and teach me right from wrong. Everything their kids did, I got to do. We went places like museums. They had a movie camera to film birthdays and things, and when I was there they made sure I was in the movie. One time it was a rocket launching and they filmed everyone in the front room and asked them their opinion, and when they got to me I was embarrassed. No one, not even my aunt, had made me feel important. I started to like school, which was new to me. I didn't know how to read or write at all before that time.

Teachers began to compliment Puppet on his abilities, and his confidence soared. His foster parents signed him up for Boy Scouts. He took to the organization and soon was elected subchief. Puppet looks back on that honor with amazement as he recalls its impact.

> I couldn't believe it when they elected me. They put my name on a plaque which stays at the camp. Even ten, fifteen years later they keep it and just add the new names each year. That was something I never had and it was important because it made me try a little more to be better. I didn't have to think I was really bad to be somebody and it made me look like I could get respect.

Despite Puppet's good behavior and accomplishments, he was removed from his foster home after about a year. He was 9 years old. To his child's mind, he couldn't figure out what went wrong. In reality, the family was going to move out of the state and couldn't take him. From that point on, as he was shuffled from one foster home or relative to another, his attitude and trust soured. His interest in school and Boy Scouts withered as well.

> That first time I never will understand what happened. Later I think I got moved around because I messed up. I tripped out a lot. I really didn't like any of my relatives or foster parents after that. Most of them just took me in to get the money. They would trip out if I wore out my shoes. Some were racist in the things they would say. Their own kids were the real children. I was basically an extra hassle for them.

Puppet has been in so many homes that he cannot remember all of his foster parents, the towns he lived in, or the schools he attended. Even with the aunt he remembers the best, it didn't work out when he stayed with her a couple of times. He was older now (eleven or twelve), and he and his cousins would get into fights and she would take their side, regardless of who was right. Another time he stayed with an older aunt (his mother's sister), but she couldn't handle him, since he would just stay out in the streets all the time.

Perpetually the new kid at the schools he attended, he often felt he had to fight to prove himself to his new classmates: "I didn't look for fights, but when someone wanted it I wouldn't back down. That was part of my tripping out." Chicanos were a distinct minority in several of Puppet's schools, and he traded insults and engaged in fistfights with other students, both Anglos and African Americans. Not surprisingly, the more Puppet fought, the worse his academic performance became.

> I always had a face on in class—a "don't mess with me" face. When I did talk, I tried to insult everyone. I never gave a straight answer, which messed up the class when the teacher was trying to get everyone to listen. When I felt like it I would get up and walk around the class while the other kids were sitting and doing their work. If I felt like doing my work, I would just copy someone's paper and then hand it in. That's if I cared to do it. Most of the time I just drew cartoons and wrote on the desk and books. I hated it so I ditched class all the time. I don't think the teachers missed me too much because, by then, the office had me in there every week. My file had papers in it that said, "This guy is a problem." I just added to my file and then I would move soon anyway to a new home and start over.

At thirteen, about to enter the eighth grade, Puppet was moved into the home of an aunt on his father's side. He doesn't remember that he was any worse or any better there. What had an effect on Puppet was the location of his new home—Pico Rivera, a barrio. For the first time, he came into contact with street gangs. It was a funny encounter at school that started his association with one. He was in class and dressed in regular jeans, "looking lame like you [pointing to me], and this guy next to me looks at my pants and says, 'Where did you get those pants?' and before I could answer the guy says, 'I'll get you some *firme* [cool, good] pants at my house.'"

This was the beginning of friendships with guys at school who were members of an established, traditional gang—Pico Viejo. Pico Viejo, which some say dates back to the nineteenth century, evolved from a rural colony of Mexican migrant workers. The colony was eventually overtaken by the sprawl of suburban housing, at which time the colony became a barrio with a resident gang. Puppet learned of this history from his new friends, who pressured him to join.

> They started offering me drugs, booze; they would share anything
> they had with me. They introduced me to other members. At first,
> the idea of being in a gang was too weird for me. These guys were
> always hanging out together. I thought to myself that if you ever got
> one by himself he would be a big pussy. It just seemed like they were
> running in a pack. At that time I was getting beat up in school,
> which was not a new thing. I started to think maybe I could be part
> of the gang and get left alone. Plus, part of me was attracted to trou-
> ble and they were always getting into trouble. One day I got beat up
> by ten guys, and that's the day I made my decision to join.

Puppet began to actively seek membership in the gang. He became friends with more members of the gang. When they needed something, he was always there to be useful. In school especially, it was fun to be egged on by the guys to do something wrong that would get their attention. It showed you were a good listener and follower, someone who knew how to act with the group. They spent most of their time together hanging out at the park, committing petty theft, and experimenting with marijuana.

After several months of this, it was time for Puppet's formal initiation.

They jump you in. I had to fight four guys at the same time. The
rules are you can only use fists and feet. No weapons allowed. It's
just a few minutes but they don't hold back too much. They beat
you pretty good. I was swinging wildly and I hit one of the older
guys and he got mad. So he started hitting me with some good
chingazos [hard blows] and bloodied my nose and blacked my eye.

The blows were real and painful, but Puppet withstood the beating without crying or giving up. After the fighting was over, according to the
gang, Puppet was a man, a formal member of Pico Viejo.

It is perhaps not surprising that Puppet found stability in the gang,
given his early life of instability and the lack of regular and consistent
parental and other adult guidance. His homeboys became his surrogates,
both fathers and brothers to him. They taught him how to think, act, and
feel. They provided many of his best adventures and "manly" experiences. "They taught me how to keep my *palabra* [word] and they would
always watch my back. Man, they had a lot of *cora* [heart]."

> To me, these were the good guys. I didn't care how they looked to
> anyone else. My aunt didn't like what was happening. She and her
> husband thought all cholos were just bums and punks, but my
> homeboys were good to me. To me, that was the only thing that
> mattered.

Puppet's aunt and uncle ("husband" is what Puppet always called him,
because they were not on good terms) tried imposing harsh discipline in
hopes of curtailing his involvement with the gang. They insisted that he
be home before dark each night. Ignoring them, Puppet spent even more
time away from home. He ran away several times. As he says, they "were
doing what they wanted, so I was going to do what I wanted like all my
other friends." What his friends wanted to do was live by impulse and
"act crazy." They would dare each other to get into fights or hit a
teacher. Their craziness gave them a feeling of power, a pretty heady feeling for junior high students.

> When we were together, nobody could tell us what to do—not
> teachers, not nobody. We even jumped the gym teacher once. This
> teacher was always messing with us, saying we were no problem for
> him, just some little kids. He was always saying threats—"I'd love

to have a chance" and stuff like that. The chance just came. It was dark outside and we waited and kicked his ass. He had a good idea who it was and we got suspended for a while. Because the teacher had threatened us was the only reason we didn't get expelled.

Once Puppet entered high school, his gang involvement intensified. He started dressing even more in the cholo style: khakis, cutoffs, white T-shirts, and athletic shoes—B.K.'s. He had kept his hair short at first, but now he started to shave it like the other guys. At age 14 his style of dress was so important to him that it precipitated a pivotal event.

> I wanted to get some khakis. I had never had any—I always had to borrow them, so my friends and I decided to go to a department store. I found some I liked and just rolled them up under my jacket and walked out. I left them at my house, and when I went out I guess my aunt found the pants and she knew that's what cholos wore so she tore up the pants and threw the pieces in the trash. When I got home, I got into it with her. I was tired of other people telling me what to do. I got my stuff and went to live with some older cholos from the gang.

Puppet speaks of his khakis and choloization in almost reverential tones. This is not surprising because group expectations are extremely intense within the gang. In order to be accepted by his peers, Puppet had to conform to the gang code of the cholo.

The cholo style is a distinct reflection of a subculture that derives from the poor, working-class background of the barrio populace, so the clothing Puppet wore was all part of the standard style of his time and place. However, clothing is only one part of the cholo style. Puppet also had to learn to put up the "cholo front." He had to learn to walk and act in a methodical, purposeful manner with a detached demeanor. Conforming to the code, he exchanged the *firme* arm salute with his homeboys (arm up as though to block someone, but with elbow bent, and held rigid to show confirmation). Anyone failing to meet the gang standards had to pay *levas* (sanctions) to his homeboys. Once the homeboys had each other straightened out, they looked for other targets.

They harassed "schoolboys," as only "sissies" did homework. Insulting teachers and anyone associated with the educational system was expected by gang peers and considered to be great fun. In fact, Puppet got his moniker because of his clownish classroom behavior. By November of his freshman year, he had dropped out and moved in with one of his homeboys. Puppet's high school education ended almost as soon as it began.

Living with his older homeboys only sped up the process of Puppet's choloization. The older *veteranos* (veterans), of course, wore the right clothes, affected the most powerful postures, and often gave Puppet money to buy his own clothes.

> Aside from the money, those cholos taught me a lot of things they thought I needed to know. They taught me how to hot-wire a car, for one thing. The best thing was, I could do whatever I wanted—come home, go when I wanted. No discipline. It seemed better to me than my life with other people. I sometimes sold a little yesca [marijuana] and learned how to take money from the other kids.

Fights between Anglos and Chicanos were common around Puppet's new home. He happened to live on the border of the barrio that was located next to a lower-working-class Anglo enclave. Since he was now a resident, this presented a challenge. Youths from the two ethnic groups often came into contact and exchanged numerous insults and blows. At first, Puppet welcomed the opportunity to defend his ethnicity and his homeboys.

> I looked forward to taking them on when I first moved there, standing up for my boys, but I got tired of fighting every day. I started hoping, just to myself, that there would be a way to get out of the situation.

The way out for Puppet came from people he had all but forgotten. After he ran away from his paternal aunt's home, the authorities tracked down his maternal aunt and alerted her. She and some of his mother's relatives looked for Puppet and, as he hadn't gone far, found him. His aunt reluctantly offered Puppet a place to stay. Still cherishing memories of his long-ago family, Puppet accepted and moved to her home on the other side of town.

For a few months, Puppet stayed with his aunt and was able to avoid trouble. During this time, he saw his mother several times but, sadly, by now she was addicted to heroin and Puppet was unable to have any meaningful communication with her.

Puppet managed to spend a great portion of his time visiting and hanging out with his homeboys. During one visit, he got involved in a fight and was arrested for assault with a deadly weapon. Puppet and twelve homeboys had attacked another cholo in the front yard of the cholo's house. The guy had insulted and challenged one of the homeboys, and when called out of his house came out with karate sticks, ready to do mortal combat. Predictably, "he got his ass kicked, rat-pack style—all thirteen to one."

> We went over to his house to get him. It was some crazy guy. I forget the exact reason. We weren't drunk or on any drugs. He did something and that's why we were there. He needed to get his ass kicked and we were the ones to do it.

Puppet was quickly released from jail and went back to live with his aunt, but there was always the impulse to violence. In another incident, he and a homeboy were walking by a local beer joint that catered to undocumented Mexican workers. Some of the workers were outside, talking drunkenly among themselves. One of the workers shouted a challenge, or was just talking boisterously and aggressively without aiming his words at anybody. Puppet turned to his homeboy and asked, "Does he want to get down [fight]?" and the answer from the homeboy was "Yeah." So they quickly grabbed a stick and beat the challenger—and his fellow workers who had run out of the bar once they heard the commotion. Then the two walked away. This was conducting business as usual.

Puppet and his friends often fought for no special reason and to little benefit. Bored, frustrated, and eager to prove their machismo, they viewed fighting as an outlet. Sometimes when nothing exciting was happening, they would box among themselves, usually without gloves. They fought to win the respect of their peers, with little regard for their own safety or that of their victims. Acting crazy, or *loco*, generated esteem among the homeboys. To back down or act like a coward was to ask for ridicule and banishment.

> It makes no difference who started the fight. It doesn't even have to be a one-on-one fight. We are always ready, and all it takes is for something to start it out. It can be a get-even thing, or someone who wants to get revenge on someone, but all gangs fight, and we just get into it because help is needed.

If there was a reason for a fight, it often centered on defending or protecting one's neighborhood. Many of the fights began when one gang tried to invade the turf of a rival gang. A barrio gang jealously guards its territory; another gang expresses defiance by cruising through it in their cars, viewing each invasion as a coup. This is the basis for many confrontations. Puppet describes one incident in which he and his homeboys were ambushed as they drove through the neighborhood of a rival gang.

> One Thursday afternoon we were just driving. Sometimes we liked
> to cruise through a neighborhood that we didn't like. This time
> some guys saw us and went after us. They got us hard and smashed
> our car with rocks and bricks. One of the *vatos* [guys] was real
> messed up and needed stitches. The rest of us just got beat up a lit-
> tle. I got a bump on my head and a scratch across my nose.

Puppet and his friends avenged the attack by "busting in" on parties in the rival neighborhood. During this time, Puppet never really bothered to reflect on the violence and the danger and heavy price that it exacted.

> Only later did I begin to think about how we used to be. Back then
> we didn't care. We felt we were doing the right thing. Those *vatos*
> had it coming to them for what they had done to our homeboys. I
> just wanted to act *loco*.

Puppet often did *loco* things to defend his sense of honor. He could not tolerate insults, even those that were more imaginary than real. For example, Puppet often got into fights with recent Mexican immigrants (he refers to them as *mojados*, "wetbacks"), who he felt looked down on him for being Americanized and unable to speak fluent Spanish. In fact, aside from the time when he lived with the older cholos, Puppet usually got into fights only with other Chicanos or Mexican immigrants. It may seem a paradox to an outsider that Puppet fights those who share his ethnicity, but it doesn't strike Puppet as unusual. He thinks little about ethnicity. His fluency in Spanish is minimal, which of course is due in part to the fact that he grew up in different homes with parents of varying cultures and languages. His biological parents were bilingual, yet they had preferred speaking to their children in English. He can understand a little Spanish, but he cannot use it to articulate his thoughts. He does not seem particularly embarrassed by his lack of fluency.

I'm proud to be what I am. Don't get me wrong. I fought for what I
am. Even though I fought all kinds of people, I'm not prejudiced
toward anyone. I fought for my gang, not because I hated a type of
people.

He fought often in defense of his gang identity, and inevitably some
of these fights turned deadly. One summer, one of Puppet's homeboys
was shot and killed by a member of another gang. Puppet witnessed the
shooting. It was the first time he had seen a person killed. Not surprisingly, that incident set off a deadly battle of retribution. The violence
moved back and forth between the two gangs for weeks. Nonetheless,
despite all that he has witnessed, Puppet is intrepid. His attitude toward
death is fatalistic.

You don't think about it with fear. When you do you make it
easier for your enemies. Everybody is going to get killed. The only
difference between men is how they handle it.

For good or bad, these violent events solidified Puppet's commitment to
gang goals and roles.

Puppet cruised with his homeboys into enemy territory as a way to
test their commitment and bravery, a way to assert their manhood and
allegiance to the barrio. He took drugs to win his peers' acceptance and
approval and took pride in sharing his drugs with his homeboys, an act
of generosity that was highly valued within the gang. Marijuana derived
from the plant's buds was the drug most commonly used. Puppet often
smoked about ten to fifteen marijuana joints a day. He admits to experimenting with heroin, which, luckily for him, he didn't like. Nor did he
like pills and rock cocaine. He did not sell drugs on a regular basis, as he
was not particularly interested in making money.

Occasionally when he needed money, Puppet stole auto parts and
broke into homes to steal guns and other valuables. Theft was another
way for Puppet to prove he was *loco.*

At the time, that was just one of the things you did. I don't look at it
as good now, but I didn't see it as wrong then. If I could take something from you, it was your loss, your weakness, my being smarter.
We never knew if we would get in the house and someone would be
waiting with a gun. So to get in there and out with the goods and
alive proved we were *loco.*

The thrill of being *loco* grew old for Puppet. At nineteen, when many young men are deciding on their college major, he considered retirement. As is common with many gang youths, Puppet began to feel less like a warrior and more like a survivor.

> The crazy stuff wasn't for me no more. I saw other guys go down and I knew it was just a matter of time before I paid my price, you know. I met my girlfriend and she was always on me about getting out of the gang. She gave me a reason, but I was already tired. I was tired of fighting all the time, running around all the time.

In Puppet's case, his gang did not oppose his decision to leave, to "mature out" of the gang, especially since he had been a ready and able *loco*. His homeboys apparently had an understanding that eventually a man will want to settle down and raise a family. In that case, the former member of the gang is left alone and becomes a respected *veterano*. As Puppet says, "If you're older and you've got a family, most people won't even bother you. If a guy wants to settle down, that's his business and that's good." Moving away helps, but "I still thought of my homeboys every now and then."

Despite his unstable family life and lack of steady adult supervision, Puppet holds himself responsible for his life's choices. He believes that nobody pushed him into it.

> Saying no is not easy, but after a while it gets old. Saying yes becomes hard. If you wanted to do something wrong, it's up to you. All I wanted to do is have friends, have people that like me and take care of me. Nobody is pushing you and you can always say no. Some of us got out, but I know some that got into the life of more serious crimes and addiction to heroin. Those guys never got nothing going for themselves. They gave up. Maybe they wanted to make something of themselves, but they never got into it.

Puppet now lives with his girlfriend and their one-year-old son. He is working as a construction laborer and hopes to obtain his GED. Having much to learn, he has a long road ahead of him. Yet he has no regrets about his past and is thankful he did not suffer the same fate as others he has known. He is not in prison, nor is he addicted to drugs—and he is alive!

5

Blacks in Los Angeles

From Central Avenue to South Central Los Angeles

FOR THE AFRICAN AMERICAN population—now so used to being on the receiving end of negative publicity associated with street gangs and drug trafficking, including insulting gang stereotypes—it might come as a surprise that the phenomenon of black gangs is relatively recent, dating from about the 1940s. Gangs are not a part of African culture, nor are they a part of the South's African American culture. They breed in cities, and it is to places like Los Angeles, Chicago, and New York, where African Americans have migrated in this century, that we must direct our attention if we are to understand the black gang problem and implement programs to eradicate it.

Although blacks and Afro-mestizos from Mexico were among the earliest *pobladores* (settlers) in Los Angeles, arriving in 1781,[1] African Americans did not migrate to the area in significant numbers until more than a century later, at the turn of the twentieth century. These African American settlers, often skilled workers who possessed some degree of education, usually came from the South and border states. At the time, Los Angeles was considered more tolerant of nonwhites than many other areas of the country, and the small numbers of blacks who settled were not perceived as a threat.[2] As one researcher noted, "The small and relatively inconspicuous Negro population appears to have enjoyed a lessening of racial tension and a considerable degree of acceptance."[3] Perhaps the established presence of Afro-mestizos nurtured this attitude; for example, by the 1880s African Americans had the right to vote, testify in court, and attend integrated schools.[4] In addition, the real estate opportunities available to African Americans in and around Los Angeles offered a potential road to economic success that would have been denied them in most other cities of the nation, where ghettoization, discrimination, and repression were the rule.

If such practices were less severe and widespread in Los Angeles, the survival strategies that the city's African Americans developed nonetheless were the same as elsewhere. They looked to each other for guidance through troubled times, relying on mutual aid in the form of multifamily dwellings, social capital (e.g., nepotism in job networks), community organizations, churches, cultural centers, and so on. Altogether, group support proved to be a source of significant and powerful social control in the community. With such a relatively strong foundation, the African American community was not plagued by high crime rates, family instability, juvenile delinquency, prostitution, or gambling. Thus, despite the prevalent racism of the era, Los Angeles' African Americans enjoyed unity and relative economic prosperity—over one-third of the families owned their own homes.[5] As national organizations such as the National Urban League and the National Association for the Advancement of Colored People (NAACP) emerged in the second decade of the twentieth century, they quickly established chapters in Los Angeles. In short, the African American community of Los Angeles was fighting valiantly for internal strength, solidarity, and consciousness.

By the 1920s, unfortunately, the cohesiveness of the community had begun to break down. The breakdown is often blamed on the influx of new African American immigrants who came by the hundreds of thousands in the "Great Migration" of 1915–1929. These migrants were not as well off as the earlier ones, being mostly unskilled urban workers and farmers from the poor South, what Claude Brown referred to as the sons and daughters of sharecroppers.[6] What the established African American residents perceived as the superstition and laxity of the newcomers ran counter to their own ethic of self-improvement and hard work. Unity was now becoming more difficult to maintain because of intra-ethnic differences.

Between 1900 and 1920 the African American population in Los Angeles increased more than sevenfold[7] and new devices for racial confinement, such as restrictive housing covenants, emerged in tandem with the population growth. Although local courts had ruled these practices either illegal or unenforceable just a few years earlier, the white community quickly adopted them—and they remained in place for decades to come.[8] As a result, African Americans continued to be restricted largely to a few isolated areas that constituted a spatial ghetto. By 1920 most were living east of downtown and west of the Los Angeles River in an area that stretched approximately thirty blocks southward from downtown along Central Avenue. Within ten years, opportunities for African Americans to live outside the boundaries of the ghetto became severely limited.[9] Three of the city's twelve assembly districts held 75 percent of the African Americans, whereas in five districts their population was less than 1 percent.[10]

In addition to the influx of African Americans, hundreds of thousands of Mexican immigrants entered Southern California in the 1920s, as did a steady but much smaller stream of Japanese immigrants, until the Exclusion Act of 1924.[11] Consequently, jobs that paid well became even harder to find. By the end of World War I, in fact, both foreign white and Japanese immigrants seem to have displaced blacks in all industrial jobs, and they threatened to do the same in domestic occupations. Trained English servants succeeded blacks as valets and butlers, and Greek immigrants invaded even the seemingly unapproachable shoeshine trade. At the time, of the 106 local unions in Los Angeles, African Americans were members of only eleven, the two with the largest black membership being the waiters' and musicians' unions, and even these were segregated. Therefore, African American workers typically had little wage and benefit protection and often were forced to work in substandard conditions.

When real estate prices rose in the 1920s, most African Americans found that the more desirable homes were financially out of their reach. Moreover, as both the African American and Caucasian populations had continued to grow, so had segregation. Whites at this time built miles of residential tracts along the coast and into rural lands adjacent to the city. African Americans were barred from this expansion. The result was "increased ethnic concentration, a deterioration of property values, and a less optimistic view of their community on the part of some blacks."[12] The tightened residential segregation was tremendously damaging to the economic health of the African American community in Los Angeles, paving the way for massive overcrowding and the institutionalization of the ghetto.[13]

Housing has always been a problem.

The 1920s saw a rise in the prominence of the Ku Klux Klan (which in 1920 erected a cross at 109th Street and Central Avenue),[14] and also heightened discrimination on the part of more moderate elements; the Los Angeles City Playground Commission segregated municipal swimming pools and several coastal communities prohibited African Americans from visiting their beaches. The ultimate insult was a sign placed in the waiting room of the Pacific Electric Railroad in Compton. It read: Negroes! Be Out Of Compton By Nightfall. Motivated mostly by the desire to maintain all-white neighborhoods, such actions were not uncommon throughout the decade. Klan violence would recur for another thirty years or so, but the 1920s were perhaps the last decade in which such virulent sentiments were so widespread and overt in Southern California. Whatever the extent of actual Klan activity, however, "white Angelenos displayed a distaste for black neighbors, prompting black businessman H. A. Reeves to claim that ninety-five percent of the city's housing in the 1920s was restricted against blacks."[15] By 1929, many of the older areas along Central Avenue had the structural characteristics of a slum: few sanitary conveniences, leaky pipes and roofs, patched windows and doors, and general neglect of maintenance and repairs.[16]

Following the depression, another wave of African Americans moved westward with the state of California as a primary destination. Overall, from 1940 to 1950 the African American population in Los Angeles grew by more than 100,000, with most newcomers arriving from the rural Deep South.[17] Unfortunately, Los Angeles had little to offer them late in the 1940s, and African Americans suffered the highest unemployment rate of any group in the city.[18] Racial discrimination continued to flare up in the early 1940s as blacks began to spill out of the Central Avenue strip into nearby areas.[19] For example, white students at Fremont High School threatened their African American schoolmates in 1941, burning them in effigy and displaying posters declaring "We Want No Niggers At This School." The infamous Zoot Suit Riots broke out in June 1943, during which white servicemen and civilian mobs staged at least five nights of terror, attacking Latino and African American zoot-suiters, beating them and ripping off their clothing while the police followed behind, arresting the victims.[20]

Such incidents were the primary catalyst for the formation of Los Angeles' first African American street gangs, which emerged during the late 1940s as a defensive response to white violence in the schools and streets.[21] Racial gang wars erupted, for instance, at Manual Arts High in 1946, at Canoga Park High in 1947, and at John Adams Junior High in 1949. Whereas Chicano gangs were generally turf-bound, based in tiny enclaves, black gangs tended to surface in the marginal areas close to whites and drew members from a larger social space. Black youths thus were able to vie with whites over the social space of schools and entertainment areas.[22] In the mid-1950s South Central gangs such as the Businessmen, Slausons, Farmers, Parks, Outlaws, Watts, Boot Hill, Roman Twenties, and later the Gladiators and Rebel Rousers, served as the architects of social space in the new, usually hostile, settings. There and in neighborhoods of the ghetto's Eastside (i.e., along Central Avenue), where tens of thousands of 1940s and 1950s black immigrants were crammed into the overcrowded, absentee-landlord housing, youth gangs offered "cool worlds" of street socialization for poor young newcomers from rural Texas, Louisiana, and Mississippi.[23]

Unfortunately, these gangs did not have the power to create jobs. The unemployment situation remained critical until war plants finally decided to hire a large number of African Americans to remedy the shortage of local labor created by the draft and war effort during World

War II.[24] The shipyards and aircraft industry opened their doors to thousands of black workers. However, many other industries and businesses continued to refuse to hire African Americans for the duration of the war, and many well-trained African Americans could obtain only janitorial or other menial jobs. Blacks comprised a disproportionately large number of workers on night shifts,[25] almost never received jobs that gave them authority over white workers, and were largely excluded from higher-paying positions of responsibility.

After the war, when the white soldiers returned home, there was a marked increase in discriminatory hiring practices in civilian industries, and housing discrimination once again intensified. As the African American population in the city grew (it more than doubled in the 1940s), so did the use of restrictive covenants, so that most African Americans remained confined by prewar boundaries, a containment that only served to worsen already congested living conditions.[26] African Americans faced housing discrimination in other ways as well. In Watts, for example, African American home buyers almost always had to pay more for a home or apartment than a white buyer. To meet the higher prices, black families often had to take in boarders, a social capital custom that placed a burden on everybody. In addition, blacks paid more for mortgages, fire insurance, and home repairs, and found it extremely difficult to secure credit for the equity in their homes.[27]

The entrance of blacks into surrounding communities was also resisted in other ways after the war, some highly visible. For example, the rejuvenated Klan burned crosses on the lawns of blacks who had moved into white neighborhoods. Ultimately, African Americans were able to escape the ghetto to surrounding communities, but in doing so they merely widened the ghetto's boundaries.[28]

Interestingly, housing and residential barriers created a different type of African American organizational tradition, making social boundaries more important than spatial arrangements. Social linkages between residents of different residential areas affected the structure of black gangs. As noted, territorial boundaries were less important than the social connections and relationships among gang members, who easily encompassed a wider area, creating gangs that were more confederations than single entities.

It was also during this time that serious juvenile delinquency among black youths became a widespread problem. In addition to the barriers and obstacles mentioned above, recreational opportunities and playgrounds for children in this overcrowded environment were scarce, and such facilities were often located near dangerous streets. Dedicated men started scout units for these youths. Nevertheless, even in the scouts or such organizations as the YMCA, opportunities for African Americans remained very limited. In the summer, the municipal swimming pools only admitted African Americans and Latinos on special days, after which the pools were drained and then refilled.[29] Furthermore, with no enforcement of zoning codes, warehouses and junkyards sprang up all over, creating an unsafe, dirty, and vermin-infested environment.[30]

In 1940, females made up 44.1 percent of the African American workforce, but the corresponding figure for whites was 35.8 percent. The larger percentage of working females in the black community is still a problem that reflects the difficulty black males have always had in finding work.[31] Prolonged separation from children on the part of the working mother may have fostered juvenile delinquency and later the formation of female gangs,[32] which mirror the tradition of self-reliance on the part of African American women. In contrast to other ethnic groups, whose notion of tradition means the old-country customs, tradition for blacks implies a long history of survival against tremendous odds, with females fighting alongside males from the beginning.

Watts, which became famous in 1965 for the first urban revolt of the turbulent 1960s, serves as an excellent example of the process of community deterioration resulting from discriminatory practices. In the post-Depression era, it was a blue-collar community which depended on other areas for service providers such as doctors, lawyers, and schoolteachers. There were few businesses in Watts and virtually no government agencies or institutions. As a result of the limited economic base, the infrastructure and environment began to gradually worsen. Homeowner unemployment and low-paying jobs caused many mortgages to be foreclosed, and whites residing in the area began to flee to the outer suburbs. African Americans, however, were forced to stay because of economic discrimination and restricted housing elsewhere. African Americans continued to move into the area because of the lower rents. New home-building could not keep up with demand, and overcrowding became the standard. The community nearly doubled in size between 1940 and 1946, with 11,817 African Americans moving in and 1,661 whites leaving. Whites in Watts were now outnumbered two to one. For the first time, Watts was an

African American neighborhood, and feelings of isolation and despair were high.

From 1953 to 1955 Watts was the center of an experiment in housing. During this time a number of housing projects were under construction, among them Jordan Downs (700 units housing 2,940 people) and William Nickerson Jr. Gardens (1,110 units housing 4,662 people).[33] Along with the Imperial Courts project, housing was thus introduced into Watts for nearly 10,000 people in an area with only 26,000 residents. By the end of the 1950s, more than one-third of Watts residents lived in public housing, triggering a dependency that undermined the foundation of the community. As one author wrote, "The social fabric of the community could not withstand the strain. Churches and civic groups which had been recognized in the community for years had to struggle to preserve a shred of identity."[34] The African American community found itself overburdened and without the social and professional infrastructure to tend to needs of the residents such as medical care, school curricula, transportation, crime, and housing. Ironically, public housing was introduced to counter the effects of racism by providing decent, affordable housing, but the results only complicated the initial difficulties associated with racism. Furthermore, admission to the new projects was dictated by financial need, thus mandating a uniformly low economic level for new residents, who were mostly "aid seekers" and largely strangers to the community, with no ties to anyone or anything local.

Efforts were made to combat community decay, of course. In areas where the small numbers of middle-class and well-to-do blacks resided, spacious, well-kept homes were the rule, and throughout the community individual homeowners and neighborhood associations did their best to ward off a group sense of malaise. Larger organizations such as the African American churches, the Young Men's Christian Association, the Urban League, and the NAACP also persevered. Nevertheless, there was a continuing, seemingly inexorable decline. Indeed, "in the cramped clubs [of Watts], people . . . drank alcoholic beverages, played cards, and generally tried to escape the worries of the preceding week."[35] On the streets, homicides, stabbings, shootings, and fistfights became less uncommon.

Political leadership was also a problem, since virtually no African American elected officials lived in Watts. Residents had almost no access to the power structure to bargain with whites. Unemployment was high. Public transportation was too slow and inefficient and incomes too low to make automobiles affordable, which precluded use of the freeways to reach jobs outside the city's perimeter. All these factors acted on and reacted to one another to ghettoize the African American community. As one researcher noted:

> Los Angeles did not preserve its mid-twentieth century ghetto by
> legal or physical barriers, but by economic constraints. Residency in
> the bulging ghetto was maintained and enforced by the cost-segrega-
> tion of shelter along with the price of transportation.[36]

African American buyers found that the new tract houses, once they were legally available, were cheapest in the suburbs, but the cost of traveling to work each day tended to offset the bargain prices. Furthermore, new housing required prior savings for the down payment, the outlying sites were served exclusively by automobile transportation, and financing policies were largely exclusionary and based on race. Oliver and Shapiro (1995) have underscored how a lack of assets has plagued the black community for decades.

Integration in the 1950s perhaps paradoxically hurt the African American community in Los Angeles by eroding much of its remaining cohesiveness.[37] As racial barriers were relaxed and broken, especially through challenges in the courts in the late 1940s, social restrictions were eased but not economic hindrances. The African American community continued to deteriorate. African Americans with the money, education, or means to take advantage of the new opportunities were now able to move out of ghetto areas. With this flight of the middle class, no longer did the poorer African Americans have the benefit of direct and indirect contact with successful African Americans. As one author writes:

> As long as these communities reflected every strata of economic
> achievement, children, though still exposed to the criminals, gam-
> blers, and drug addicts, developed a greater sense of career and edu-
> cational possibilities. Also as the more affluent departed, the per-
> centage of home ownership declined and the physical structures
> began to reflect the decay that often accompanies landlord neglect.
> And so begins the cycle that leads to poverty and despair.[38]

The segment of the African American community left in the ghetto

Storefront church reaches out.

was forced to adapt to an increased level of marginality and neglect. African Americans continued to be excluded from the growing number of blue-collar construction and aerospace jobs, which required little education and were learned on the job. Thus, youths who had gone to high school—whether graduates or dropouts—could not take advantage of an expanding local economy. Median incomes in South Central declined by nearly a tenth, and African American unemployment rose from 12 percent to 20 percent overall, and to 30 percent in Watts, between 1959 and 1965. In 1964 two Watts residents wrote of the kind of impact such an environment had on the youth:

> It has often been stated that the number one motive for juvenile crime is not necessity, but sheer lack of anything else to do. Therefore it can safely be concluded that if there was more for idle hands to do, there would be less juvenile crime, resulting in less upset in the life of ghetto individuals. . . . Cultural depression, lack of pride, resulting in mass feelings of inferiority, all together make an excellent setting for the role that the many social problems play in the lives of the people in Watts.[39]

In the 1960s the civil rights movement and the War on Poverty brought a glimmer of hope that grew from within and without the black community. As the civil rights movement became more widespread and achieved successive victories, more militant elements, such as the Black Panthers in 1967, began to attract and recruit street youths and gang members; the latter were ready-made fighters. Concurrently, the War on Poverty created many programs for youth in Los Angeles, as elsewhere in the nation. Among them were Teen Posts and Neighborhood Youth Corps (NYC), both of which kept street kids in over 135 neighborhoods, barrios, and ghettos off the streets and involved in constructive activities, even working and earning a modest income. Harnessing gang members' energies in these militant and constructive ways effectively redirected them away from gang goals and routines. For a few years in the late 1960s the gang phenomenon seemed to have reached a plateau in the Los Angeles area.

For law enforcement, the involvement of youths in civil disobedience, protests, and the like changed matters very little, as they were still considered lawbreakers. Even the constructive Teen Posts and NYC did not help matters, because police looked on all poor, marginal neighborhoods as on the side of the bad guys. For the youths themselves, it meant everything. Instead of fighting among themselves or falling into a life of crime, the youths now felt they had a purpose, a higher meaning. They thus joined with others to fight the social system that kept them down. Ironically, it was that same social system's War on Poverty that helped them spend time constructively, do work in the community, and earn some money.

During one protest at a local whites-only drive-in restaurant, for instance, it was the timely arrival of the Slausons gang, based in the Fremont High area, which saved the protestors from an attack by whites. In this way, gangs such as the Slausons and the Gladiators (from the 54th Street area) became a crucial social base for the rise of the local black liberation movement.[40] The ideology and example of the Black Panthers Party (BPP) permeated the streets, as many black youths became involved in the movement and focused much of their energy on addressing police brutality.

> Ex-gang members such as Ron Wilkins created the Community
> Action Patrol to monitor police abuses and William Sampson (ex-
> gang member of the Slausons) along with Gerald Aubry (ex-gang

member of the Orientals) started *Sons of Watts*, whose key function was to "police the police." The BPP [Black Panther Party] organized the *Black Student Union* on several high school campuses in Los Angeles and the *Black Congress* . . . for Black residents [concerned with] community issues.[41]

Following the Watts revolt of August 1965, rival gang hostilities were put aside to some degree for a period of three to four years. Many street gang members, males and females, focusing on their shared hostility toward the police, started speaking of the 1965 disturbances as the "Great Rumble." The Black Panthers were especially popular among street youths who immersed themselves in the "Black Power Revolution," including young women, who became prominent among the local leaders of this movement. The abrupt destruction of the Panthers and the cutbacks in War on Poverty programs probably contributed to the acceleration of street gangs in the early 1970s. With the decline of the Black Panthers and other street-based black-identity groups, "youth looking for a new identity began to mobilize as street gangs . . . as they did in the 1950s and early 1960s."[42] The first Crips gang was formed in 1969 and soon caught the attention of the authorities and the media; Crippettes soon formed as the female counterpart.

By the 1970s "Crippin'" (i.e., taking part in Crips activities) had spread through the city as Crip "sets" were established.[43] The first of these, the 107th Street Hoovers, were based in a somewhat unique socio-ecological niche, an interstice created by the preparations for the Century Freeway, which brought a traumatic large-scale removal of housing and destruction of neighborhoods. Many likened it to the effect of a natural disaster, but without the well-wisher sentiment and aid that usually accompanies destructive acts of nature.

A number of independent gangs—e.g., the Brims, Bounty Hunters, Denver Lanes, Athens Park Gang, Bishops, and Pirus (some of them descendants of the pre-Watts gangs)—became federated as the Bloods in response to pressure from the Crips gangs (identified with the color blue). The Bloods (red, obviously) became particularly strong in the black communities in South Central—especially in places on its periphery like Compton—and in outlying communities such as Pacoima, Pasadena, and Pomona. Media attention on the group's activities generated new members and rival gangs for the Crips. By 1972, "three years after the first Crip gang was formed, there were 18 Crip and Blood gangs in Los Angeles."[44] The Crips and the Bloods were the largest of the more than 500 gangs active in Los Angeles in the 1970s, and close to 95 percent of the members of these two confederated gangs were African American. The housing projects built in Watts in the 1950s—Jordan Downs, William Nickerson Jr. Gardens, and Imperial Courts—became the neighborhoods for the Grape Street Crips, the Bounty Hunter Bloods, and the PJ Watts Crips.

The Crips inherited the Panther aura of fearlessness and transmitted the ideology of armed vanguardism. In some instances in the early phases, the Crip insignia continued to denote Black Power, as during the Monrovia riots in 1972 or the Los Angeles school busing crisis of 1977–1979. But too often Crippin' came to represent an escalation of intraghetto violence to Clockwork Orange levels (murder as a status symbol, and so forth).[45] Such behavior was unknown in the days of the Slausons (veterans from that time can't believe how contemporary gangs have broken the moral code of the past) and anathema to everything that the Panthers had stood for:

> If they began as a teenage substitute for the fallen Panthers, they
> evolved through the 1970s into a hybrid of teen cult and proto-
> Mafia. At a time when economic opportunity was draining away
> from South Central Los Angeles, the Crips were becoming the
> power resource of last resort for thousands of abandoned youth.[46]

The proliferation of gangs from the 1970s to the present has been an end result of the breakdown—or absence—of social control by the institutions that should have provided it.

What began as a relatively promising life for African Americans in Los Angeles has been transformed. Human will and social resources can compensate only so much for limited economic opportunities and access to power. Once, extended family support systems had helped with the care of children, job networks had ensured that work was made available for relatives, and homeownership instilled pride. Then came an unraveling of social control institutions, including family and schools.

Economic discrimination began to undermine the family. Over the years, overcrowding and competition for jobs among the sharply increasing ghetto population strained social life. Migrant newcomers who arrived just before, during, and after World War II were poorer, less skilled, and mostly rural. Racial discrimination and the widespread economic downturn of the 1930s brought very high rates of long-term unemployment to the community. Black women often felt forced to seek work, since the men could not find jobs. As a result, tensions between working wives and unemployed husbands often led to marital discord and separation, while unmarried women who found work grew wary of linking their destinies to men who were not working.

In more and more households, fathers were either absent or only tenuously connected with their children, which led to a lack of positive male role models for such children. Working women who spent considerable time away from their homes and children often were able to manage their mother-centered households satisfactorily and inculcate in their sons and daughters a positive sense of self-worth and gender identification, but unfortunately if understandably not all fared so well in such circumstances.

When racial barriers were relaxed after World War II, upwardly mobile skilled and professional blacks left the ghetto for more upscale neighborhoods.[47] Even though William J. Wilson focused on Chicago, his research can be applied to how Central Avenue was transformed when time and place are considered. These demographic changes over time robbed the ghetto of its successful members, leaving youth with few conventional, socially mobile role models. As these changes gradually unfolded in combination with other factors, street socialization took its toll and compelled more youths to join gangs. The introduction of public housing into the ghettos to fill the need for affordable housing, as well as the concentration of poor and low-income peoples in such areas, further contributed to an increase in the number of unsuccessful residents, thus ensuring that available positive role models were kept to a minimum and that the role models who were around belonged to the street.

The educational establishment historically has a poor record in training and preparing black youth for the future. Since the demise of slavery, African Americans have struggled mightily to right the wrongs of the past, including the schooling obstacles that have plagued blacks from the beginning: segregated and inferior schools; inadequate and shoddy materials; undemanding, culturally biased (and downright racist!) curricula; insensitive, poorly prepared, and unaccountable teachers; ability tracking; inferior testing; and poor counseling. During the 1970s, the Los Angeles Unified School District was ordered to desegregate its de facto racially separated schools with busing. This course of action would bring poor black and other minority children to schools in affluent areas where teachers and students were better and more advanced and thus, it was inferred, would help to raise the educational levels of transferred students.[48] The study habits and learning abilities of the good students, it was thought, would rub off on the poor students. This did not happen, however, because busing damaged the traditional concept (and benefits) of community schools. Neither children nor teachers were adequately prepared to deal with the obstacles that the children's different backgrounds presented, and were unable to overcome it. White parents pulled their children out of newly integrated schools, and thus the busing remedy probably caused more problems than it solved.

Resources for our school systems continue to dwindle—the per capita student expenditure has fallen and the Los Angeles Unified School District (the nation's second-largest district with over 700,000 students in the late 1990s) has a dropout rate of 30 to 50 percent in the inner city. Sadly, schools take a backseat to the criminal justice apparatus. The contrast between the two institutions, certainly key to how social control is established and maintained, is astounding, as many more billions of dollars are spent on criminal justice operations than on educational matters. Currently, African American males from South Central Los Angeles are three times more likely to end up in prison than on a University of California campus.[49] Increased numbers of violent street-socialized youths often change local schools from safe havens into new breeding grounds for gang conflicts.

Although family and schools often have failed black youth, the criminal justice system has been an even worse offender, ensuring that the population remains out of control. Police, courts, and prisons have historically practiced an unofficial type of racism when dealing with the black community—harsher treatment, uneven application of the law, and higher incarceration rates. It is a nationwide record, and in recent decades Los Angeles has been one of the leading centers of this institutionalized legal inequality. This is evident from a recitation of only the well-publicized outbreaks of police-community hostility: the Zoot Suit Riots, the Watts revolt, the Panther shoot-out, the Symbionese Liberation Front shoot-out, the Eula Love killing,[50] and the Rodney King riots. The current Los Angeles Police Department's Ramparts Station scandal is a reminder of this bleak record.[51] Statistical data also reveal the disparately high proportion of blacks arrested, convicted, and imprisoned.[52]

For gang youth, so recent in Los Angeles' history, the stories throughout the decades signify hostility, harassment, brutality, and a general trend of "hook and book" with little provocation. For blacks, it is the Napoleonic law that applies: guilty until proven innocent. This is evidenced further by Driving While Black (DWB), the widespread practice of racial profiling that infuriates the black community. Police patrol cars stop and question black auto drivers for no reason except that they "look suspicious"—because they are black.

The attitudes and behavior of some members of the African American community have changed for the worse, especially in the poorest, most rundown sections of town. In the past, job barriers and discrimination shaped the attitude "Why try if they won't hire me anyway?" More recently, a related attitude has been emerging: "Why behave if they're going to charge me for something I didn't do?" A vicious cycle has resulted, with bad attitudes held by both police and community generating miscommunication, misunderstanding, and a sense of persecution.

The two largest law enforcement agencies in Los Angeles that patrol and police the streets set up specialized units to focus exclusively on gangs and gang members. The Los Angeles County Sheriff's Department had Operation Safe Streets (OSS) and the Los Angeles Police Department its counterpart, Community Resources Against Street Hoodlums (CRASH); the former is now Safe Streets Bureau (SSB), while the latter was disbanded in the wake of the Ramparts police station scandal. These units were designed to infiltrate gangs and gather intelligence on street affairs (sometimes bending the law to do so), with the goal of preventing gang violence and apprehending known gang members who were violently out of control. Such streets units have been augmented and supplemented by similarly gang-focused prosecutors (e.g., Operation Hardcore, created by the district attorney's office), parole and probation officers, and prison functionaries. The Los Angeles Police Department even purchased an armored, quasi-military vehicle, the Hammer, to break down doors and walls of alleged gang drug dealers' strongholds.

Yet the harnessing and concentration of so many resources on street gangs has not effectively curtailed the growth and spread of street gangs throughout the city. After the 1992 Rodney King rioting, black gangs in

Street socialization affects females, too.

particular attempted with considerable success to impose a moratorium on gang conflict. These peace initiatives helped reduce gang homicide rates for a time, but the pleas of gang members and reformers for social, recreation, and economic alternatives for street youth have gone largely unheeded.

In the context of all the problems in the home, in the schools, and with law enforcement, and given the absence of training and employment opportunities, it is inevitable that many youths will embrace gangs as a buffer to help them negotiate adolescence and street life. Female gang members, who face pressures and obstacles similar to those that males do in a life of exclusion and poverty, are affected in ways that compound their sense of hopelessness and despair. Within the street-socialized gang group, they must also deal with the aura of dominance that permeates the street, a place that males feel is their own. Working within the tradition of self-reliance that is their history, black female gang members strongly follow a sisterhood ethic that helps them to navigate through various friend or foe networks.

For many of the youths I interviewed, the initial attraction to the gang was an older role model, perhaps a brother or an uncle. I have heard too often the refrain, "I wanted to be like my brother, so when he joined the gang I decided then to join the gang too." Later, after being acclimated to gang life, youths speak of the gang, not in terms of an organization or a physical entity, but of feelings of love, camaraderie, and support. For example, one youth defined the importance of a gang as

> a feeling of knowing that you can always call on people. . . . Most people have this thing about gangs. They think it's about turf, and money and shooting. It ain't—it's about respect.

Peer pressure also is an important factor in understanding the attractiveness of gangs.[53] The youths fear being "marked out," that is, accused of being afraid to join the gang or not supporting their homeboys in tough situations. Sometimes meetings are even called to have the marked youth explain his failure; if his response is unsatisfactory, he faces a beating or being kicked out of the neighborhood. Finally, in understanding the reasons why youths are attracted to gangs, we should not underestimate the basic human desire to be known, to be recognized, to be applauded for one's prowess or accomplishments. Frustrated in school and with few economic opportunities, many youths turn to gangs to fill their longing for self-esteem and the esteem of their peers, to become a ghetto hero, as Shakur (a.k.a. Monster Kody) (1993) states. Gang youths often simply say, "I joined the gang because I wanted to be known. I wanted to be somebody."

In the 1980s, the unemployment rate for African American youth was a staggering 45 percent. How can it come as a surprise that the underground economy, particularly the illicit drug industry, became a major problem in these circumstances? Although we cannot say with certainty that drugs fueled the rise of gangs, or vice versa, it is clear that these two factors—drugs and gangs—share a close symbiotic relationship. Numerous youths I interviewed repeatedly brought up this relationship. For example, one youth told me:

> I started getting in gangs because of the money, you know, selling drugs. I started hanging out a lot with drug dealers that used to gangbang a long time ago, but they started selling drugs.

Another youth simply said:

> I started to sell drugs because it was the only thing I could do.

Of course, an integral factor in the attraction of the drug trade is strictly economic; drugs are a ghetto opportunity structure. During the 1980s, for example, 40 percent of African American children lived below or barely above the poverty line. In addition, politically motivated attacks on programs instituted during the War on Poverty led to the end of most of them, leaving inner city African American and Latino youth with nowhere to turn. Indeed, with the dismantling of the Neighborhood Youth Corps (NYC) and the termination of the Comprehensive Employment and Training Act (CETA), as well as the ending of Job Corps, this retreat from the inner city had obviously ill effects only slightly offset by the Clinton administration's reintroduction of programs such as Ameri-Corps. In any event, for gang members there are still virtually no job alternatives to choose from. As one social worker noted, "You could pull 80 percent of gang members, seventeen years old or younger, out of gangs, if you had jobs, job training and social alternatives."[54]

Although economic rewards are a strong incentive, just as with other ethnic groups in this book, there is tremendous variation in the level and purpose of involvement of each gang member, and the multiple functions that a gang serves. Of course, protection and friendship are always men-

Being a part of a set

tioned, both very practical reasons for joining gangs. However, sometimes the motivation is revenge (when a brother was shot), survival ("it kept me alive"), adventure ("it was fun and free"), fear ("I felt better with my homies"), ego boosting ("I liked the power"), spontaneity ("we could do anything, anytime"), or an outlet from the boredom of a life filled with unstructured time (e.g., one with no home or school supervision or obligations). All of these motivations reflect the fact that, for a disturbingly large proportion of African American youth, street socialization has prevailed over conventional institutions of socialization.

Mookie, whose case history is the subject of the next chapter, is a youth whose life reflects the effects of street socialization and racism over time. It certainly shows how race was a factor in where his parents lived, what school he would attend, and whether he would be able to find a decent job. His parents struck out from Texas to leave a life of blatant racism and extreme poverty. In California they became socially mobile, and like so many parents, they attempted to recapture a youth that had passed them by. They moved several times, eventually residing in an area that was farther west of the black Central Avenue district of earlier

Taking a militant stance

decades. However, this formerly all-white neighborhood had become by then an extension of the ghetto and was rife with Bloods and Crips sets. Mookie's problems stem more from parental omission than commission. He and his brother were farmed out to his grandmother and day care centers. As a young child, Mookie had a lot of freedom and spent an inordinate amount of time in the streets. Play antics soon metamorphosed into gang affiliations and serious trouble, leading eventually to prison.

6

"I Noticed the Problem but Never Had the Cure"

Mookie's Story

THE CALIFORNIA SUN ascends well above the horizon. The tidy neighborhood smells of newly watered earth and cut grass. An elderly woman in a housedress examines her roses with the intensity of a diamond cutter. Folks who work for a living are long gone and those who are left—the preschool children, the retired, and the unemployed—enjoy the long yawn of morning. There is no rush, no road rage, and no need for alarm clocks.

Mookie, a young Crips gangster, sleeps peacefully until his friend appears at the door, a quart of beer in hand. It is sometime between eight and nine o'clock, time to wake up.

After much door pounding, Mookie gets up and opens the door wide for his friend. Accepting the beer, he sits on the couch, ready to make plans for the day.

Mellow from the beer, the friends work up a breakfast of chorizo and eggs. After reviewing the previous evening's activities, their gentle entry into the day is over. It's time to get out and about.

The first stop is a clothing store at Manchester and Vernon. When there's money, it is not unusual for Mookie to ignore his closet at home and buy a new outfit—gang attire, of course. Right now, the right gang style includes khakis, DC pants, DC overalls, Converse All-Stars, and Pendleton shirts.

Around noon, Mookie and his friend finally get to Helen Keller Park, one of their main hangouts. They meet up with four of their homeboys.

Shouting, laughing, joking, they fill each other in about what's going on with the gang (who had a party, who was seen in the neighborhood, rumors of sightings and rumors of rumors). Basically, this is a real kick-back time, a homeroom-orientation period.

The young men stroll home for a late lunch and then they're out again, just walking around. This evening, there is a neighborhood barbecue. After the barbecue, Mookie and his buddy chip in to pay for the food. About nine in the evening they head to a corner not far from Mookie's home to sell some dope. They hang out with some "hood rats," a.k.a. "pussy broads." These young women are typically hooked on drugs and, eager to obtain more, usually willing to barter their bodies. The two "brothers" manage to sell dope worth $100 for $200. They stay at it on this occasion until 2 A.M. Tonight there are no parties, so the night ends when the selling is over.

Shortly after Mookie was born, in 1966, Mookie's family moved from Texas to South Central Los Angeles. He has one brother, several years younger. They live in gang territory. Nevertheless, the homes there are generally appealing, and most in the neighborhood are owned. Mookie's three-bedroom home is no exception.

Mookie's family life is exceptional in at least one way. In a time of high divorce rates, his parents have stayed married. High school sweethearts, they married after graduating (his mother also attended college for a time). She gave birth to Mookie when she was twenty-three. They have worked hard to attain home ownership and their current socioeconomic status. During an interview, she relates:

> Even though I've known for quite a while about my son's problems, I'm still surprised to hear about certain things in court. I wonder why we didn't know more, notice more. Maybe it's because he always kept it out of the house. He knows his father and I grew up poor, both from big families. Our answer was to work, struggle to get out. I work as a clerk and my husband is a machinist. We didn't teach our sons to go this way. We used to spend Saturdays together—shopping, going to the park, all of us, horseback riding. I look back again and again—what happened? I can't see much except to say my son had a lot of peer pressure. He's known those young men since they were all small boys.

Who could foresee gang involvement in the life of a small, quiet, respectful boy?

Mookie's preschool years were unexceptional. He lived with both parents. For four months his grandmother lived with them, and during this time she baby-sat Mookie. Except for this brief period, he was in day care, full-time at first, and later part-time.

> I don't remember much when I was real young, but when I was coming up and it was time for school I remember my mom dropping me off at day care in the morning, and she picked me up there too. I was there maybe three hours a day.

In kindergarten, his teacher wrote:

> He has shown tremendous growth in all academic areas, above average ability, needs to improve effort, enjoys physical activities.

Despite his mother's hectic work schedule, she made sure Mookie attended church and Sunday school weekly. He participated in Pop Warner football for four or five years, his father coaching him. In elementary school he played with the drum corps and orchestra. A neighbor who has known Mookie since he was an infant recalls:

> He was obedient, did what he was told to do. . . . He always showed good manners.

Beneath this picture of stability and harmony, there were real problems. Mookie's father worked long, hard hours and often was not home. He never used drugs but did drink. As with so many other drinkers, alcohol transformed him into an angry person. At times, he got carried away.

> My father, he gets drunk, we knew we better stay out the way. All the things me and my brother do, just running in the house, it didn't normally cause him anger. But when he drank in those days, we knew he'd whup us easy.

Several sources reveal that there was another problem. Apparently, Mookie's father through the years has had numerous affairs. Several women even called the house when Mookie's mother was home. Both parents made efforts to conceal these marital problems, but the impact was real and observable. As Mookie elaborates:

I noticed when I was little that my mother had her friends and my father had his. They went to different events and took separate vacations. Either way, us kids didn't go. Now that I'm older, I realize that's not a normal way to be married and all, but then that's just the way it was. They weren't together much.

As a result of the absences of their father and the frequent vacations and social events of both parents, Mookie and his brother were often in the care of others. Left with friends or in day care, they were safe but notably without consistent, daily parental interaction and supervision.

Mookie and his brother were nevertheless the only children in the neighborhood to live with both parents. His family had a middle-class socioeconomic status. Deeply religious, his mother had the desire to raise her children properly, yet her relationship with her husband was weak and both had poor parenting skills. They occasionally cracked down on their sons, but in between these outbursts would be long periods of benign neglect. The parents provided food and clothing but ignored or did not notice signs that would have alerted many parents—late nights, questionable friends, behavioral and academic problems at school, and involvement in violent incidents.

My parents didn't know most of the things that were happening. When I was about seven, a bully three or four years older used to threaten me, push me around, punch me. Usually he got me when I was walking home. I was scared and crying. I used to hide in my house. Another thing, there was this O.G. [veteran gangster]. Everybody in the neighborhood, they was scared of him. He drinked every day—an alcoholic, you know. He used to make us steal beer for him. He always told us he would whup us if we didn't listen to him. The funny thing is, even though we had to do what he said because we was scared, he would still give us a dollar sometimes. Then we would go buy some ten-cent candy—buy some Now and Laters.

Mookie's parents were law abiding and hardworking, but what positive influence they could offer was diminished because they spent little time with their sons. Mookie and his brother found themselves drawn to the streets. Mookie explains his situation then:

I grew up in the streets. I saw drug dealers, winos, and prostitutes. It wasn't the street people who messed with me the most. It was other kids. My parents thought it would be better if I went to a Catholic school. That was a big mistake, but it didn't last long. Now everybody in my own neighborhood started chasing me because now I was different, you know—funny clothes and all.

The gang subculture was an omnipresent component of Mookie's life. The immediate area is home to at least nine gangs; most are African American. They include the Athens Park Boys, Payback Crips, G13, Shotgun Crips, Raymond Crips, Harvard Gangster Crips, 111th Street Neighborhood Crips, 112th Street Hoover Crips, Denver Lane Bloods, and South Los. Some are allies and some are enemies.

The gang I joined is one part of the Crips. They've been there as long as I can remember. It just seemed that as I got older, that's the thing you would do—join up one day.

Despite his good start in school, Mookie began to adapt to the street behavior he absorbed daily.

Finally, I got tired of being chased. When Pirate, who later on became one of my homeboys, slapped me in front of an O.G., I jumped on his bike and took off. Later that day I saw him at the arcade and I knew he was going to get me, so I kicked his ass first. That was the first time I fought and it was out of fear. After that, I got a little respect and I even started hanging out with some of the guys. I actually started to do some crimes—mainly to have fun and be with my friends. Like we shot up some pigeons at the water tank with a BB gun. We did get caught, and some worker from the Department of Water and Power brought us home. We got in trouble from our parents. I got put on punishment that time. I had to do my brother's chores for a week plus mine. I remember we used to go to Ascot Racing and stole bikes to get the parts. We didn't get caught on that, though.

Mookie brought his new behavior with him into the classroom. By fifth and sixth grades, his teachers consistently noted this change. One report describes him as having a "defiant, impudent attitude" and being "easily provoked by peers."

Mookie began to smoke marijuana and drink regularly. At fourteen, he was drinking a quart of beer and smoking two to three joints a day. At age 15, he began using cocaine. About this age he also was introduced to the moneymaking potential of dealing drugs.

> I was kicking at my friend's house. His big brother was there, doing some kind of deal. I think it was cocaine. After the guy left and everything, big brother asks me to count his money. When I was done, he peels off six hundreds for me. Man, all I knew was that was when I wanted to sell dope. I saw what it could do. Why make a couple bucks an hour? Make more, easier job.

Mookie's academic performance, already poor, now deteriorated significantly. He attended three different junior high schools because of behavior problems. Regularly involved in conflicts with other students, he had a reputation as a troublemaker. His grades were C's and D's.

At this time, Mookie embarked on a very interesting relationship. A coworker of his mother stopped by one evening. Cathy was a white woman ten years his senior. They chatted for a while. She offered Mookie some work; she needed just a little help moving furniture. From that time on, Mookie, and sometimes a few of his friends, would stop by to visit. They would tell her their troubles, and she would give them advice. Cathy, during an interview, remembers:

> In those visits, I never saw a rough, tough character. He was just a young boy who was so helpful. If he saw my trash was full, he would take it out. I'm married, but during that time I was having some trouble and Mookie encouraged me to stay with my husband, to work things out. I tried to help him too, to tell him to stay out of trouble. He would always listen politely. He told me his mother didn't approve of us being friends, but it was a good friendship.

Mookie's mother did not approve of the relationship. She bristled when she was asked about it.

> I feel that that Cathy betrayed me. I had told this so-called friend that my son was skipping school. Later on, I find out that she is lending Mookie her car during the school day! Later on, Cathy doesn't know this, but I discovered pictures she sent my son, and I am certain the relationship was not what Mookie said it was—just a friendship.

Unable to stop the relationship but hoping to help Mookie's academic situation, his parents sent him, once again, to a suburban Catholic school, a high school with only a few African Americans. Mookie was taunted and ostracized.

> They thought my clothes were funny, the way I walked, everything.
> So I tried to look like it didn't bother me, so then I was "Mr.
> Bigshot." There was no way going to be a friendship and no girls
> neither. At least in my other school, the girls wanted to be with me.
> They liked to be with a gangbanger 'cause they knew if anybody
> messed with them, they could tell their boyfriend. I hated it at my
> new school, so I started ditching class and just spending time with
> my homeboys in the neighborhood.

One night when Mookie was fifteen, just fooling around with his friends, they noticed an empty house.

> You've got to realize, I keep my lives separate. I never had any trou-
> ble at my house, no parties, no messing up in my parents' home. So
> we were in the street, at the park a lot, you know? When we saw
> this house, it was like an opportunity to just kick back out of the
> night. We turned on a radio and that's when some neighbors called
> the police. So we were arrested, but they just talked to us and let
> us go.

At sixteen, Mookie was arrested twice for theft. The first time, he was apprehended outside an Alpha Beta store and accused of petty theft. He denied stealing anything and was released.

Since Catholic school had failed to redeem their son, Mookie's parents gave in and allowed him to transfer, in eleventh grade, to a South Central high school. This high school, however, had a substantial rival gang population that was happy to spend time harassing and challenging Mookie.

Mookie spent much of his time with his friends in his neighborhood—they knew each other very well. All the little boys from the neighborhood were growing older. In a steady march, childish pranks and petty crimes gave way to more serious, even deadly, crimes. Mookie's efforts leaned more and more toward achieving an image in the arena that counted for him, his gang.

I saw the older homeboys. I saw who had the money, girls, whatever they wanted. Shit. That was my inspiration.

"Jumping-in," the traditional initiation event for a new male gang member, involves the initiate's getting beat up by his future gang brothers. He shakes hands with a circle of youths and then, for about ten seconds, they all punch and kick him. He can try to fight back, but the most important thing is that he stand tough, take it like a man, and he'll be okay. He'll be one of them, they'll be one with him. Since Mookie grew up in the neighborhood, he was not jumped into the gang. Instead, to join it Mookie had to participate in a drive-by shooting.

One night his homeboys drove him to the house of a rival gang member. They asked him if he was ready to "go blast." They told him when to shoot. He obeyed and, to this day, neither Mookie nor his friends know if the shots fired that night caused damage or injuries.

I just closed my eyes and started shooting. Then we just drove away. I don't know if I hurt anybody. I knew I was going to do it so, at that time, you try not to think too much.

Just a few months later, still 16 years old, Mookie and some friends were arrested on a felony charge—grand theft auto. On a mild March evening, Felipe, a neighbor, pulled up to his home a couple of blocks from Mookie's house and parked his cousin's motorcycle. Exhausted from his job at a body shop, he was grateful to have transportation. His own car was out of commission and his cousin had been kind enough to loan him the bike.

Opening the front door, he heard a car door slam. Turning, he spotted his friend Manuel arriving. They had plans to have a beer together and watch a basketball game on TV. Felipe welcomed his friend inside and they were soon parked on the couch, watching the game and eating sandwiches.

Their relaxation was interrupted by a knock at the door. Felipe opened the door to a complete stranger. The middle-aged man looked nervous.

"Excuse me. Did you have a motorcycle out front?"

"Yes," Felipe replied, immediately looking past the man to the empty spot at the curb. "What happened?"

"I just saw four black guys take it."

Felipe exploded out the front door, with Manuel following. They jumped in Manuel's LTD and started searching. Sure enough, driving south on Hoover Avenue, they caught sight of the four juveniles. Mookie was sitting on the bike and the others were pushing.

When the teens realized they were being pursued, they dropped the motorcycle and ran into an alley. The LTD followed them into the alley, where Felipe witnessed the thieves running between the backyards of two houses. He directed Manuel around the corner, so they were positioned at the front yards of the houses. There was Mookie, standing in one of the front yards.

"Hey, punk, what were you doing with my motorcycle?" yelled Felipe.

"What motorcycle?" replied Mookie.

"You just jumped off of it and ran. Why're you sweating, man?"

"I don't know what the fuck you're talking about. Get off my property, asshole!"

"Okay, smart guy. I'm calling the cops," Felipe stated as he got into the car. Mookie then picked up a brick and threw it at the LTD, leaving a six-inch dent on the roof.

"Go ahead and call them, motherfucker!"

Felipe and Manuel left the residence and recovered the motorcycle. Returning to Felipe's residence, they kept their promise and called the police. After hearing the details, the arriving officers, with Felipe and Manuel, returned to Mookie's residence. When officers knocked on the door, Mookie answered. After the officers asked him to step outside, Felipe was able to positively identify him as the motorcycle rider and brick thrower. Mookie was quickly arrested and handcuffed.

Mookie denied any participation in the theft. His mother, home at the time, talked with the officers.

> I've warned him so many times about hanging out with the wrong
> kind of people. Now, if he was guilty here, I would not defend him,
> but I think he has been falsely accused. I've still got to say, though,
> that this might be the lesson he needs, and if it gets him on the right
> track, well, maybe it'll be good for his future.

Mookie's future did take a turn at this point. He was charged with a felony for the motorcycle theft, along with a misdemeanor charge for damaging the car with a rock. Since he was never caught in the drive-by shooting, this was his first felony charge and conviction, and he was sent to a California Youth Authority (CYA) facility.

Mookie arrived at Karl Holton School shortly before his nineteenth birthday. He told a social worker:

> I know the way I go off is wrong, and I know I've got to work on it. I'm ready to do that and, hopefully, finish high school and do some college too.

He was assigned a counselor, who sat down with Mookie and helped him to set some goals. The goals included managing his anger and stress, attending drug and alcohol counseling, and stopping his delinquent, gang-related behavior. They wrote up contracts and Mookie attended group counseling sessions. Mookie told his counselor:

> I live two lives. The drugs and gang is one life. The other life is with my family. My gang life was always important to me because, since I was young, they were the best friends I made. The drugs I took for fun. I'm starting to see I can't do them if I want my mind to stay strong. I hurt my family, too, so I guess I didn't do a good job of keeping those lives separate.

Over the next eight months, Mookie made real efforts to change. He had few behavior problems. He took the General Education Development (GED) test, a high school equivalency exam, and passed. Counseling sessions continued and Mookie attended regularly. He began to write weekly letters to his parents. Nearing the time of his parole, he wrote:

> I know I acted like I didn't care about you and I don't know if I can ever make up for what I've been before, but I am sorry to you. I don't want to be that person anymore. I feel strong about it, but I know coming home is a test. I want to start over.

Mookie's parents, knowing that serving his parole in the old neighborhood was risky for him, contacted relatives in Texas with a proposition. Would they be willing to let Mookie stay with them while he was serving parole? After much discussion, including expressions of concern for their young children, his cousins agreed. Mookie could come to Longview, Texas.

Eight months after his stay began, the CYA released Mookie to serve his parole. His case was assigned to an officer in Longview. There are no records that Mookie had any serious problems while he was outside of California. However, less than two months after his arrival, Mookie concluded that he was unhappy with Longview.

> I just didn't like Longview. My parole officer was crazy, acting scared of me all the time—L.A. gangster and everything. The weather was nasty. I guess I was homesick. It had been a long time since I was home.

Actually, more than two years had passed since Mookie had lived with his family. Since he hadn't found any job whatsoever in Texas, with his parole officer's official permission, he returned to California.

Assigned a new parole officer in Los Angeles, Mookie began, as required, to look for a permanent job. He claimed he was "hoping for maintenance and warehouse work." He wasn't very successful, most likely due to his spotty effort. One parole board report states, "He wasn't seriously seeking employment." Over the next two years, he held three jobs, lasting from one day to three weeks. His shortest stint was as a high-rise window washer. Hanging on the side of a building from a few cables was more than Mookie's nerves could handle. The agency found him another job, as a warehouse worker for a stereo manufacturer. Unfortunately, they needed him for only three weeks.

After a few months at home, Mookie began to have a hard time adjusting to family life. For the first time in his life, he fought frequently with his parents. Because of all the conflict, his parole officer decided to move him into a group home.

> After I got out of CYA, when I got home I got more respect from the homeboys. I got recognition. Even though I thought I was done with it, I really wasn't. I meant to stay out of it, but I started to get drawn back. Also, it was a lot harder to get along with my parents. I wasn't used to living with them and them telling me what to do.

The group home was less restrictive than his parents', so Mookie had a lot of time between his infrequent jobs to further renew old friendships and habits. He reconnected with his set in the Crips and began, once again, abusing drugs.

Seven months after his release from custody, during a routine drug test, Mookie tested positive for cocaine. He claimed that, even though he had used cocaine in the past, he had only used it this one time since his parole. He stated that he found some cocaine on the bus bench and put it in a cigarette and smoked it. The parole board ordered him to spend sixty days in jail for this violation of parole. When his release was imminent, the board reviewed his case and history and judged that Mookie should continue on parole and be required to return to the home of his parents, "as they provide structure and discipline." He was also ordered to attend an outpatient substance abuse program and an employment preparation program.

After he returned home, Mookie contacted his old friend Cathy. She hadn't seen him in over two years. She was glad to hear from him, but was shocked when he showed up at her door. Gone was the false bravado, the little boy. The 20-year-old man who stood before her didn't look like he was acting the part anymore. He was as respectful as ever but seemed set on who he was, no longer trying to maintain two personas. When they talked, Cathy told him it was her turn now to encourage him to do right:

> I told him maybe he wasn't trying, like he used to, to respect his parents. They hadn't changed, whatever problems they had. He had changed. Maybe that's why now he had fights with them. That never happened before.

Mookie listened, behaving just like his old self, thanked her, and left. He took another temporary job as a parking lot attendant. This job only lasted ten days. Mookie did not make much effort to find a new one.

The CYA can order confinement of a youth for only so long, and Mookie became even more lax in his efforts to fulfill the requirements of his parole. When he had only two months left, his parole officer placed him in the county jail for one week because of his failure to seek employment. After his release, the officer ordered Mookie to wear an electronic bracelet at all times. He thought that he would then be more likely to look for a job. However, Mookie, knowing that the CYA's hold on him was expiring, began to do as he pleased. Even though he had a 7 P.M. curfew, he stayed out later whenever he wanted to. He violated curfew on seven occasions over a few weeks' time. The monitor reflected that on some evenings Mookie would be home by his curfew but would leave the house at midnight and return at four or five in the morning. Another drug test came back positive, again for cocaine. One month before the expiration of CYA's authority over him, Mookie was arrested at his home for violating his parole. Since time was running out, the violation was not taken to the parole board.

By this time, drug use and drug dealing had increased exponentially in South Central. In Mookie's neighborhood, strangers sometimes would bring their wares to sell to locals and to other outsiders who drove through the neighborhood looking for a chance to score. Local gang members would often insist on a cut of the outside dealer's revenues, which occasionally would lead to a conflict. One day a younger gang member killed such an outside dealer.

Like other sidewalk shootings, the crime scene within a few moments was vacant save for the dealer's body. A neighbor, hearing the shot, called the police. In a few minutes, curious neighbors, now sure the shooting was over, began to come out. The police arrived at an all-too-common scene: the body was surrounded by people, including children, but not one witness could be found.

No witnesses and the lack of evidence suggested that this case would remain unsolved. The loss of the dealer did not exactly raise an outcry in the community. Nevertheless, detectives decided to canvass the neighborhood, hopeful that someone would talk. They were lucky—a witness to the murder turned up, a street person, a fixture in the neighborhood. When interviewed by detectives, the witness named one of Mookie's friends as the shooter.

Before the case could come to trial, however, the witness was murdered at a friend's home. The friend, with support from others, identified Mookie as the man who they saw running from the home after hearing the victim's screams.

Mookie's friend was never convicted of the murder of the street dealer. However, there was a murder trial for Mookie. This time, the witnesses remained alive to testify and, in short course, Mookie was sentenced to life in prison for murder in the first degree. Mookie was 26 years old.

Looking back, Mookie laments his gang involvement:

> The gang shit fucked me up. I could have done the probation if it weren't for that. I did the program. I had a top job. It's just the gang stuff. . . . I want to stop banging, but it's hard when you're around gangbangers. It was mostly the Hoover Crips that have been against me. They swore that I shot one of their homeboys. This has been most of my problem here in prison.

Mookie no longer feels close to his homeboys:

> At first they seem like your best friends for life. They risk their lives for you, push you out of the way of a bullet. . . . that's why we call them homeboys. But when you get locked up it all changes. They move on with their lives. I don't get packages or nothing. They don't even write.

So Mookie remains in prison, now estranged from his homeboys but still threatened because of his past gang activity. Sometimes he turns for consolation, as have countless prisoners, to song—in Mookie's case, to rap music.

Deep Thoughts in My Mind
By Mookie

Sometimes I think back on those days when I was a kid—
I can never go as far back as when I ate from a bib,
But I can strongly remember how my life used to be.
And I remember those days when I used to be free
From the pain and agony of a family mess.
I used to pump myself up, try to stick out my chest
And try to handle it the best way I can,
But then I realize I was just a boy, not a man.
As time went on I grew more mature—
Sometimes I noticed the problem but never had the cure,
Times I didn't have to look for it, 'cause it found me.
I used to look for my parents just to set me free,
But see, they were the problem and now I'm glad that I know.
Sometimes it hurt so bad that I thought I had to let go.
And if my thoughts were a knife, you take a look and go blind
'Cause it's too hard to comprehend these deep thoughts in my mind.
Comparing now to then is like a dream come true—
The sorrow, the pain, I never thought I'd get through,
But I succeeded and seldom sometimes think back
On this day when I was young and how my life was whack.
But you see, you gonna pull through eventually some day,
But don't take life too fast 'cause you just might pay.
And if you think I ain't real, then check me out these days—
These deep thoughts that I remember can never go away.

7

Vietnamese in Southern California

CHICANO AND AFRICAN AMERICAN gangs have long been part of the Los Angeles scene, where families with deeply rooted histories often include several generations of gang members. Our understanding of street gangs would be incomplete, however, if we did not take into account a much more recent addition to the gang culture— Vietnamese. As immigrants, they are comparative newcomers who did not begin to settle in the Los Angeles area until 1975, after the end of the Vietnam War. Consequently, we do not have much data on the Vietnamese gang phenomenon and even less on female associates. Nevertheless, Vietnamese gangs in the Los Angeles area can be understood in terms of the same multiple marginality framework that has been applied to their African American and Chicano counterparts, for they occupy the same piece of the socioeconomic sidewalk.

To assess the rise of Vietnamese gangs, we need to look back to the Vietnam War and understand some of its ramifications. The Vietnamese presence in the United States prior to the war was minimal—only a few Vietnamese students and scholars. The fall of Saigon to the communists in 1975 set off a chain of events that led to a sudden, massive influx of Vietnamese people into this country. When news of the imminent communist takeover first spread through the streets of Saigon, rumors of an impending bloodbath generated desperate efforts to escape. Many thousands left Saigon to flee Vietnam by boat, leaving behind most of their possessions. Under chaotic circumstances, over 130,000 were able to escape to places of safety in Asia.[1]

These refugees, which have been labeled the "first wave," were later brought to the United States and distributed among four refugee camps.[2] Camp Pendleton, a Marine base located south of Los Angeles, was the site of one of the camps. It housed approximately 40,000 refugees.[3]

The refugees in the first wave were not typical of most Vietnamese. They were generally well educated and came from the elite ranks of Vietnamese society.[4] Many were fluent not only in English but also in French (a vestige of French colonialism), and were remarkably urbanized. They included military officials, politicians, academics, and businessmen, many of whom had ties to the United States through family or professional relations. In addition, and of extreme importance, most of them were able to escape with their families. In Vietnamese culture the family is the central social unit, and its importance to the refugees cannot be underestimated. As one Vietnamese refugee remarked:

> To Vietnamese culture, family is everything. There are aspects which help us readjust to this society. It is easy for us because of [the] tradition of helping in the family.[5]

With their united families, linguistic skills, and socioeconomic and educational background, the first wave of refugees arrived with important assets that would help them acculturate to U.S. society. Yet they did face serious problems, including discrimination. Gallup polls at the time showed that over half of the U.S. public opposed resettlement of the refugees, and opposition was particularly intense in California.[6] As the first-wave refugees from Camp Pendleton moved into the Los Angeles area and their presence increased there, so too did native resentment.

Given the general opposition to these first-wave Vietnamese refugees, President Gerald Ford adopted a policy of dispersing them geographically on their arrival in the country, to prevent imposing an economic burden on any one city.[7] The policy backfired because most Vietnamese felt out of their element in colder climates and in areas where few Asian Americans resided. Many of the dispersed refugees quickly headed to Southern California, attracted by the warm climate, the large numbers of Asians already there, and, most important, the rumored abundance of jobs. A massive secondary migration to California was underway.

Unfortunately, while Southern California did have warm weather and

A thriving mall in Orange County

a growing Vietnamese enclave, it did not have the high-paying jobs the refugees were expecting. A national recession that hit California hard during the late 1970s, coupled with racial discrimination, pushed the Vietnamese to the bottom of the economic ladder. Many of the first-wave refugees, including doctors and professors, were unable to find work, and those who were employed were often working in menial jobs. Nevertheless, many Americans believed Vietnamese refugees were taking away scarce jobs.[8]

Under these circumstances, many Vietnamese turned to their families and extended kin to start their own businesses. Relatives pooled their money and worked in family enterprises from twelve to fourteen hours a day to support themselves. After many long hours, much sacrifice, and united family effort, refugees frequently attained economic prosperity, as evidenced by the number of booming Vietnamese-owned businesses in the Los Angeles area. In particular, the growth of Little Saigon, a business enclave located in Orange County, is dramatic testament to their economic success. Today, Little Saigon alone has more than 2,000 Vietnamese-owned businesses, including several large shopping malls, and generates over $50 million in annual sales.[9]

COSUMNES RIVER COLLEGE
LEARNING RESOURCE CENTER
8401 Center Parkway
Sacramento, California 95823

While refugee parents were working, their children were studying. In time, they flooded into California's universities. Southeast Asians made up over 12 percent of the 1989 freshmen class at the University of California, Irvine (located in Orange County), and they remain a sizable presence throughout the University of California system.[10] Thus, despite their early struggles, the first-wave refugees apparently have overcome barriers and successfully adapted to U.S. society. But the story is not that simple, nor is it completely accurate, for while they were busy working and studying in this country, many other Vietnamese—tens of thousands of them—were still longing to escape from Vietnam.[11]

After listening to refugees talk about life in communist Vietnam, it is not difficult to understand why they were desperate to escape. They tell of their businesses being confiscated by the government and of being arrested after the war. According to one survey, one in four refugees in Orange County reported spending time in Vietnam's prisons, where the police tortured many of them.[12] Economically, life in communist Vietnam was abysmal, and refugees also tell stories of children becoming prostitutes, robbers, and cigarette vendors in order to survive. In response to the situation, more and more Vietnamese attempted to escape, creating multiple waves of refugees. In total, nearly 500,000 people escaped from Vietnam and resettled in the United States.

Escape left many scars on the later refugees, who are known as the "boat people." The vessels they used to escape in often were only minimally equipped for sea travel. Many were grossly overcrowded, subject to engine failure, and without sanitary facilities or an adequate food supply. To make matters worse, the threat of typhoons and pirates was ever-present. Under these conditions, it is small wonder that nearly one-third of all the boat people apparently perished in the open sea.[13]

The boat people who survived found safety in refugee camps located in Thailand and Malaysia. From the camps, many came to Southern California, where an estimated 40 percent of the Vietnamese American community lives today.[14] The influx of waves of refugees added to the overall economic health of the original Vietnamese American community and helped consolidate the existing Vietnamese commercial enclaves.

A remarkable number of the boat people (over 50 percent) were mere children or teenagers, and many of them came without their parents or other family members.[15] Escaping often entailed paying an expensive fee to smugglers who made their living transporting refugees, and parents too poor to pay for their own escape might send their oldest child in hopes that that child would be able to achieve honor and success for the family in the United States. Many of the children have succeeded, in spite of enormous obstacles, and are often referred to by those in gangs as the "schoolboys" and "schoolgirls." But not all have succeeded. One young man committed suicide in his late twenties when he realized that he had failed in the mission set by his parents. Other refugee children, traumatized by war and ill equipped to handle the socioeconomic pressures in the United States, fell into the subculture of the streets and have become streetboys and streetgirls.

Resentment against the refugees was still high in the United States in 1979, when a Gallup poll showed that opposition to refugee resettlement had increased to 60 percent.[16] This anti-refugee sentiment contributed to incidents of discrimination and numerous altercations between the Vietnamese and other ethnic groups. Compared to first-wave refugees, who also had encountered anti-refugee sentiment, the boat people, as a group, were less prepared to handle their new situation in the United States. Generally from the lower socioeconomic classes of Vietnam, they were poorer, less educated, and less urbanized.[17] For example, in 1982 the first wave of refugees, who arrived in 1975, had a poverty rate of 25 percent—a figure that is high but not in comparison to the 90 percent poverty rate of refugees who arrived between 1980 and 1982.[18] By 1989 the first wave refugees had achieved income parity with the general U.S. population, but the unemployment rate and poverty rate for the boat people were twice the national average.[19]

In Southern California, poverty in the Vietnamese community appears to be especially intense. Data from Los Angeles and San Diego Counties indicate that the annual family income of Vietnamese refugees in the late 1980s was only $9,000 per year, similar to that of female-headed African American households.[20] Tellingly, the Vietnamese have a disproportionate number of single-parent, female-headed households compared with other Asian Americans.[21] Even in the mid-1990s nearly 36 percent of Orange County's adult welfare recipients were Vietnamese.[22]

Given the background of the boat people, these poverty levels are not entirely unexpected. Many refugees were severely hindered by their inability to speak English, and employment opportunities often were limited to menial, part-time work that offered little in the way of future advancement.[23] Massive government cutbacks in job training and English as a Second Language (ESL) programs did not help the situation. As a result, many refugees found themselves dependent on welfare. Government estimates of refugees in the Vietnamese community who were welfare dependent were as high as 50 percent. Only 31 percent of all Vietnamese refugees were totally self-supporting.[24]

It must be recalled that many of the boat people do not have the presence of their family to help buffer economic stress. As a result, the spirit of the family, the socioeconomic core of the first-wave refugees, often is painfully absent in the lives of the boat people. For those refugees who do have family in the United States, a myriad of other sociocultural forces have acted to severely weaken the spirit of the family.

> The traditional Vietnamese family has faced tremendous changes in gender roles, family expectations, generational perspectives, and family relationships since arriving in the United States. . . . The loss of economic security, social status, and self-esteem often creates depression, and the role reversals which may occur have placed stress on marriage relationships.[25]

Most notably, intense generational and cultural problems have erupted between Vietnamese parents and their more Americanized children. The wanton liberalism and openness they find in the United States often shocks parents who have only known the strict ethics of the Vietnamese culture.[26]

One of the family experiences recounted by both males and females is the physical abuse they received at the hands of parents, mainly their fathers. In instances cited, when the child stepped out of line the parent would go into a rage and punch or beat the child into conformity. Some youngsters have reported their parents to social service agencies in order to protect themselves from further harm.[27] Many individuals referred to this treatment as the impetus for running away from home.

Children, less bound to the cultural ethics of their homeland than their parents, find themselves pulled both ways in a cultural tug-of-war between their parents and the outside society. This cultural tug-of-war also plays into the internal formation of the youth's identity. Culturally the gang youth may be more U.S.- than Vietnamese-oriented, but racially the youth will never be able to escape her or his ethnic background. This culture conflict undermines the formation of a youth's identity, causes family strain, and exposes youths to racial harassment by their peers.[28]

Interestingly, there are instances when the street gang has become the culture carrier. New gang members, including females, who have undergone Americanization have relearned Vietnamese language and culture through gang members. In this way the gang appears to protect and preserve aspects of the culture and to resist dominant influences, thus complicating the processes of self-identification.

The cultural clash is often manifested in language and, unfortunately, often results in a breakdown of parental control. Parents can speak only Vietnamese, but the children can speak English as well. As one Vietnamese social worker told me, this discrepancy can create problems:

> I've seen a lot of parents who are very ignorant of the American culture, or are illiterate even in the Vietnamese language. . . . They cannot control their children because they cannot speak a word of English. The children are the ones calling the shots, not the parents.

This point is underscored by the story of the child who, interpreting for the principal, tells his parents, "I am given three weeks off for good behavior," when in fact he is being suspended from school.

Harsh economic situations also take their toll on the family unit. When parents work in menial jobs up to fourteen hours a day, seven days a week, in order to support their family, the parental presence in the home is minimal and children resent the fact that their parents are workaholics. Several gang youths interviewed reiterated this complaint:

> "When I live with my family, it's no fun . . . you have to work everyday."

> "When they opened up their shop, we never had time for each other."

> "The only time we see each other is when we eat."

> "My parents were never there for me."

One youth put it this way:

> I look around and say, "What's wrong with my family? How come my friends' parents take them to movies, to the game? Why are my parents always working?"

Vietnamese parents will often justify their long hours by arguing that they are working for their children's future; specifically, the parents harbor hope of being able to afford sending their children to college. This places enormous pressure and expectations on the student, and unfortunately many Vietnamese youths, especially the later-wave refugees, do not have the social skills needed to perform well in school. Many had missed several years of schooling due to dislocation and transitions between refugee camps.[29] Often the youths resent their parents' expectations and are angry about their parents' long working hours. Also, children are often embarrassed by their parents' low-status jobs and dependence on welfare.[30] These feelings affect attitudes and result in youths' poor performance in school. This in turn leads to loss of self-esteem and rejection of their parents' values. As one gang youth emphatically declared:

> I just don't look at them [classmates who do well in school] or nothing. . . . I don't like those people. Man, they're too smart. They get A's, and you can't get no A's like that. I get mad. I get jealous. You're in your world, I'm in my world.

That some Vietnamese students do not do well in school may belie the stereotype of the Asian whiz kid, but the truth is that although many Vietnamese students get straight A's, a significant number drop out of school.[31] Many of these children find themselves in the double bind in terms of age and grade placement. Upon entrance to school, parents will state their children are two to three years younger than they are so that school officials will place them in a lower grade, thinking that this will aid them. Instead, it creates havoc for the children, for they know they are living a lie. Unfortunately, the problem of poor performance is complicated when a child's learning deficiencies go undetected and teachers expect that child to achieve at a higher grade level.

Racial harassment at school is clearly another factor that helps explain poor academic performance. With their smaller physical stature and obviously different racial features, Vietnamese youths are often a target. Feelings related to the Vietnam War still ran strong in the late 1980s, and despite their anticommunist background, many Vietnamese youths found themselves identified as the enemy. As one gang youth we interviewed said:

> When I was going to school, white people always be calling me "Nip" and "gook" and "shit." And it hurts. I didn't go to school, didn't want to get into fights and stuff, so I stopped going to school.

Other youths resort to bringing knives and guns to school for protection. Law officials interviewed reported that semiautomatics are among the guns they regularly confiscated from Vietnamese students. For many youths, acquiring weapons is the first step toward the gang subculture.

The shock of a youth's first encounter with the U.S. school system can also inhibit future academic performance. Some youths, accustomed to the teacher-dominated mode of Vietnamese learning, are confused by the give-and-take of the U.S. classroom.[32] Moreover, cultural factors complicate the child's educational experience in more subtle ways. In Vietnam, for example, parents receive notes primarily when children are misbehaving or performing badly—but since U.S. students frequently come home with innocent notices and progress reports, Vietnamese parents often believe their children are in trouble.[33] When English proficiency is limited, the student is unable to understand the teacher's instructions and normal classroom procedures. One youth related his experience:

> I know nothing in school. I just go there and they say, "Sit there, sit there." . . . I don't say a word. . . . I didn't know a single word of English. . . . They pass out work and I just sit there and stare at the work. I couldn't do nothing. I'm tired of that. I got bored.

For youths who drop out of school because of boredom, frustration, or racial harassment, the gang lifestyle offers an exciting and accommodating alternative.

Females often find that in the streets this freedom is a double-edged sword. It provides a respite from the gender expectations of Vietnamese culture and also allows for inclusion and almost equal status with males. Unfortunately, such a reconstitution of their gender role exposes young women to added risks of victimization. Young women who frequent male-dominated areas, such as coffee shops and pool halls—considered inappropriate female behavior in traditional culture—often encounter men who attempt to seduce them or coax them into potentially harmful activities. Nevertheless, seeking and finding this freedom is enticing and empowering to many young women.

In sum, considering the background and socioeconomic conditions of many refugees, it seems inevitable that a Vietnamese gang subculture has arisen. Many gang youths have vivid memories of their difficult, often traumatic life in Vietnam and as a fleeing refugee. The effects of these traumatic experiences are difficult to gauge, but certainly they are com-

Friendship and camaraderie formed in the streets

plex and strong enough to undermine secure and stable patterns. Life in the United States, being free from communist oppression, is a definite improvement for refugees, but many young refugees experience the oppression of being marginalized because they are poor and racially different. Even within the Vietnamese community, class tensions and boat people's suspicions of earlier refugee leaders' corruption add to youths' sense of marginalization.[34] Parents and family are not always able to help them cope with the pressures of U.S. life, and the youths find themselves bored, alienated, and isolated at school.

It stands to reason that the emergence of street gangs in Vietnamese communities coincided with the influx of the later wave of refugees, and it is not accidental that most Vietnamese gang youths are boat people refugees. The traumas of their refugee experiences, the poverty and racial harassment they have encountered in the United States, and their family conflicts and poor schooling experiences have all fueled the growth of Vietnamese gangs in Southern California.

Pushed to the margins in terms of socioeconomic status, culture, and language, many of the youths have been pulled into street life. There was little to pull them back. The social welfare system initially was not prepared to handle the influx of the Vietnamese and their unique problems. Jobs were few and inaccessible. The education system offered many youths a forum in which to excel, but for youths who could not keep up the schools were catalysts for gang formation: For example, because Vietnamese students were often harassed by their classmates, the first Vietnamese gangs were formed at school as a means of protection. One of the first to appear was the Nip 14.

The history behind the gang name itself is instructive. Vietnamese students were often called Nips (short for "Nipponese"), a racial slur that originated in anti-Japanese sentiments. Perhaps as an ironic show of their power, the youths adapted the racial slur as part of their gang name. The number 14 was derived from the fact that the Chicano gangs, which often harassed the Vietnamese youths, had claimed the number 13. Thus, the Nip 14 was one up on the Chicano gangs.

This theme of forming or joining a gang because of racial discord is one that comes up repeatedly when talking to police officers or with the gang youths themselves. "I needed to protect myself" is a common phrase that is heard when youths explain why they first joined a gang. As one law enforcement agent I interviewed explained:

That's what it started out as, and what happened was that the Asian kids were banding together for protection, much like the Hispanic kids banded together, and that's basically how [Vietnamese gangs] got started.

In essence, the hate and prejudice of others appears to have been a powerful motivator for youths to join a gang. A nineteen-year-old gang member told me:

It's just that I was thinkin' I'm Vietnamese, so I should be hanging with other Vietnamese better. . . . I knew that white people were prejudiced. . . . They hated me and I hated them.

Other researchers have come to similar conclusions in other communities: Southeast Asian youths in San Diego and San Jose also identified the need to protect themselves from other youths as the reason they joined a gang.[35]

Forming gangs for protection in and of itself is relatively benign. However, Vietnamese youth gangs quickly developed a criminal subculture based on their desire for money and material goods. Some later used their youth gang activities as an entrée into the established adult illicit economy, including organized crime. Having seen their parents toil long hours for relatively little gain, gang youths are hungry for financial independence and the freedom to live life on their own terms in the streets.

The relationship between desired goals and roles and access to them is important in U.S. society. A significant disjunction between future goals and access to those goals serves as a catalyst for criminal behavior, and the street subculture provides a means for alienated youths to achieve desired status. Thus, what starts out as a group of friends who merely join together to protect themselves can escalate to more malignant behavior.

Many youths start by stealing cars but quickly progress to higher levels of criminal activity. As one youth explained:

> I didn't want my parents' money . . . I feel like maybe they need the money. I always tried to get my own money. . . . I got a job [as a hotel bellboy] to save money. But the money was too slow. I didn't have enough money . . . so I quit. . . . With my homeboys I could make $10,000 in a day.

Several youths we interviewed bragged about "earning" thousands of dollars; some of that may be exaggerated but not entirely unrealistic. According to law enforcement authorities interviewed, Vietnamese gangs can acquire massive amounts of money very quickly via home invasion robberies. Unlike African American or Chicano gangs, Vietnamese gangs do not usually deal drugs for money. Rather, they prey on other Vietnamese who for various reasons keep large amounts of cash and valuables in their homes.

The Vietnamese have a long, traditional distrust of the banking system. In Vietnam, inflation and wars turned many people's life savings into worthless pieces of paper. In the United States, many refugees are unfamiliar with the Western banking system and so are wary of it. Therefore, many Vietnamese keep cash and gold bars in their homes (gold is valued as a stable, nondepreciable form of cash).[36]

Unfortunately, Vietnamese gangs are all too aware of the home savings system in their community. Acting on tips from friends and other sources, they will target the home of a victim, almost always Vietnamese. Gangs will often survey the home for several days to obtain information such as the number of people in the house. When they feel the situation is safe, the gang will raid the home and force their victims to reveal the location of their valuables. Various methods are used to gain entry. For example, the gang will sometimes have one of their female companions knock on the door (a female arouses less suspicion), and then the rest of the gang will invade the home. Automatic weapons are often used during these home invasions, as well as other cruel methods of persuasion. One youth told me that during a robbery, he held a victim's infant over a toilet bowl and threatened to drown the child if the victim did not reveal the location of his valuables.

Home invasion robberies can be highly profitable—there are some police reports of victims losing over $100,000. These immense profits are usually shared among gang members and friends and used to support a lifestyle that values fancy cars, fancy clothes, drugs, gambling, girlfriends, nightclubs, restaurants, and overnight stays in motel rooms. For refugees who lived in squalid poverty in Vietnam and found more poverty, plus discrimination, in the United States, the home invasion robberies provide a quick fix to their shattered dreams.

Unfortunately, victims do not often seek recourse in the U.S. judicial system. They are often fearful and intimidated by the U.S. legal system and reluctant to bring their case to the police. Conversely, Vietnamese gangs are reluctant to invade homes of people who are more likely to seek retribution through the legal system, namely Anglos. As one gang member told me:

> We believed that they [the victims] was scared of us and the law. But we scared of whites, [of] any other race 'cause they know a lot of law and they don't keep cash within their home.

A victim's fear of the law also may be explained by the fact that often the victim is also violating the law. Many gangs especially like to target victims they know are committing welfare fraud or who have substantial amounts of unreported income. As another gang member explains, these victims are less likely to report the robbery to the police.

> It's easier. Most of the Oriental, they don't go to the police unless they rich and stuff. Most of them [the victims] are on welfare and they make money on the side.

A victim's reluctance to report a home invasion robbery is heightened by threats of physical retaliation. Many gangs will threaten to kill victims if they are ever caught. This is a real fear for many Vietnamese because of the U.S. bail system, which allows suspects to leave jail after being charged with a crime. Complicating the situation is the belief of many Vietnamese that law enforcement is corrupt, a belief that stems from their experiences with police in Vietnam. Thus, when gang members are released on bail, many Vietnamese interpret that as meaning a bribe was paid for the gang member's freedom. Over time many refugees have learned to trust police officers, but they still do not trust the legal system. Among the problems cited by Vietnamese refugees in Los Angeles were the authorities' untimely responses to calls, poor communication with law enforcement officials, prejudice, and linguistic and cultural barriers.[37] One prominent Vietnamese community leader told me:

> You have to think about your family. I know the police are good guys, but they are not going to protect me. Within seventy-two hours the criminal can be out on bail. . . . So am I going to tell the police? No way!

Law enforcement officials in Southern California estimate that as many as 90 percent of all home invasion robberies go unreported. Consequently, for Vietnamese gangs, such robberies are an all-too-tempting way to make quick money, even if it comes at the expense of their fellow Vietnamese. The success of home invasion robberies has also meant that Vietnamese gangs do not usually turn to activities such as selling drugs or extortion. Indeed, home invasion robberies are a defining trait of Vietnamese gangs.[38]

To cast a wider net for home invasion robberies, gangs will often roam all over the United States and even go into Canada and Mexico. It is not uncommon for a youth gang to commit a robbery in Los Angeles and then drive the next day to Seattle or even Canada to meet friends and wait for the situation to cool down.[39] Highly mobile street groups composed of both males and females often rent motel rooms to party and lay low. Law enforcement officials claim that Tijuana, Texas, and the East Coast are especially popular areas for Vietnamese gangs on the move. Obviously, the highly mobile nature of Vietnamese gangs makes them much more difficult for local law enforcement agencies to apprehend (and for researchers to study). Many have suggested that Vietnamese youth gangs may have an organized national network for communicating, but research seems to indicate that Vietnamese gang networks are

Partying at the motel

informal.[40] Vietnamese gangs are certainly street gangs, but their street is often an interstate highway.

For youths who have struggled in school, the street lifestyle is appealing. Even among good students, it is not uncommon for some individuals to strike a balance between being a schoolgirl/boy and a streetgirl/boy. The male dress style often reflects movement between the two identities. They dress regular with Levi's and sports shirts and then go New Wave with dark (especially black) clothing and trench coats. Some Vietnamese youths adopt a baggy pants, white T-shirt style that parodies the Eses, as the Vietnamese refer to Chicanos ("Ese" in Chicano parlance means "Hey, you"). The young women tend to favor fancier clothing in mod, Hollywood-influenced styles.

Many youths have not been able to build their self-esteem through academics, and so joining a gang is one way to seek self-esteem. A youth who has been bullied by bigger classmates and has flunked out of school can join a gang and find that he automatically acquires an air of notoriety, of danger, and of respect. A twenty-year-old Vietnamese gang member points out this need for some sort of recognition:

> The majority of kids want a name. . . . They want people to know them. That's why most of the kids doing what they are doing.

Thus, the gang lifestyle is highly attractive to youths who are searching for self-esteem and yet struggling in what is probably their most important social forum, their school.

Ordinarily, the stability of a strong family could counteract the temptation of the gang lifestyle. But many gang members have no stable counterforce in their lives. Culture conflict, poverty, and the lure of the gang lifestyle undermine parental authority, and youths find that they can defy even the strictest forms of control. One gang member told me:

> See, my dad—he know if he going to hit me, it ain't going to hurt me, 'cause I'm still going to go back and do the same thing.

For Vietnamese parents, the loss of their authority is often shocking. They come from a cultural ethic that treasures filial obedience and parental discipline. This ethic is the foundation of the traditional Vietnamese family. Unfortunately, youths have been able to find a new family in their new country—their gang.

The Vietnamese gang members' claim that the gang is a family echoes what we have heard from members of other ethnic gangs. But the family analogy is especially apt for Vietnamese gangs, because they live and travel together rather than just commit crimes together. During their extensive travels, as many fifteen or twenty of them may share one motel room. In their struggle to survive, even if by criminal means, the gang members do form genuinely intense personal relationships. As one gang member told me:

> [My homeboys] were family to me. . . . I love 'em. Something come down. . . . I'd die for my homeboys.

Another gang member told me:

> I'm just trying to survive. People my age, I try to help them survive because they help me survive. We're family, we're not a gang. White people say we are a gang, but we are not a gang—we family.

The above quote illustrates another point—Vietnamese gangs may not be gangs in the traditional sense of the word. The word *gang* implies a structure, an organization. Yet Vietnamese youth gangs are highly disorganized and often do not even have an appointed gang leader. Overall, there is little role differentiation or status hierarchy, no declared turf, and an open and always changing gang membership.[41] Moreover, it is not uncommon for a youth to participate with several gangs in their criminal exploits or to jump from gang to gang. Indeed, gang membership is not determined by any code or orientation rite (such as jumping-in), but merely on the basis of interpersonal relationships. As a nineteen-year-old gang member explained,

> Somebody look like your good friend, they look like they cool, they not stab you behind your back and you know them well, so you just kick it [hang out] together.

Thus many Vietnamese gangs do not have the typical traits of a gang: a turf, colors, graffiti, gang tattoos or hand signs, or even a gang name.[42] However, as the Vietnamese youth gang subculture has evolved over time, it shows signs of beginning to mimic its African American and Chicano counterparts. By the mid-1990s, gang names had become popular, names like Natoma Boys, The Chosen Brothers, Orange Boys, and NIP Family (female associates were known as NFL, the NIP Family Ladies). Gang size, which had been from 6 to 10 members, changed to close to 100 in some instances, though the age spread remained between the ages of 12 and 25.[43] Vietnamese youths in San Jose adopted gang symbols, tattoos, and colors.[44] Their many tattoos are more decorative and highly personal. Three dots forming a triangle symbolize three words, La Vida Loca ("The Crazy Life"), taken from Chicano gang members. Five dots (four corner dots and one in the middle) approximately mean "I stand alone at the center of the world" and represent a traditional Vietnamese five-word saying taken from a Chinese tattoo ("Trust No Man," in Chinese). The tattoo T T T T stands for "thoung, tien, tu, toi" ("love, money, prison, crime"). Many Vietnamese youths have adopted the 4 T's as a slogan; originally it was probably learned from older criminals. The 4 T's symbolize all too well the life many Vietnamese youths have created for themselves in this country. Of all Asian groups, Vietnamese Americans had the highest rate of institutionalization in 1990.[45]

Regardless of the gang monikers or slogans they use, Vietnamese gangs are sophisticated and pragmatic.[46] Their sophistication is evidenced by their home invasion robberies, which are well prepared and organized to overtake their victim and escape from police. Their prag-

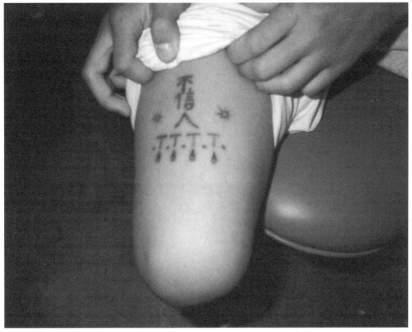

4 T's (thoung, tien, tu, toi: love, money, prison, crime) and Chinese translation of "Trust no man"

matism can be seen in the fact that they realize the lack of a turf and identifiable monikers makes it much more difficult for law enforcement officials to apprehend them. Similarly, Vietnamese gangs will not waste their time and energy on activities that do not profit them. For example, Vietnamese gangs have little use for the kind of persistent intergang fighting that is seen in Chicano or African American gangs. One youth explained to me:

> Black and Ese [Chicano] gang, they . . . fight for neighborhood.
> They shoot each other for nothing. For us, we try to make money.
> We don't fight for a little neighborhood 'cause that's stupid.

The sophistication of Vietnamese youth gangs has led some to suggest that they may be tied to Vietnamese organized crime groups. While there may be some organized criminal activity in the Vietnamese community that engages in high-level extortion and drug smuggling, youth gangs usually are not involved.[47] As one youth told me:

They [the Frogmen, a reputed group of ex-Vietnamese soldiers that engaged in extortion and drugs] don't kick with us because we just boys.

Organized crime groups, however, do have some influence on Vietnamese youth gangs, as the gang appropriation of the 4 T's slogan attests.

The Vietnamese gang phenomenon offers us an unprecedented opportunity to explore cross-cultural issues among ethnic street gangs. Yet as a society we (including academicians and law enforcement personnel) have not yet taken advantage of this new opportunity to study the cultural complexity of the street gang phenomenon. Rather, the novelty of Vietnamese gangs has given rise to the distorted myth of an exotic, sinister Vietnamese underworld, which has heightened only our fear, not our understanding, of street gangs in general.

At first glance, Vietnamese gangs appear to be an exotic addition to the street scene. In many ways, they are entirely different from the gangs that have already been extensively studied—they often avoid gang monikers, their criminal behavior is very different from the street drug dealing that typifies African American and Chicano gangs, and their mobility and fluid structure are remarkable and distinctive. While numerous African American and Chicano youths come from extremely disadvantaged backgrounds, few have backgrounds that can compare to the trauma and horrors that many Vietnamese youths experienced at an early age. The inner rage stemming from these experiences generates attitudes that result in acts of aggression. Such intense feelings can affect female youths too, who sometimes break the gender barrier of their culture to form female gangs, some with their own gang names, such as Innocent Bitch Killers, South Side Scissors, and Midnight Flowers.

Within the Vietnamese community, gangs seem to be considered an exception. Media focus on the economic success and prosperity, as well as academic prowess, of the Vietnamese suggests that gangs in the Vietnamese community are a gross but rare aberration. Indeed, in interviewing Vietnamese community leaders, I found that many Vietnamese themselves are adamant in denying the existence of a gang problem. Clearly, we cannot refute the success that many Vietnamese have achieved, but neither can we deny that there is a significant Vietnamese gang problem in the Los Angeles area or that it needs to be addressed.[48]

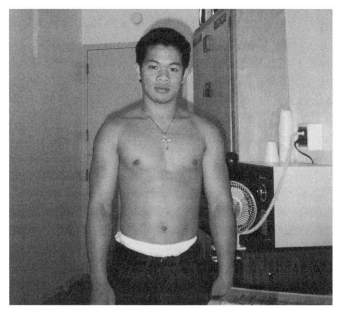

Learning the culture of the jail

Vietnamese gang members have the same bleak prospects as their ethnic counterparts. Many will eventually be killed or jailed. Some will go on to organized crime. At best, they will mature out of the gang, only to again face the very problems that caused them to join the gang in the first place.

The story that follows is of Huc, a young man who perhaps has weathered the worst effects of a street life, although the possibility of rejoining a more advanced criminal life style still remains. Huc's horrendous experiences before entering the United States provide an explanation for his life as it unfolded in this country; acting out rage and aggression is easily understood in this context. The destabilizing events in Vietnam and at sea were compounded in Los Angeles by more disruptions and fractures, and ultimately led to a life of group mobility in which criminal activities dominated the agenda.

8

"You Couldn't Hang by Yourself"

Huc's Story

HUC'S GREAT-GRANDPARENTS had immigrated from northern China to Cholon, a village near Saigon populated by many Vietnamese Chinese. The family had accumulated some money over the generations so, like most Vietnamese Chinese, they were relatively prosperous. Huc's father was a forest ranger and had spent some time in the South Vietnamese military. His mother, a homemaker, took most of the responsibility for raising the children.

Born in 1973, Huc was the oldest child in the family and had two brothers and two sisters. His early life was not easy and not without fear. His father sometimes drank heavily and became physically abusive, with his mother usually bearing the brunt of his father's rages. After the fall of Saigon in 1975, police violence against civilians was common and soldiers often took what they wanted from private homes; once they came to Huc's home and demanded food and money. Huc recalls that when he was five he saw a man shot to death in the street by communist soldiers. Even Huc's recreational activities were affected by violence, for the Vietnam War had left behind grim reminders of those deadly times: numerous munitions, including grenades. Huc and his friends played with these "toys" often, and sometimes an old grenade they found would unexpectedly detonate.

When the communists confiscated a great deal of the money and wealth Huc's family had accumulated, the family became relatively poor for the first time and Huc's father had to perform manual labor on farms in order to support them all. Perhaps because of his military experience, he also was sent to a communist reeducation camp for almost a year, where the reeducation consisted of hard manual labor and daily beatings. After his release from the camp, Huc's father was convinced that he and his family had to escape from Vietnam, and he wanted to escape to the United States, the "land of gold streets." Huc's father told them that the United States was the land of freedom and opportunity and, best of all, not ruled by communists.

Escaping from Vietnam was illegal, of course, and expensive. To buy his family space on a smuggler's boat, Huc's father gathered what money they had left and converted it into gold bars. Sometime during 1979, in the middle of the night, Huc and his family escaped.

The smuggler's boat was far from suitable for sea travel and, since all the available space on the boat was filled with people trying to escape, there was no room for supplies or food. Huc remembers having barely enough room to sit down and being hungry and thirsty most of the time. Typhoons and other sea storms often hit the Vietnamese coast; on their third day at sea, a particularly vicious storm capsized the boat. Huc's father grabbed him in the open water, and together they clung to a piece of wood for survival. They were rescued by another boat that was in the area, but Huc's pregnant mother, siblings, and aunt drowned. Huc was only six when he lost most of his family. His story is not unlike those of most boat refugees and, indeed, even worse horror stories have been documented.

Huc and his father were brought to a refugee camp in Thailand, but the loss of his mother and siblings tormented him daily. He had vivid nightmares for a year after the incident. Even today, the memories still stir up great bitterness and regret.

> I lost my whole family trying to get over here. . . . That's the part where I have anger for me to come over here. . . . To me, I grew up [thinking] it's not worth it to come over here. . . . It's not worth it.

After several months in Thailand, Huc and his father were allowed to come to the United States. With the help of a church, they first settled in an area of Los Angeles that Huc cannot recall. He and his father subsequently lived in East Los Angeles and the Hollywood area. In Hollywood, Huc's father found work as a janitor and married another Vietnamese Chinese refugee. The addition of a stepmother created a huge problem for Huc, especially when she tried to discipline him.

> I never let [my stepmother] touch me to discipline me. . . . I even hit her back. . . . I never accepted her. . . . I hurt her, but that's how I felt when I was younger. I hated the whole world.

A few years later, Huc and his new family finally settled down in Highland Park, which Huc remembers as a bad area because there was a lot of graffiti and litter. The neighborhood was primarily Chicano, although a small population of Vietnamese refugees lived there.

With both Huc's father and stepmother working long hours in a variety of manual jobs, Huc was left alone most of the time. He did not attend school the first two years he was in the country, because his father did not feel he was mentally ready. Huc spent those years sitting at home alone watching TV, which is how he eventually learned to speak English. For most of the day no one was around to prepare his meals and therefore, Huc remembers, he ate only a late dinner with his father when he returned from work. The few friends Huc had then were also from Vietnam.

When he finally did go to school, Huc was eight or nine years old. He started in kindergarten but was able to progress rapidly, and after a few years he caught up with peers his age. For the most part, Huc enjoyed school because many other Vietnamese and Vietnamese Chinese children were in his class, and he did very well in elementary school. His parents were not able to supervise or help him with his homework, though Huc's father made it clear that he had to do well in school. If he got even a B, his father would beat him. As Huc says, "I got my ass whopped. That's one lesson I learned real badly—you had to do well in school." When Huc started attending junior high school, however, things changed.

Huc's junior high school had several well-established Chicano gangs. Their presence created an immediate and urgent problem for Huc and the other Asian students. As Huc says, "At that time you trying to find where you belong, who you are, and you face a lot of racial prejudice." One day Huc got into an argument with a Chicano student who had taunted him with a racial epithet. They agreed to meet after school to settle their differences. Huc came alone; the Chicano came with eleven of his homeboys. The results were predictable: "I got my ass whopped. . . . They jumped me. . . . You couldn't hang by yourself."

After that incident, Huc carried a knife to school. He also began attaching himself more closely to other Vietnamese American students. They formed an informal group and later were able to exact revenge on his Chicano tormentors. But even at this point, Huc and his friends were not a cohesive enough group to be called a gang and, other than petty shoplifting, Huc did not engage in significant criminal activity or drug usage.

Huc's peers began taking precedent over his parents. He began staying out late sometimes to avoid his father and not even bothering to come home other times, staying instead at a friend's house. In response, his father started beating him more often, but the beatings seemed only to reinforce his rebellion.

Huc's grades started to slip, and in the eighth grade he received several failing grades. Despite his problems, he never went to his parents or teachers for help. He felt alienated from his parents, especially his stepmother, and didn't feel comfortable talking to his Anglo teachers. He preferred trying to handle things by himself: "I think it's my trouble. I never tell my mom or dad about my problems at school. I think I can take care of myself."

In high school, Huc's problems worsened. He attended Lincoln High School, which also had many established Chicano gangs. Huc got into arguments and fights often, and because he was a good fighter, he soon gained a reputation among the other Vietnamese:

> Too many people fuck with the Vietnamese people, so I help 'em out and I fight a lot. . . . I fuck a lot of people up. Then the Vietnamese know me 'cause I fight a lot and I beat up a lot of people. So I got more Vietnamese friends and more Vietnamese come from another school and we talk and kick back.

Having new friends and popularity, Huc experienced a lot of pressure to skip school. He was at first somewhat reluctant to start skipping school on a regular basis, but peer pressure won out and eventually he stopped attending classes altogether. At this time, Huc also started to experiment with marijuana and alcohol.

Huc and his friends began forming what the police at least would label a "gang." Huc never thought of himself as a gang member and still doesn't. In his mind, he was merely hanging out with his friends. One of their favorite hangouts was a local park. One day, the police came to

Alpine Park and started taking pictures of Huc and his friends. They asked him what gang he was from. Huc recalls:

> We're not doing anything. We just wanted to kick back. . . . We
> don't gangbang, we don't have a name. . . . But [the police] want us
> to have a name. Well, we just said, "Alpine, Alpine Kids." Yeah,
> that sounds good. That's the funny part—the police is setting up,
> helping us build.

Despite the efforts of the police, the Alpine Kids never developed into an organized gang. They merely ditched school together and spent their days in pool halls, dance clubs, and coffee shops. All this entertainment became relatively expensive, and Huc began to realize that he needed a source of cash, so he starting learning from several of his friends how to break into cars and steal them. Learning to steal cars was relatively easy; Huc says that he actually had a more difficult time learning how to drive one with a stick shift. At one point, Huc claims that he was stealing up to two or three cars a night. Either he would strip the car himself and sell the parts, or via connections he made through friends he would sell the car to a fence for about $800.

After six months of stealing cars, the police finally apprehended Huc. His first arrest for grand theft auto came during his freshman year in high school. He showed the police how he managed to break into cars, and he remembers one detective telling him, "Hey, this is sophisticated. How'd you learn to do that?" Huc was put on probation and managed to avoid significant detention.

Several times Huc again was apprehended for grand theft auto, but each time he gave the police an alias and pretended to be dumb. The police, assuming that the car theft was Huc's first offense and not knowing the semantics of Vietnamese surnames, released Huc as a first-time offender and so he was able to avoid trouble with his probation officer.

One afternoon, however, Huc decided to visit his now former high school, as he had dropped out after only a few months of attending class. He got into an argument in the school cafeteria with some Eses (Chicanos) who were trying to "mad-dog and race-talk" him down. To retaliate, Huc simply pulled out his gun and started shooting. Fortunately, like most other gang youths, Huc had a bad aim and no one was seriously injured. The shooting led to a wild police chase that ended with Huc being caught. This incident was the first time Huc had actually used his gun, recently acquired, and it was also the last straw for Huc's parents.

Up until this time, Huc's father had tried to discipline him by yelling, screaming, and hitting him. After this incident, he withdrew and refused to even talk to Huc. While awaiting trial, Huc decided to leave home. He spent his nights with friends in motels.

Leaving home was the culmination of all Huc's problems in relating to his family. His relationship with his stepmother had been horrible, at times even violent, and he had felt abandoned by his father, who was always busy working. Huc says:

> I never felt wanted or loved by my family. . . . Family in America change, it's not like 'Nam when they care about each other and stay together. Over here, it's like they care about money so much and have nothing to do with family at all. Everything is always money— they would backstab their own family.

Huc also had problems with the culture conflict he experienced at home. By this time, he was Americanized and had lost some of his fluency in Vietnamese and Chinese, although he is still able to speak Vietnamese and two Chinese dialects moderately well. His father, however, still retained a strong Vietnamese identity and was not able to speak English. Sometimes even when Huc said something harmless, his father would misunderstand and hit him. Once Huc referred to his stepmother as "she" and his father hit him, because using "she" is disrespectful in the Vietnamese culture. Huc says:

> There's a lot of pressure. There are changes between culture and the way you talk. You don't know what you are really because you came from Vietnam . . . the confusion about what you want to be trying to convert yourself into American. You're stuck in between, you don't know where you supposed to belong. So alone. You don't know who you are.

For the shooting incident, Huc spent six months in a juvenile camp in rural California, an experience that he actually found relatively pleasant: "It was fun over there. I liked that place because I hate cities. I like more country."

After his release, Huc did not make the effort to reconnect with his family. Instead, he immediately went back to living with his friends. His nuclear group consisted of three very close friends, but Huc also had a larger group of about thirty Vietnamese and Vietnamese Chinese friends. The age range of this group was between 14 and 25, and the individuals came from not only the Los Angeles area but also from San Diego, San Jose, and as far away as Arizona. Together, they formed a loosely organized gang. They spent most of their time in motels and gambling houses and often drove to cities all along the West Coast.

Huc's gang was cohesive but very loosely structured, as is typical of most Vietnamese gangs. They did not have gang monikers, gang turf, or even any formal gang name (although they sometimes gave themselves a "generic" name like "the V-Boys"). Although there was a significant age range within the group, there were no formal gang leaders. As Huc says, "Even the old homeboys, I give him respect but he don't want me to call him old brother, he just like him to call you and me the same." Nor was there any initiation rite or jumping-in ceremony. Joining the group was casual and depended only on interpersonal friendship: "If somebody like your good friend, and they look like they cool . . . you just kick it together." In fact, members joined the group and left it so frequently that the membership was never constant. Individuals were free to do as they pleased, and could even join another group.

Despite its loose structure, the members considered their group to be a tight family. Huc explains:

> That is the only family you know. You grow in the gangs. You might start out with five or six friends, then suddenly you have twenty friends. It's a happy family. . . . We don't consider ourselves a street gang. That is really disrespectful.

Huc's group was a gang, however, in that they committed crimes together. Their crimes centered on home invasion robberies. Huc and his homeboys would target a particular residential household, one that they knew had a lot of money. They would survey the home for several days, and when they felt the timing was right, they would invade it, coercing the victims into forfeiting their money. Since many Vietnamese keep substantial amounts of money in their homes, Huc and his homeboys often were able to obtain large amounts of money, sometimes as much as $40,000.

Huc usually picked his victims carefully. The first criterion was that the victim had to be Vietnamese or at least a recent Asian immigrant. In particular, they would try to target victims that Huc says were not Americanized, because if they were Americanized the victims were more likely to report the robbery. Huc intimidated his victims by threatening to harm the victim's family if they tried to go to the police. Huc realized that this threat would carry more weight with those that were not very familiar with the U.S. legal system.

In choosing relatively prosperous victims, Huc and his homeboys usually acted on information given to them by friends. Several times, though, they followed a prosperous merchant to his home. Either way, Huc and his homeboys invaded homes that they knew had money.

Huc usually worked with his three closest friends—working with any more than that would have aroused suspicion. After a successful robbery, Huc would share his money with his three friends and the rest of his homeboys. Money was spent on motel rooms, cars, clothes, nightclubs and gambling, girlfriends, guns, and travel. Some money was spent on drugs, mostly marijuana and crack cocaine, but Huc and his friends generally stayed away from drugs, like heroin, that they considered dangerously addictive. (Huc felt confident that he could stop using crack at will.) The money was quickly spent, and once it was gone Huc began looking for another victim.

By living on the streets and traveling up and down the West Coast, Huc built an impressive, albeit informal, network of friends. If he needed to, he knew he could leave Southern California and obtain assistance from other Vietnamese youths in Mexico, Canada, Denver, Arizona, Oregon, and even parts of the East Coast and Texas.

After nearly a year of committing home invasion robberies, Huc was introduced by one of his friends to a criminal who was about thirty years old. Huc started doing odd jobs for him and soon considered him to be his "dai lou," a Chinese word that signifies the person is an older brother, a leader, a man who is considered to be above the level of youths such as Huc. The dai lou ran a gambling house, where Huc acted as a security guard at the gambling den and was used to threaten gamblers into paying their debts. Huc would also give his friends inside information on gamblers who he knew had a lot of money. Later, those gamblers would be victims of a home invasion robbery.

Huc's dai lou also engaged in extortion, and he would send Huc to collect payments from businesses in Los Angeles' Chinatown. Huc claims that just by saying his dai lou's name, businesses would give him a protection fee. Huc claims that at one time, his dai lou "owned" an entire block in Chinatown.

Huc's dai lou knew many older organized crime figures, because they frequently gambled at his establishment. Through these contacts, the opportunity to transport cocaine from California to Colorado was once offered to Huc by several reputed Frogmen, a Vietnamese organized crime group supposedly made up of former Vietnamese military officials. Huc, after consulting with his friends and his dai lou, turned down the offer.

Huc and his dai lou both used drugs, but they made a decision to not sell drugs. They generally looked down on drug selling as a risky business that was, in their thinking, inferior to robbery or extortion. Also, they had no need to sell drugs—they made more than enough money from their other illicit activities.

Huc and his homeboys also did not generally focus their activities on intergang warfare. Huc saw the need to defend gang turf as stupid:

> Most we try to make money. We don't fight for a little neighborhood 'cause that's stupid. If you shoot, you shoot . . . if you need money or if [someone] shot your homeboy.

More often than not, Huc did not spend his time looking for a gang fight; rather, gang fights (usually with other Vietnamese gangs) tended to be accidental. As Huc explains,

> Santa Ana Boys and Nip 14, those were two gangs we were enemies with. But it's not like we look for each other and kick each other's ass. That's not our main thing. It's just that we see each other at parties.

Most of these fights tended to center on competition over girlfriends.

Other fights centered on money. One time a Chinese gang tried to take over the gambling house where Huc worked; that is, the Chinese were loaning gamblers money so that they didn't have to borrow money from Huc's dai lou. Rather than settling their differences in the gambling house, the two groups decided to meet later in a restaurant. Words and insults were exchanged at the restaurant, and guns were drawn. With bullets flying over his head, Huc managed to escape unharmed with his dai lou.

In exchange for his work and his loyalty, Huc's dai lou provided him with enough money to continue his gang lifestyle. During the time he worked under his dai lou he did not actively participate in home invasion robberies, since his dai lou took care of all his monetary needs. The dai lou's reputation also gave Huc a degree of protection and respect: People would think twice before "dissing" (disrespecting) Huc because they knew he had his dai lou's support behind him. Although they had a close relationship, Huc and his dai lou never kicked back, nor did they spend their nights together in motel rooms. A dai lou simply had too much status and prestige to bring himself down to the level of Huc and his homeboys. This status hierarchy was understood and accepted by Huc and his other friends who worked for the dai lou.

Huc's relationship with his dai lou ended abruptly, however, when his dai lou died from a cocaine or heroin overdose. Actually, Huc was not surprised by the death of his dai lou, although he had been expecting it to be by assassination. Huc felt that his dai lou had been too easy with his other "little brothers," and he had sensed that one of the more aggressive "brothers" would try to kill his dai lou to take his place. Regardless, with his dai lou's death, Huc turned again to home invasion robberies to support his lifestyle.

Huc was successful in avoiding apprehension until 1991, when his luck ran out. He and three of his friends had staked out the home of Thai immigrants in West Covina. After several days of observation, they felt confident and invaded the house. There were five occupants, three of them children. They locked the children in the bathroom, at which point their father tried to fight Huc and his friends. In response, Huc's homeboy shot the father five times, nearly killing him. They then quickly took the victim's stereo equipment and nearly $3,000 in cash.

Huc and his friends brought the stolen goods back to their motel in Norwalk. They did not realize, however, that law enforcement officials had been staking out their motel room, and they were subsequently arrested. Although the victims had filed a police report, they refused to testify in court. Huc nevertheless was sentenced to three years of detention.

Unlike his experience in the detention camp overseas, Huc's jail time was not pleasant. He was bothered by recurring nightmares of his mother's death, and he also often dreamed about his own violent death. As he reflected on his life history and his time in jail, he expressed remorse and guilt. His father visited him regularly and would sadly remind Huc about all the sacrifices he had made to bring the youth to the United States. He would repeat over and over again the trauma of their escape from Vietnam and the long hours that he worked in the United States in menial jobs to support him. Huc now claims that he finally realizes what he has done to his father and stepmother, and he says the "most important thing right now" is to reestablish his relationship with them.

Although Huc is ethnically Chinese, his life history is typical of many Vietnamese youths involved in gangs. Ethnic Chinese had a long and established presence in Vietnam before the war that resulted in so many refugees from that nation. As they had done in Vietnam, many ethnic Chinese, including Huc, have successfully assimilated into Vietnamese American culture. Huc apparently was comfortable with both Vietnamese and Vietnamese Chinese friends, and members of his gang came from both ethnic groups. He seems to make no distinction between being of Vietnamese or Vietnamese Chinese descent. It should be noted that there is a Vietnamese Chinese gang, the Viet Ching, composed only of Vietnamese Chinese youths. Informants have told me the Viet Ching behaves in a manner similar to that of other Vietnamese gangs, although they apparently formed in response to a Chinese organized crime group, the Wah Ching. The Viet Ching may be more actively involved with organized crime than other youth gangs are. However, the Viet Ching did not appear to play an important role in Huc's life, although his dai lou was at one time a member of the gang.

Regardless of Huc's specific ethnic background, the trauma and aftermath of the Vietnam War have clearly affected his life. The tragic loss of his mother and siblings clearly was devastating, and at the time that I came to know him (he was then twenty), Huc was still struggling to cope with the anger and bitterness created by his mother's death.

The loss of his mother severely dashed any hopes that the United States would be the land of golden streets for Huc. His situation was exacerbated by his inability to psychologically accept a stepmother. Moreover, Huc had no other family support mechanism to help him cope with his problems, as his father was often busy working and Huc was often left alone. It should be no surprise, then, given the pressures of friends and, most importantly, racism at school, Huc started steering toward the gang lifestyle. Huc's stories about the police fueling the creation of his gang, the Alpine Kids, are also interesting, because similar stories are told by other Vietnamese, African American, and Chicano youths I have interviewed. In a society that is paranoid about youth gangs, it is perhaps ironic that our paranoia has helped create the very thing that we fear.

Huc's relationship with his dai lou is somewhat unusual—most Vietnamese youths I have interviewed did not have a dai lou. Here, Huc's ethnicity may explain his ability to establish a relationship with a dai lou. Huc was comfortable in both Little Saigon and in Chinatown, and consequently he was exposed to more individuals than the average Vietnamese youth. As should be clear by now, who you know is extremely important in the Vietnamese gang subculture. Huc was able to meet his dai lou, as well as members of the Frogmen and youths from all over the country, because of his extensive network of contacts.

As for Huc's future, I am guardedly optimistic. Like most detained Vietnamese youths I have interviewed, he is extremely and, I believe, sincerely remorseful and guilt laden. Three years in jail is a long time for a teenager, and Huc appears to have matured during this time. My conversations with law enforcement officials and anecdotal observations seem to suggest that the recidivism rate among Vietnamese youths is low, or at least lower than that of African American and Chicano youths; more importantly, since large-scale immigration from Vietnam and Southeast Asia has dwindled, I suspect that we will see fewer gang members from this ethnic group in the future. Nevertheless, Huc will still have to struggle to rediscover the United States, the land of golden streets.

9

Salvadorans in Los Angeles
The Pico-Union Area

RESIDENTS OF THE PICO-UNION area west of downtown Los Angeles once were mostly Anglo office workers and retail salespersons. The structures they lived and worked in—stores, four-story office and apartment buildings, and a sprinkling of single-family houses—dated from the 1930s and 1940s.[1] The structures are still there, but in the 1960s large numbers of Mexicans moved into the area, and in the late 1970s and early 1980s large-scale Central American immigration brought in a new group of Latinos. By the 1990s a majority of the population was Latino, predominantly of Mexican, Salvadoran, and Guatemalan origin, in that order.[2]

The neighborhood has become one of the most densely populated areas of the city. The Ramparts Division of the Los Angeles Police Department (LAPD), which includes the Pico-Union neighborhood, had a population density in 1998 of 33,790 people per square mile, almost twice that of the division with the next-highest population density.[3] Overall, the population of the area is youthful: The most recent census figures show a median age of 25 years. The Salvadoran immigrant youths of the area are the concern of this chapter, but their circumstances in Los Angeles cannot be understood without first knowing something about the circumstances that prompted so many Salvadorans to leave their native country and come to the United States.

A middle- and working-class Salvadoran migration to the United

States occurred in the mid-1960s, and between 1976 and 1978 a second wave of migrants also came to this country for economic reasons. However, it was the civil war in El Salvador that brought about the first massive flight of Salvadorans to this country, in the early 1980s. The civil war had been brewing for over 100 years and mostly revolved around government land policies that favored plantation and coffee latifundio owners over the masses—peasants and the Nahuatlan Pipil.[4] A watershed event in the background to the war was La Matanza (The Massacre) in 1932, in which over 30,000 peasants and Indians were killed by government forces. Peace imposed by the oligarchy and military marked the ensuing decades, with sporadic uprisings and protests indicating that the situation remained volatile.

But from 1980 forward, the El Salvadoran government attempted to crush leftist revolutionary forces. In the constant war waged against the revolutionaries, the government indiscriminately tortured and killed priests, peasants, church workers, teachers, students, health care workers, union members, and anyone else who could be accused of communism or subversion, or who simply got in the way. On May 14, 1980, for example, at least 600 defenseless Salvadoran peasants were slaughtered as they fled a military operation intended to flush out guerrilla activity. In the same year, the security forces indicated their displeasure with the church through the death-squad assassinations of four U.S. nuns and Archbishop Oscar Romero.[5] More than 30,000 Salvadorans had died in the civil war by 1982, out of a total population of 5.1 million. By 1985, 40,000 were dead, another 3,000 had disappeared, 750,000 had fled the country, and 500,000 were homeless or displaced within the country. By 1987, 50,000 were dead, and by the 1990s some 60,000–75,000 had been killed. In the ten years after 1979, as many as 1 million Salvadorans may have fled the country.[6]

Approximately 94,000 Salvadorans were living in the United States at the beginning of the 1980s, whereas only five years later they may have numbered around 500,000. The figures for legal immigration reflect this growth: 5,895 Salvadorans entered the United States in the decade from 1951 to 1960; 14,992 from 1961 to 1970; 34,436 from 1971 to 1980, and almost that many (32,666) again in the half-decade from 1980 to 1984.[7] However, the vast majority of Salvadorans and other Central Americans who migrated to the United States in the 1980s were undocumented and therefore never officially counted. Apparently this is

The civil war drives families out of El Salvador (© Donna DeCesare).

still the case; recent estimates of undocumented Salvadorans suggest that 335,000 came to the United States in 1995 alone.[8]

Today, Salvadorans make up perhaps 750,000 of the approximately 1.5 million Central Americans in the United States, and most of them reside in Southern California.[9] Although Los Angeles has been the primary destination of these Salvadoran migrants, sizable Salvadoran populations are found in a number of other cities, including San Francisco, Phoenix, Tucson, Dallas, Houston, Chicago, New Orleans, New York City, Washington, D.C., and Miami.[10]

The existence of a large community of Salvadorans in the United States to some extent can be attributed to the policies of Ronald Reagan as U.S. president. Direct U.S. military assistance to El Salvador soared from zero in 1980 to $424 million in the 1981–1984 period, the years of Reagan's first term in office. The new funds led to a rapid escalation of the war in that country and major disruption of the economy and the livelihood of many Salvadorans.[11] The new levels of violence and higher levels of economic hardship led to massive Salvadoran emigration to the United States.

The United States officially denied Salvadorans asylum, despite having issued a travel advisory warning that El Salvador was too dangerous for U.S. citizens, who presumably were in less danger than Salvadorans. Politically, the U.S. government was reluctant to declare that the Salvadoran government was unable or unwilling to protect its own citizens.[12] The other principal asylum provision established by the courts, which allows granting temporary asylum to immigrants from countries experiencing extreme hardships, was not extended to Salvadorans until 1990.[13]

Most Salvadorans did not qualify for amnesty under the Immigration Reform and Control Act (IRCA, passed in 1986), known earlier as the Simpson-Rodino Bill, because they arrived after the January 1, 1982, cutoff date set by the legislation, which provided that the illegal status of those who arrived before then was to be ignored and that they were to be eligible for citizenship. Furthermore, since the Salvadoran government has been considered friendly (i.e., anticommunist) by the United States, few Salvadorans (particularly among the poorer masses) were granted political asylum during the years of that country's civil war.[14] From 1980 to 1985, in fact, less than 3 percent of Salvadorans applying for political asylum were successful in their efforts. Immigration officials contended that, instead of being political refugees fleeing in terror from an oppressive regime, they were simply economic immigrants seeking a higher standard of living in the United States.

Thus, as administered, the U.S. asylum process suffered from a number of biases. Persons from communist countries were routinely allowed to remain in the United States, even though their cases were far less compelling than those of Salvadorans. Cuban boat people, for example, were granted blanket permission to remain in the United States; none of them had to demonstrate personal danger. A 1990 Commission on Refugees report noted, "There appears to be a systematic practice designed to secure the return of Salvadorans irrespective of the merits of their asylum claims. This would appear to be the result of a deliberate policy established by the U.S. authorities."[15]

Until very recently, illegal status characterized the great majority of the Salvadoran population in this country and forced them to live clandestine lives. Living in continual fear of arrest and deportation (the United States deported approximately 48,000 Salvadorans from 1980 to 1986), they have existed psychologically in a "prison without bars," which inevitably has had negative consequences for them and the com-

An old private residence in the crowded Pico-Union neighborhood

munities in which they live. Throughout the period in which large numbers of Salvadorans have resided in the Pico-Union area of Los Angeles, it has experienced high levels of such socioeconomic problems as unemployment, poverty, and illiteracy, as well as a high degree of crime and gang activity.

Because the neighborhood is somewhat cut off, bounded by major freeways and streets as well as by physical structures, opportunities for culture contact and acculturation with the majority Anglo American culture are limited. In fact, many people rely on television and radio for virtually all of their exposure to Anglo culture. Some of the additional problems faced by Salvadorans are culture shock, separation from family, lack of medical care, racial discrimination, language barriers, crowded living conditions, lack of recreational opportunities for youth, and family instability.[16] When apprehended by Immigration and Naturalization Service (INS) authorities, Salvadorans apparently have sometimes encountered physical, psychological, and emotional abuse from officials at detention camps throughout Southern California. Detained immigrants and their advocates also have alleged camp conditions that included rotten food, poor medical care, overcrowded and unsanitary living conditions, racism on the part of the guards, difficulty obtaining legal representation, virtually no access to visitors, and threats of criminal charges intended to intimidate them into signing voluntary departure forms. In California, private security companies hired to hold illegal immigrants have even been charged with handcuffing prisoners to motel beds for days on end.[17] The specter of deportation hangs continually over the heads of undocumented Salvadoran immigrants in Los Angeles.

All the pressures and strains of life as illegal immigrants foster personal and group pathology that leads to domestic abuse and child neglect. Female street youth are especially affected by these forces. Their personal backgrounds often include major ruptures and destabilizing events that occurred in the home country, such as separation from family members or the loss of parents or close relatives to death squads. As a result of these experiences and the problems in their lives before they even reached the United States, they are especially vulnerable. Once they are neglected and left unsupervised in the pressure cooker that is the Pico-Union community, the street life envelopes them and they become closely affiliated with regular gang members. Occasionally, young females have been known to splinter off and fashion cliques of their own.

Because of their illegal status, undocumented Salvadorans have been effectively without access to governmental social services and, for the same reason, many are afraid to contact the police in times of need for fear of being deported. Thus, they are often victims of crimes such as rent gouging by landlords who have the power to evict them. Similarly, Salvadorans make a reliable and docile workforce because of their fear of detection and deportation. They are commonly overworked and underpaid, and are assigned to jobs with long hours and unhealthy, degrading working conditions. The jobs Salvadorans can acquire most commonly are in industries such as furniture manufacturing and apparel or as farm laborers, gardeners, construction workers, dishwashers and busboys in restaurants, baby-sitters, care providers for the elderly, street vendors, and building maintenance workers or janitors.

The single most occupationally "niched" people in the city are Salvadoran women. They are fourteen times more likely than average to be found in domestic service, almost all of which is performed by women. Interestingly, this job does create the opportunity (indeed, the necessity) for them to learn about differences between their own cultural habits and child-rearing practices and those of their mostly Anglo American employers. Tensions often arise, for example, when a Latina thinks a baby should be held, while the Anglo mother wants the baby to move about more and to explore.[18]

Women motivated to seek a job often discover that it requires them to find child care and transportation as well. These dynamics of working complicate matters but do force the women to interact with established Angelenos, both Latinos and non-Latinos. What is interesting in this regard is that, to a greater degree than in other ethnic groups, street-raised Salvadoran females mix work and street life. Family or survival forces this choice on them. With their family support system often back in El Salvador, they have less social capital to draw on, and so have to work to survive and take care of their children. It should be underscored, though, that low-skilled, low-paying jobs are available in abundance in the area, and thus these young women can readily move in and out of such jobs.

Overall, work-related interactions between Salvadorans and Anglos have shaped cultural attitudes and contributed to stereotyping. The great majority of both women and men in the Salvadoran community are in the labor force and make up a disproportionately large part of the working but underemployed poor. The jobs they can get are mostly low-wage, dead end jobs with little opportunity for promotion, raises, benefits, or status. Their low economic status has made them look inferior in the eyes of members of the dominant group, even though many Salvadorans enjoyed higher status in their home country and came to this country with an education. The average household income reported for Salvadorans in Los Angeles in the middle 1980s was about half the poverty level.[19] The predictable effect is increasing poverty, low self-esteem, and growth in drug trafficking and crime, as well as participation in the informal economy (vending food and trinkets on street corners, holding yard sales, and the like) in the absence of more remunerative legitimate job opportunities.[20]

Today, Los Angeles has the second-largest urban population of Salvadorans in the world, next only to San Salvador. In fact, because there is safety in numbers, many Salvadorans feel safer in Los Angeles than in El Salvador. Absorption into an established community for nearly two decades has made the situation of new arrivals easier than in other sections of the United States. Nevertheless, many on arriving in the city have

The best pupusas *(rice-dough quesadillas) in town*

had to survive as best they can, sleeping in parks, under freeways, or in abandoned vehicles. Some have managed to locate friends or family members and live with them in overcrowded apartments in run-down neighborhoods for the first month or two, occasionally finding this to be their first introduction to gang life. Oftentimes, these crowded apartment buildings become small villages and the hallways teem with children at play. Teenagers and young adults gather at the ends of hallways or in stairwells to carry on private conversations. In cellars and on rooftops, as in East Coast and Midwestern tenements, the most intimate contacts and actions sometimes take place; young children, especially girls, are exposed to the danger of sexual advances or molestation in such closed community buildings.

In other instances, newcomers who find it difficult to contribute financially to settled families are either forced or feel compelled to leave, creating a large population of "urban nomads, moving about from place to place, secure in none of them."[21] Not surprisingly, many Central Americans continue to hope for a return to their homeland: Only 51.5 percent of men and 49.4 percent of women would choose to stay in the United States. Although many women have achieved a greater degree of self-reliance here, they often say they are drawn to returning to El Salvador because many of their children are still there. Thousands of families are similarly divided and unsure of what to do as they wait to learn the fate of those who fled during the civil war and later returned home.[22]

Often young immigrants whose parents sent them to the United States for safety have been traumatized by their experiences and eventually become resentful. Never truly knowing what their parents were like, they have been deprived of important role models to emulate. For young males in particular, the lack of a meaningful father figure, and perhaps of the discipline and authority that come with one, can have a very debilitating effect. Young men who grow up too quickly in a highly male-dominated culture may develop feelings of inadequacy, subsequently turning to destructive or self-destructive acts as a way of proving their masculinity. At least some young women gang members of Pico-Union become almost as angry and aggressive as the men, as in the case of two women, both gang members, who shot a cab driver.

The new immigrants who most directly suffered the inhumanities of the El Salvador civil war have sometimes needed years to become comfortable enough with their new surroundings in Los Angeles to stop being afraid. To make matters worse, in the late 1980s Salvadoran death squads, or people purporting to represent them, began threatening refugees in the Los Angeles area. Many Salvadorans received anonymous phone call threats or death-threat letters signed "E.M." (Escuadrón de la Muerte [Death Squad]). The situation became so bad that Mayor Tom Bradley issued a $10,000 reward for information about the death squads, and the Los Angeles City Council called for a congressional investigation into the attacks and threats.[23] One can readily see how the culture of violence created by war, including its by-products (such as corpses in the city streets), may have desensitized many young immigrants to the pain of violence and may play some role in the legendary savagery of Salvadoran gangs.[24] As Manuel Contreras, a psychologist for the juvenile courts, put it, "The desensitization of the war had its effects in the most vulnerable group, which are the children."[25]

In these circumstances, many organizations have mounted efforts to help alleviate the problems facing the Salvadoran population of the city, especially the refugees. In general, community organizations provide services such as health care and education, places to meet, English-language training, legal advice, job training, scholarships, funds for hometown projects in El Salvador, and family counseling. Many of the programs target young people specifically.[26]

Youth coming from a characteristically violent homeland confronted a new environment of violence, and together these experiences of violence seem to have converged to facilitate violent behavior. Also, "the younger generation and children of Central American immigrants, growing up impoverished in a society of relative abundance and a culture that prizes material possessions, are more likely than their parents to be dissatisfied with a survival standard of living,"[27] and more likely, therefore, to join gangs.

Sadly, many of the mothers of these children came to the United States to improve their economic fortunes and to maximize educational opportunities for their children. A study by two leading Latino institutes indicates that Salvadoran immigrants in Los Angeles believe strongly that inadequate schools are their children's most pressing problem, ahead of language difficulties, poverty, and immigration status.[28]

In Pico-Union, despite the increased number of children who arrived in the 1980s, no new schools were built. Schools in the area are now so crowded that, in order to utilize the schools fully year-round, children are placed in alternating "tracks"; they attend school for two months, then are off for a month before repeating the cycle. Belmont High School is the most crowded secondary school in the Los Angeles Unified School District, and the diverse student body reflects many of the social and economic strains mentioned earlier.[29] In fact, a school police officer recently was shot at on that campus and students were forced into a day-long "lockdown" as police cleared the campus.[30] Berendo Middle School has close to 3,000 students on staggered tracks, more than 1,000 students over its intended capacity. Nearby Hoover Elementary School has more students for its campus size than any other comparable school in California. With recent mandated reductions in class size, some children have had to switch teachers and classes two or three times in a few months, with learning progress adversely affected. A shortage of teachers has made for quick or temporary hiring solutions. These new teachers often lack adequate training and experience and are thrust into a lose-lose situation in which they are always trying to catch up. Busing to more affluent areas and schools is an option that many parents have taken, but for the wrong reasons. The nearly hour-long bus ride in the morning and again in the afternoon becomes a type of baby-sitter, allowing less time

A fast-food spot for a hangout (© Donna DeCesare)

for the child to waste at home or spend on the streets before the parents get home from work.

Yet schools must compete with the streets for the commitment of many young Salvadorans. Increasingly over the last two decades, street involvement has led to involvement in drug trafficking. Soon after Salvadorans began arriving in large numbers, Salvadoran youth became aware that they could earn more selling drugs on the street than by staying in school or working in the low-paying jobs available to them. They also came to realize that while engaged in street drug activities they ran no greater, and perhaps less, risk of being detained and deported by the INS.[31] It is thus not so surprising that an estimated 2 to 10 percent of the Salvadoran community's youth formed gangs of their own, such as Mara Salvatrucha, or joined existing gangs, in particular 18th Street, which emerged in the Pico-Union area in the 1960s. Originally 18th Street was a Chicano gang, but it now has a sizable number of Central Americans, especially Salvadorans, since they are now the predominant immigrant group. The gang is now considered by police to be the largest in Los Angeles County, with an estimated 20,000 members. How many of them are Salvadoran nobody knows, but I would guess that more than half are. The 18th Street gang is dispersed throughout the county from Pico-

Union to the San Fernando Valley, the San Gabriel Valley, the South Bay, and South Los Angeles.

Members of the gangs created in the 1980s included immigrants fleeing from various Central American countries,[32] some of whom were homeless, some former military members, and others guerrillas. Many young girls fell into the homeless category, or at least were without their families, and they were street-socialized alongside the boys; later, as young women, they joined the young men as gang auxiliaries. There are now more than thirty gangs operating within the eight square miles that comprise Pico-Union.

The name of the Mara Salvatrucha gang is derived from *mara*, a local street-Spanish term for "gang"; *salva*, short for "Salvadoran"; and *trucha*, slang for "watch out" and also the Spanish word for "trout," a fish that swims upstream and thus symbolizes the fight for survival. The gang was formed by mostly Salvadoran youth to fend off and protect against 18th Street and other smaller Chicano gangs in the area. In the 1990s, Mara Salvatrucha proliferated into the Pico-Union and adjacent neighborhoods to form other cliques, still roughly age-graded like traditional Chicano gangs but with each unit staking out a different territory or hangout (about fifteen cliques exist in and around Los Angeles, according to the Gang Task Force of Los Angeles). This territorial practice approximates the more dispersed territory pattern of African American gangs, a pattern also adopted by many 18th Street cliques that have spread throughout the county.

With both Mara Salvatrucha and 18th Street in Pico-Union, it became the gang hotspot of Los Angeles by the mid-1990s. Other local gangs include the Drifters, the TMC, the Playboy Players, and the Crazy Riders. As the names suggest, gang lifestyles tend to differ. In the 1980s, for example, the Mara Salvatrucha youth were mostly stoners, that is, adherents of hard-rock music who were known for heavy drug use. The other gangs just named tended to favor disco music and dressier clothing.

Mara Salvatrucha is considered by police to be one of the most violent of Los Angeles' street gangs. Some gang members have begun to affiliate with the notorious prison gang La Eme (The M; The Mexican Mafia) to operate criminal and drug-sale rings. The Los Angeles city attorney has suggested the Mara Salvatrucha gangs have extensive ties to the Mexican Mafia, which through such ties exerts its control over drug trafficking well beyond the walls of state prisons.[33]

As drug trafficking in Pico-Union grew and came under the control of rival street gangs, the normal antagonisms between such entities rapidly increased and resulted in new levels of violence. In particular, Mara Salvatrucha and 18th Street engaged in continual conflict over the control of particular areas. The fighting included ambushes and drive-by shootings in which bystanders more often than gang participants were injured or killed. The response of the Los Angeles Police Department to this complex tangle has been aimed principally at suppressing the gangs by force. Police armed with court injunctions—which recent news reports suggest may have been obtained through the false testimony of certain police officers[34]—have blocked off streets in the neighborhood, raided suspected gang hangouts and homes of suspected members, and arrested gang youths who were publicly meeting with one another when they were under court orders not to do so. In their own descriptive terms, police adopted "rock'n'roll" and "kick-ass" tactics.[35] Other injunctions prohibited specific individuals from using pagers, cell phones, and other devices police believed were being used in drug trafficking.[36] Similar injunctions have been used by the county sheriff's office, for example, against a Mara Salvatrucha unit in Hollywood.[37]

As an example of the LAPD targeting of Salvadoran youth in other ways, it is recorded that when the Joffrey Ballet in 1988 offered some free seats to Salvadoran youths studying dance at a local church center, the LAPD warned the Ballet that the kids were the most "ruthlessly violent in the city," and that the church was little more than a gang hangout. As a result, no free tickets were given out.[38] Similarly, the LAPD launched a new offensive against members of Mara Salvatrucha with the initiation of an elite unit called the Community Resources Against Street Hoodlums (CRASH) program. This unit is the focal point of the LAPD scandal concerning the Ramparts Division, which polices Pico-Union.[39] The Ramparts Division scandal focused on widespread corruption, including officers stealing impounded drugs, framing suspects, and beating and even unlawfully shooting suspects and then lying to cover up their actions.

Many Salvadoran youths in the area have been targeted for arrest and subsequent deportation. Eight teams of federal immigration agents

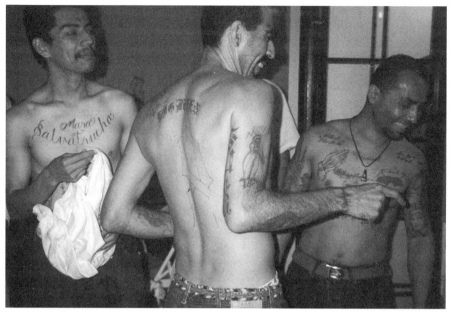

By deporting delinquent youths, the United States exports gang culture. Members of the Homies Unidos in El Salvador

were recruited to work with the LAPD in identifying and deporting gang members, and 56 of the 175 youth deported at the time were returned to El Salvador—"to uncertain fates at the hands of the military and death squads."[40] Many of those deported left families behind.

One former Mara Salvatrucha member, after maturing out of the gang, became the director of the Homies Unidos program in an attempt to help current gang youths stay out of trouble. He now faces deportation because of earlier problems. In an interview with a student, he lamented the "challenges" he faced "with the crooked law enforcement on the streets. It's almost like they resent having an ex-gang member try to make other gang members become better people."[41]

During the 1992 Rodney King riots, the Pico-Union area was especially volatile.[42] Hordes of gang members led the charge on businesses and retail stores in the looting and mayhem that followed. Later in the same year, the civil war in El Salvador came to an end, while the campaign for Proposition 187 in California heightened anti-immigrant feelings.[43] (Proposition 187 denied government-sponsored medical and welfare program access to undocumented immigrants.) Law enforcement and immigration authorities thereafter decided to intensively track and apprehend gang members who were in the United States without documents.[44] A deportation program was instituted that sent Salvadoran and Central American youth gang members back to their respective countries of origin.[45]

The move also created another phenomenon: the exportation of U.S. gang culture and lifestyle, in particular to El Salvador.[46] Many deported gang members, moreover, continued to keep in touch with those in Los Angeles by phone, fax, and e-mail.[47] The diffusion of this social problem now seems to be affecting other regions of Latin America as well. As of January 1995, the Gang Task Force had deported more than 780 gang members. San Salvador's mayor, Hector Silva, in addition to seeking more U.S. financial help, also requested assistance in controlling gang violence in San Salvador. "All over San Salvador," he says, "you see the graffiti [of Los Angeles] gangs."[48]

Today in Pico-Union, small businesses such as stores, markets, restaurants, and street vendors service its growing population. They provide special foods, services, and products and "contribute to the bustling street life and ethnic identity of the neighborhood."[49] Salvadoran shops coexist with those operated by entrepreneurs of other ethnicities. Along with the thriving business community—on Olympic Boulevard, Pico Boulevard, and Alvarado Street, for example—there are many residential areas. Some of the locations are well kept and the appearance of the housing is clean, but in a greater number the housing is run-down, dirty apartment buildings with graffiti-painted walls, held by absent owners. In some sections, road blocks erected by the police to curb drug trafficking give the neighborhood the appearance of a war zone.

The story of Arturo in the next chapter, both before and after his arrival in the United States, captures some elements of his people's history. It was violence in El Salvador that led to the uprooting of his family and their flight to the United States. It was violence that greeted him when he started off his life in the Pico-Union area of Los Angeles, an area in which gangs were extremely active. Arturo's gang, Mara Salvatrucha, arose in defensive reaction to the harassment and attacks of Chicano gangs. Arturo acted out of a personal rage that brought him close to serious trouble as he went along with the gang. Fortunately, his life was not without positive accomplishments that finally led him out of the gang and to the university.

10

"Where Is My Father?"

Arturo's Story

ARTURO WAS FINALLY in the United States, patiently enduring yet another bus ride, anxious to see the mysterious place where his mother had lived for a long time. He had spent many hours imagining what his mother's house looked like, imagining her wrapping up the toys she had sent to him in El Salvador—brightly colored plastic action figures and containers of Play Doh. Toys like that were only the beginning of the 7-year-old's dreams. There were supposed to be even more good things in the United States—fancy houses and money. This trip would give him a chance to see it all himself. Mickey Mouse lived here. Thinking about these things occupied him as the bus bounced north. But his biggest and best dream kept sliding into his thoughts: "I'm going to meet my father."

Arturo was born in San Salvador at a time when the civil war in El Salvador was beginning to intensify. Yet it was not the war that dominated his early life, but an unusual congenital heart condition. Arturo was born with a disease called the tetralogy of Fallot, which severely limited his physical activity.

Having a large extended family somewhat made up for Arturo's physical condition. He lived with his aunts, uncles, cousins, and grandparents—about fifteen relatives in all—in a large house. Arturo remembers that all his relatives pampered him, even those who were younger than he was. They carried him from place to place because he could not walk long distances, much less run.

Members of Arturo's extended family, who had stable factory jobs, were better off than their neighbors. They pooled their money in a collective fund and helped take care of each other, especially Arturo. In general, Arturo has pleasant memories of his early life in El Salvador.

But Arturo's secure family life could not protect him from two threats that loomed darkly in his life. One was the civil war and the fear it created, which was always in the background. Cousins he had known from birth disappeared overnight. He was told the government could take them like that if they needed them for the army. His relatives wouldn't sing certain songs at parties because they were revolutionary and censored by the authorities. He remembers sitting anxiously with his family and listening to the radio for news about the war.

The other problem that Arturo had to confront early in his life was the absence of his father. He had left Arturo's mother shortly after Arturo was born. Arturo's mother refused to talk about his father, and so Arturo could learn nothing from her. This bothered him tremendously as a young child because he saw his cousins and friends with their fathers and always wondered, "Where is my father?"

At age five, Arturo was separated from his mother also. Although his family was more comfortable financially than their neighbors, they were nonetheless poor, and they all dreamed about life in the United States. One day, Arturo's mother left the family to go work in the United States. She regularly sent Arturo toys and gifts and he was well cared for by his relatives, especially his grandmother, but still he felt somewhat abandoned and alone.

Of course, his health remained another issue that confronted Arturo. By the time he was seven, his heart had deteriorated considerably, to the point where he had difficulty breathing and performing basic tasks of daily living. Doctors told the family that he needed surgery desperately. The state of technology and expertise in pediatric cardiac care in El Salvador was not adequate to deal with his condition. Arturo would have to leave the country to have his surgery.

Consequently, Arturo's mother returned to El Salvador to take him to Los Angeles for the operation. Because they did not have the necessary immigration papers, they would have to enter the United States illegally, as Arturo's mother had the first time she went there.

Their journey started with a long bus ride from San Salvador all the way through Mexico to Tijuana. When they reached Tijuana, Arturo and his mother separated. His mother would have to enter the United States by crossing a river. Arturo, because of his health, would be smuggled across in the back of a truck. Arturo doesn't remember being scared or apprehensive about his journey:

> I wasn't scared to go with the man in the truck because it was an adventure to me. My mother had tricked me and told me I was just going for a visit. I didn't know about the surgery I would have. I didn't even know I needed to have surgery. So I wasn't anxious about anything except how fast I could get to Los Angeles. My mother said we would meet in a short time anyway, so I went right to the man who was going to take me there.

Although the issue was never discussed with his mother, Arturo assumed he would meet his biological father in Los Angeles. He had no reason to doubt it. After all, he had heard his mother talk about the "male friend" who lived with her. He was so excited and anxious about the prospect of being with his father that he could not bear to ask his mother directly about this "male friend" but kept his dreams to himself.

Crossing the border was easy and uneventful, although he experienced culture shock when he saw Anglo people.

> I had never seen a white person in my life. As far as I was aware, tan was as light as one could get and a person only looked white whenever they were sick.

Once he was in San Diego, Arturo reunited with his mother. From there, they traveled to Los Angeles, where his mother lived. After all his dreaming on the bus, he was disappointed by the reality of her life in the United States.

> I imagined that people in this country made money as easily as they breathed in the air. I thought my mom was doing well. If she could buy and send me toys, I figured she had to be doing real well, and that she maybe owned her own house or two.

Instead of a house, his mother lived in an old, decrepit apartment building. The dingy apartment of three rooms (if one counted the bathroom) was stuffed full with six people. Arturo was accustomed to living with a large group of people, but they had a large house. Worst of all, despite his hopes, Arturo soon realized that his mother's male friend was not his father. Understandably disillusioned and disappointed, he deeply resented his mother's new husband.

Happily, Arturo's journey accomplished its main purpose. Arturo did get the operation he needed, at Children's Hospital of Los Angeles, and he made a dramatic recovery. For the first time in his life, Arturo was now able to run, climb trees, and, in short, act like a normal 7-year-old.

Despite Arturo's recovery, life in the United States was difficult. His mother and stepfather were very poor. His mother worked ten to fourteen hours a day, seven days a week, cleaning houses for people in West Los Angeles, a long trek from their Pico-Union apartment. His stepfather was working in a steel shop when Arturo arrived, but unfortunately he soon lost his job and was unable to find a stable one for several years. Still, although Arturo knew that they didn't have as much as other people in the United States, he didn't really think he was poor. That changed when he started going to school.

School brought big changes for him in many ways. First of all, when he started going to school he realized that he wasn't going back to El Salvador. He became intensely homesick. Second, he had to go to school alone, and negotiating his way through the city streets terrified him. His mother had accompanied him for the first several days, but because she had to work she had to let him go by himself after that. In El Salvador, his grandmother or aunt had always accompanied him places. Third, when he started going to school he began comparing himself to his classmates, and he soon realized that he was indeed poor.

This realization hit him the hardest one day when it was raining particularly hard. Because he did not have a rain jacket or an umbrella, his mother fashioned him a rain jacket out of a large garbage bag. At first, he liked his new rain jacket—to him it looked like the one soldiers wore in the movies. When he got to school, however, and proudly took off his jacket and placed it next to his classmates' umbrellas and rain jackets, all his classmates began pointing at him and laughing. Even the teacher seemed to be smiling at him.

> That was the first time I felt ashamed of being poor. I didn't wear the bag on my way home and got drenched for it. That was the last time I ever let anyone point at me and laugh. To this day, I can't stand it when someone smiles at me for no reason.

Somewhat surprisingly, learning English was not a difficult task for him. The transition was aided greatly by a bilingual education teacher who worked with Arturo one on one. In addition, most of Arturo's classmates were Mexican, and so they were often in the same position that he was in terms of learning the English language. They all managed to communicate despite their different Spanish dialects.

Learning English was important to Arturo because he realized that his mother needed his help. On weekends and vacations, Arturo would go with his mother to the homes where she worked. Arturo soon realized that some of the people she worked for would call her stupid because she had difficulty pronouncing some words or had misspelled something in the notes she had left for them. Arturo took it upon himself to learn English as rapidly as possible so that he could translate for his mother. In a way, his determination to do this characterized their general relationship: Arturo felt that he had to protect his mother, while his mother depended on Arturo to act as her guide. At the same time he protected her, Arturo was ashamed of his mother. He said:

> It didn't seem very cool to clean houses. When my friends asked me
> what she did, I had to tell them she cleaned other people's houses.

Overall, Arturo did quite well in school. He first started when he was nine, in the second grade in the middle of the school year (thus he started out one grade behind). Understandably, he did not do well his first year and flunked all his courses. But as his English improved so did his performance in school, and thereafter Arturo received good grades.

While Arturo was learning English in school, he also was learning about life in the streets of Pico-Union. Because his mother and stepfather worked long hours, Arturo was often left alone after school and spent most of his time on the streets. His neighborhood was a comfortable place for him in that virtually everyone came from El Salvador. The sounds of people speaking and the smells were all familiar. In the hallways of his apartment building, children would play games he remembered from his childhood. On the fire escape, Salvadoran music would blare while people ate watermelon. Arturo himself would roam the streets of his neighborhood or box on the roof of his building with his friends.

Arturo soon learned to gain the respect of his friends by demonstrating that he had no fear. Of course, his friends placed a great deal of value on not backing down from a fight. Even if Arturo knew an opponent could "kick my ass," he acted unafraid. Willing to take on anyone and perform any daring challenge, Arturo soon gained a reputation for being tough.

> I was not a good fighter, but I didn't mind the pain and would always get up when knocked down. Also, if I managed to get the other person on the floor, I'd bash his head on the floor till he started to cry.

When they weren't fighting, Arturo and his friends spent their time in the neighborhood on skateboards or grabbing car bumpers and stealing rides. They would drag their skateboards to the top of a hill and speedily coast down through traffic lights and intersections. One time Arturo flew through a red light and a car hit him. Fortunately, he sustained only a broken arm. Soon after he recovered, he was out coasting down the hill again.

Spending so much time on the streets, Arturo also came into contact with police. One of his first contacts occurred at a movie theater when Arturo was 12 years old, just starting junior high school. Arturo and his friends had been watching the movie when police with riot gear began storming the theater. Arturo had no idea why they were there. He saw people getting hit over the head by the police, even though they were already handcuffed. Everyone was yelling and crying. Prior to this incident, Arturo had not had much exposure to the police. He thought that they only picked up the bodies of dead people. As limited as this seems, he had never seen them do anything else.

> I became very afraid of the police. It was like I woke up that day and didn't trust them. If they could do what they did to people that day, I didn't think they were good.

Overnight, neighbors and friends would disappear and the gossip on the streets was that they had been deported. Disappearing people were a part of Arturo's memories of El Salvador that he would just as soon have forgotten. These missing people added to his distrust of the government. Arturo quickly decided, then, to place no trust in any government authority.

Up to this time Arturo had been a relatively good student in school, even though he did not have much parental support. Arturo's mother would often emphasize the importance of an education to him, but she was unable to follow through and help him because of her long work hours. Arturo remembered bringing home notices to his mother about parent-teacher conferences, and he always hoped that his mother could come. Inevitably, his mother would be too busy, and so Arturo would have to go with his friend's parents. Eventually, Arturo stopped giving the notices to his mother. Although disappointed, Arturo could never get mad at his mother, because he knew "if she didn't work, we didn't eat."

Bused to a junior high school in the suburbs, Arturo had a daily commute of two hours round-trip. He felt like an outsider in a school where most of his classmates were Anglo and from families that were better off. Believing he did not fit into the suburban school environment, he resorted to fighting to gain respect.

> There were a few Latinos who already lived there, you know. But they were like Anglos to me, the way they were. They were embarrassed by us poor city Latinos. So that made it even a worse place. I was ready every minute to take anyone on.

After he fought several times, Arturo noticed that using his fists to make a statement had paid off with his peers.

> I instantly had friends. Girls that had only looked past me in the beginning began to speak to me. During this time I got into many fights with big, small, all types. Every time, whether I won or lost, I seemed to get more respect.

Having gained some respect, Arturo now began a quest for "power." The school was "ruled" by several Anglo kids who had flunked several grades and thus were older and bigger than the other students (yet slower academically). Eventually, Arturo and several of his friends (also bused-in Salvadorans) beat up enough of the Anglo kids to gain "control" of the school—that is, they got the best seats in the cafeteria, the best spots on the playground, and so forth.

While Arturo and his friends "ruled" the playground, Arturo was losing ground in the classroom. For the first time, he experienced difficulty in his relationships with his teachers. Teacher reports from that time dismiss him as "one of those kids who probably won't make it" or "a constant problem." One teacher made him stand up in front of the class and then directed him to pick up all the trash. Arturo recalls, "All the teachers never gave us Latino kids a break." As his resentment of his teachers grew, Arturo became more rebellious and, predictably, began spending more time in detention.

As school became more of a negative experience, Arturo began ditching it. In the morning he would take the bus to school, and from there he would leave with his friends to hang out at the mall, McDonald's, or the home of a friend whose parents were absent. During their time away from school, he and his friends would listen to music, experiment with cigarettes and occasionally marijuana, and commit acts of petty theft such as stealing bikes and candy. In the afternoon, Arturo would catch the bus home. In the evening, he hit the streets with his closest friends and together they would steal from cars in parking lots or would steal bikes:

> Just for the hell of it we would jump some foolish kid who happened to be riding his bike and then we would sell it. If the bike happened to be good, we could sell it for as much as $75. Otherwise, we took it apart and used the parts to fix our own bikes. We did this almost every night.

Arturo's mother was never aware of his behavior. Her English was still poor and so she could not understand the notices the school sent to her. Also, she simply was too busy at work to be able to discipline Arturo at home. His stepfather, meanwhile, didn't have the authority to discipline him. Arturo simply would not allow himself to be subjected to him, and if his stepfather felt that Arturo had to be disciplined, his only recourse was to tell Arturo's mother and have her impose the discipline.

It was while Arturo was in junior high school that an "uncle"—actually his stepfather's younger brother—came to live with them. At first, Arturo and his uncle, a high schooler, did not get along and avoided each other. Things changed, however, when a group on the street cornered Arturo and wanted to "jack him up." His uncle, by then a member of the Normandie Locos, rescued him. The Normandie Locos were one of the biggest cliques of the Mara Salvatrucha, a Salvadoran youth gang. At the time his uncle had joined (around 1988), the Mara were not yet very large. Mostly they were a bunch of kids who wore Vans shoes, torn blue jeans, and heavy metal shirts. Gradually, however, with the influx of Salvadoran nationals who escaped to Los Angeles to avoid the Salvadoran civil war, the Mara grew, especially in the Hollywood and Pico-Union areas.

At first Arturo was afraid of the Mara, and whenever he was on the streets he tried to avoid them. After stealing a bike, he and his friends would be especially careful to watch out for the Mara, because they would likely demand the bikes as "payment." But after the Mara members in his neighborhood realized who his uncle was, Arturo was assumed to be a member of the Mara as well and was left alone. For the first time, Arturo could cruise the streets of his neighborhood at any time and know that he was safe from being "jacked up." Arturo began to respect his uncle because of his role in the Mara, and they soon formed a close relationship.

As a member of the Mara, Arturo spent most of his time just hanging out in the neighborhood with his homeboys, experimenting with light drugs and exchanging gossip. Once in a while, their routine would be highlighted by soccer games, which were extremely important to the Mara.

> The guys from the Mara Salvatrucha loved to watch and, if possible, attend soccer games. Particularly when a team from El Salvador came to play at the Coliseum against a team from Mexico. They would arrive by the carloads to go watch the games. They would go so far as to run to the other side where the Mexican fans sat, and they would steal a Mexican flag and tear it up in front of everyone.

Other activities of the Mara centered on their hated enemy, the Drifters. Whereas the Mara were known as stoners (i.e., they favored heavy metal music), the Drifters were known as disco freaks. The Drifters had a distinctive dress—Fila shoes, baggy khaki pants, white undershirt, and a baseball cap with the letter D on it. More important, they had their own neighborhood, or turf. Violations—even perceived violations—of turf were a common reason for fights between the two groups, for they each jealously and vigilantly guarded their borders.

At one time Arturo had been friends with several members of the Drifters, but after he joined the Mara the animosity between the two groups was so strong that it took precedence over any friendships that Arturo had had.

Arturo recalled his friend, Cebolla, who was a member of the Drifters:

> Cebolla had grown up in the neighborhood and we had been friends at first. But later on he became a Drifter, so we stopped being

friends. Eventually the other guys from the Mara found out that he was a Drifter, so he would not leave his house till night and he would not show himself for days at a time. He had already been warned that if he showed up in the neighborhood claiming the Drifters he was going to get killed. One evening somebody saw him trying to sneak into his house, and the next thing he knew, about ten guys, including me, rushed after him. I really didn't want to jack him, but I was with my homeboys and he was a Drifter. So we just had to do it. Not only did we kick his butt, but we kicked his father's butt when he took out his shotgun and tried to interfere. We took the gun away from him and used it to shoot up his home. A few days later Cebolla moved away, and he never showed himself in the neighborhood again.

While the Mara had many enemies—namely, any gang that had territory near their neighborhood—they also had uneasy alliances with other gangs. One of their allies was the Fedora Locos. The Locos were not actually a youth gang but a loose collection of drug dealers who sold drugs on Fedora Street (near Olympic Avenue in downtown Los Angeles). Many of the Locos were Salvadoran, and virtually all were from Central America. They were, in general, older (over 18 years old) and sold drugs to support themselves and their families. Members of the Mara, including Arturo, would help the Locos by hiding their stash for them or by loaning them small amounts of cash. Arturo explained their "business" relationship:

> I didn't sell drugs, but I would give them some of my own money, which they would use to buy more stuff—usually weed, coke and sometimes heroin, acid, PCP, and just about any other drug you could imagine. In the next couple of weeks, they would pay me what I had given them plus some of the profit. So if I gave them ten dollars I would usually get fifty in return. This wasn't much compared to how much they actually made, but at least you didn't have to worry about getting caught selling.

Later, however, some members of the Mara began to steal drugs from the Locos. They were later found dead—each shot three times in the head—and the Mara retaliated by driving the Locos out of Fedora Street. In a short time, only members of the Mara were selling on the street.

By this time, Arturo found himself disagreeing more and more with the activities of the Mara. The incident with Cebolla had left him with ambiguous feelings about his loyalty to the Mara, and although Arturo enjoyed smoking marijuana, he hated the idea of selling drugs. The Mara was also growing dramatically. Younger youths were eager to join, and the size of the group in Arturo's neighborhood grew from about fifteen core members to over seventy, at which point Arturo found he did not have the same feeling of kinship he had originally had with his homeboys when they were like his brothers. As more and more youths joined the Mara, Arturo found himself drifting away from its core members.

During this time, Arturo was going to high school, again a school located in the suburbs, and so he still took the bus to school every morning. Students from all parts of Los Angeles were bused to the predominantly white, upper-class school, and the high school simmered with racial tensions. Daily fights between racial groups required the intervention of the school police. In one fight, Arturo remembers, a teacher was stabbed in the arm with a pencil when he tried to break up a fight.

Life in the classroom became unimportant to Arturo as he focused all his energy on simply trying to protect himself in a hostile environment. Often he was put in detention for fighting, and in the tenth grade he began to carry a knife to school for protection. Eventually, his propensity for fighting got him expelled from the high school. Arturo transferred to another high school and was soon expelled from it, and then two more schools, for fighting.

As his expulsions multiplied and his dissatisfaction with life in the Mara deepened, Arturo became increasingly depressed.

> High school was definitely the hardest time for me. I couldn't stand to be at home with my family, and I would spend most of my time alone. At times, I even thought about killing myself. Instead, I would just go sit on a bus bench and collect a bunch of bottles. I'd just sit there and wait for cars to drive by, especially if it was a fool who was trying to act cool. Then I'd just throw the bottles at the car. I'm not sure why I did it. I felt like I was dying inside. Before I would get a rush from something like that.

It was yet another beating that finally provided the impetus for Arturo to realize he had to change his life. Linky, a member of a rival gang, confronted Arturo in the school parking lot. Arturo called several of his Mara homeboys over, but then Linky called over an even larger group of his homeboys. Seeing they were outnumbered, Arturo's homeboys all ran off. They told Arturo to run too, but for some reason he stayed to confront Linky and his friends:

> Before I knew it I was on the floor. After a few minutes they stopped kicking me, and I got up. I started walking toward them again because I wanted to keep fighting. Then all of a sudden I heard this voice of a girl I knew. She was one of my best friends at school. She just kept yelling, "No, don't do it!" I just felt this sudden shame. I wasn't ashamed of losing, since I had lost a lot of times. But it just all of a sudden became clear to me that I was getting my head beat for no good reason. And where were all my friends? They all ran away so that I was left alone.

After that incident, a disillusioned Arturo transferred to still another high school, stopped fighting, and began to concentrate on school again. Critical to his turnaround was his uncle, who by this time had settled down with a steady girlfriend, a child, and a stable job. Gradually, he had turned away from the Mara, and he encouraged Arturo to do the same.

Arturo's stepfather also became an important influence in his life, especially after his mother gave birth to a son, Arturo's half-brother. After the birth, Arturo expected his stepfather to leave. He reasoned:

> My father left me when I was born. It just seemed like somebody was always leaving me. But he [his stepfather] never left my mom or me. He stayed on, even after my brother was born.

When his stepfather stayed, Arturo realized that each man makes his own choices. It was at this time that Arturo began to call his stepfather "Father."

Eventually, Arturo began getting good grades in school again. He managed to graduate from high school on time and even enrolled at a community college. About three months after the graduated from high school, Arturo happened to run into Linky, the member of the rival gang that had beaten him. This time, they were both alone but Linky happened to be in Arturo's neighborhood. Arturo describes the encounter.

> When he saw me, he got spooked because he knew he was in my neighborhood. Instead, I just went up to him and talked. He told me

he was trying to get out of the gang. We agreed that if we had lived in the same neighborhood we would probably have been friends. Then we just parted. Later I told my mother what happened and I asked her if I had acted like a man. She told me I had done the right thing. I felt like such a coward though, and I don't know why I didn't beat him up, but all I can remember is that I was fed up with all the fighting.

Maybe he didn't realize it at the time, but Arturo, like his stepfather, made the choice to be his own man.

11

Charting a New Future for Urban Youth

HUNDREDS OF YEARS from today, observers will look back to the time when the United States struggled with a serious street gang problem. From that distance, their frame of reference will not be a few of our contemporary decades but will begin around 1850 and extend into the twenty-first century, which we can only hope they will be able to see as the time when serious, scientific efforts to eradicate the problem surfaced and won the day. Then the Plug Uglies will not be remembered the way we think of them now, as quaintly removed from us, but rather as just another part of the days when there were all those gangs.

Although circumstances are different for each of the ethnic groups discussed in this book, it is clearly the difficulty of adapting and adjusting to a new culture that has led to the unraveling of social control institutions within some sectors of all the communities examined. In particular, families, schools, and law enforcement have collectively failed to develop the connections, engagements, and involvements necessary to ensure that its new members will conform to society's belief and value system. Significant numbers of youths from low-income, ethnic minority populations that have been subjected to the many combined effects of economic, social, cultural, and ecologic marginalization continue to fall prey to the streets when disruptions in parenting, learning, and sanctioning routines occur. With loosened ties to key social influences and without adequate conventional socialization, these youth are street-socialized in ways that are remarkably similar but nevertheless reflect each community's unique ethnic history.[1] In time, gang members become a street fixture in the community, an institutionalized subculture with its own set of rules and regulations affecting both males and females. The patterns and practices within the subculture derive their texture and context from the ethnic group's own subculture and its relationship with other ethnic communities. Understanding why and how this transpires can set the tone and point the direction in seeking remedies for the gang problem.

Comprehension of the process, and the gang subcultures it produces, is enhanced by cross-cultural investigation across groups along similar dimensions within a social control framework that has conformity, rather than deviancy, as its paramount focus. While the cross-cultural analysis here is set in the same place and time (Los Angeles in the 1990s), previous experiences of the various ethnic communities have created contrasting macrohistorical and macrostructural situations among the groups. Considered in the context of these peoples' histories and socioeconomic trajectories, place and time take on renewed, multidimensional significance, particularly when we look at the connections between the history of a group and the history of an individual in the group.

For the Vietnamese and Salvadoran populations, breakdowns in social control actually began before immigration to the United States. U.S. interventions in the affairs of both nations, overt and covert, were largely responsible for the uprooting of hundreds of thousands of people. These interventions were intended to save both nations from the spread of communism, a failed attempt in the first instance and an aborted one in the other. The Vietnamese and Salvadoran refugees, having found their way to the United States, and especially the Los Angeles area, both experienced difficulties maintaining control over their children. The Vietnamese settlement pattern was more dispersed, with pockets in downtown Los Angeles, the San Gabriel Valley, and Orange County. In contrast, Salvadorans were concentrated in the Pico-Union area just west of downtown Los Angeles, the neighborhood that became famous as one scandal after another, most of them involving police officers' dealings with the street gang population, hit the Ramparts Station of the Los Angeles Police Department.[2] Integral to the scandals was the revelation that police and immigration officials colluded in seizing and deporting gang members to El Salvador, which resulted in the exportation of a violent gang culture to an already war-torn country.[3]

Breakdowns in social control occurred earlier for the resident Chicano and black populations and took place wholly within the United States when, especially in Los Angeles, their respective populations reached a numerically critical mass in certain areas, generating large segments of marginalized youth. These developments, which began in the 1930s and 1940s in Chicano barrios and in the 1950s in the African American ghetto, were an entrenched phenomenon by the 1990s. Marginalization of Chicanos, in fact, dates back to the time the United States annexed California and other areas of the Southwest and thereafter treated them as pariahs. What exacerbated matters is that whites looked upon them as illegal aliens and conveniently forgot that they were native to the area. After World War I, large-scale immigration—continuous but with periodic ebbs and flows to this day—helped feed into and maintain a choloization (marginalization) process. This mostly second-generation dynamic ensured a steady crop of youths ripe for gang membership in each succeeding generation. As the decades passed and a cholo street subculture became more and more deeply rooted, even members of the first generation of subsequent immigrant families were recruited into the subculture.[4]

Blacks have a "long memory"[5] of race and racism as pivotal forces in their lives, forces that have affected their integration (or disintegration) throughout the United States. In Los Angeles, race restrictions, racist attitudes and treatment, and exclusion and isolation had a tremendous impact on the adjustment of newly arrived blacks, especially after World War II when the population mushroomed. At different times and in different ways, both blacks and Chicanos experienced an economic marginalization that was accompanied by the concentration of residents in isolated, ecologically distinct neighborhoods (i.e., ghettos in South Central Los Angeles and barrios in greater East Los Angeles).

For the Salvadorans and Vietnamese, family life often was undermined before or during their journey to the United States; for example, the two individuals whose case histories have been examined here both arrived in the company of a single parent. Once they were in Los Angeles, the constant everyday struggle for economic survival dominated the family situation. The children were "latchkeyed," left to fend for themselves while parents worked. Cultural barriers and language difficulties complicated their lives generally, but especially in the schooling situation, where conflict with teachers and classmates interfered with learning. Law enforcement was not seen as a positive force in either the Pico-

Union area or the Vietnamese communities. Both groups viewed authority figures with a jaundiced eye, partly because of experiences they had had in their home countries. The case study of Huc illustrates links between Vietnamese youth gangs and Asian organized crime networks, which Huc became a part of, later serving time in prison for his transgressions. Arturo, the Salvadoran, finally reconciled with his mother and stepfather and turned his life around, demonstrating that even youths who participate enthusiastically in gang activities can sometimes be encouraged to redirect their lives in more prosocial directions.

Statistically, blacks have the highest percentage of single-parent families.[6] However, whether a family is of the single-parent or two-parent variety, it is the strains the family is under that make for attenuated parental control, and even working-class families can lose control.[7] Mookie's parents brought their two sons to Los Angeles, provided them with a living arrangement in a refashioned garage, and then proceeded to live a life separate from each other and their sons. Mainly, the parents were grasping for the freedom and opportunities that had eluded them in rural East Texas. Schooling, which included busing and a series of new situations to adjust to, was never a smooth affair for Mookie. His checkered learning career was strongly affected by the unusual family situation that had him staying with a series of caretakers, who provided him little guidance in his education. Growing up in an area and time period in which black gang life was at its peak, he early on began to hang out on the streets and came in contact with unsavory characters and negative influences. Interactions with law enforcement also took a negative turn. Eventually, his record included CYA detentions and finally a sentence of life in prison for murder.

Puppet, Arturo's Chicano counterpart, was born into an already thoroughly disrupted family: His parents both had been raised in barrios and were affiliated with gangs in their youth.[8] They were at one time or another addicted to drugs and other substances. Puppet is one of the second-generation members of the gang subculture, a small but growing percentage of all Chicano gang members. Whereas Puppet's father had completely and totally abrogated his parenting duties, his mother struggled to adequately care for her four sons—but lost the battle. Thus, Puppet lived in a series of relatives' houses and foster homes, mostly bad ones, and wound up on the streets in practically every neighborhood he was moved to. Schooling experiences were filled with hostile and destructive events, including the time he and his friends attacked the gym teacher. Police and detention facilities figured prominently in his life, for even while still in elementary school he was learning how to break the law and run from the cops.[9]

Females also undergo the experiences outlined in the biographies included here, but the biographies do not speak of them much. The stories of Puppet and Arturo yield little information about the girls in their lives, and what Mookie had to say was mostly disparaging. These responses (or lack of responses) are common and fit the overall indifferent attitude of male gang members toward females in their set, although Huc did speak of the group solidarity among males and females. Sexual exploitation and male dominance appear to affect all the females, with variations within each ethnic group, and the *locura* (craziness) that results is expressed in diverse ways. Black female and Chicana gang members have become more "street," in that they often join their male counterparts in criminal activities—hiding weapons and drugs, setting up rival gang males for hits, and the like. This involvement stems from the longer experience both ethnic groups have had in the streets. Black females, who have a longer history of culture conflict and change, have had to develop greater self-reliance in order to survive. Among gang-associated females of the other groups, tensions between the values and norms of their traditional culture and of U.S. culture play a stronger role.

The biographies of individuals illustrate some features commonly found in their respective communities which, taken together, comprise the background that contributes to the growth of street gangs. For example, census figures indicate that single-parent families make up larger proportions of the African American (57 percent) and Hispanic (32 percent) populations than of the white population (22 percent).[10] In many of the two-parent households in marginalized neighborhoods, however, family violence can be more disruptive in children's lives than having a single parent. In a survey of 1,000 seventh- and eighth-graders, nearly seven in ten children who were exposed to abuse, violence, or neglect in their homes also reported committing "delinquent" acts themselves, and exposure to family violence increased by half the probability of children being involved in violence away from the home.[11] These home conditions are often compounded by school problems, reflected in part by school dropout rates: Whereas at the national level 7.7 percent of white youths drop out of high school, 12.6 percent of blacks and 30 percent of Hispanics do so.[12] In California in recent years, declining public funding for family assistance and schooling has aggravated the situation. Meanwhile, incarceration rates have increased and minority youths have disproportionally filled the California Youth Authority's facilities; in 1999, whites made up only 14 percent of the CYA population, while Hispanics and African Americans comprised 49 percent and 28 percent, respectively.[13]

In 1989, I conducted a summer ethnographic training seminar funded by the Social Science Research Council. As part of their training, I had students undertake a survey of youths interned at a CYA facility in Los Angeles County that included a series of interviews with the youths. Nearly all of the inmates had dropped out of school well before the incidents that led to their incarceration. Most of them indicated they had had serious problems with school before dropping out. Four of every five reported they had been raised in single-parent households, and a large majority (as many as 91 percent of the Salvadoran inmates) had been exposed to or experienced family violence. These inmate youths—almost all of them gang members and all of them convicted of serious, usually violent, crimes—exemplified the marginalized, street-socialized backgrounds that are typical of youth gang participants.

Such trends and statistics, in combination with the contextualized life histories and ethnographic evidence, enable us to formulate or revive different strategies to resolve or at least alleviate the street gang problem. Social reformers of the late nineteenth century, especially women in the suffragette movement, attempted to help "pavement children" by organizing social and recreational clubs and activities. A host of initiatives and individual efforts such as Jane Addams' Hull House and Jacob Riis' investigative reporting and photography[14] and, later, Father Flanagan's Boys Town addressed the problem. Such well-meaning efforts never had the support or continuity needed to bring about significant changes for most marginalized youth, but this spirit of helping the less fortunate certainly became enshrined in the U.S. value system. It is noteworthy, though, that these much-romanticized efforts were focused on troubled white children, not on the children of people of color, who, today as in the past, are disproportionately found among the less fortunate.

The simple fact is that the solution to the street gang problem must be based on the reason for the existence of gangs: When the institutions of social control break down, the gang fills the gap by regulating a youth's life, replacing parenting, schooling, and policing. To combat the street gang subculture and subsociety, we must look at the ways separate social control influences—family, school, and law enforcement—are integrated and interact with each other. In, for example, the life history vignettes in this book, this reciprocal connection showed an action and reaction interplay that evolved over time. The larger dynamics of poverty, cultural contrasts and conflicts, and racial discrimination strongly affected the social control institutions in the lives of the individuals portrayed.

Gaining and maintaining social equilibrium through conformity is a formidable, sometimes unattainable task. Thus it is all the more laudable when success comes for families that survive, when students piece together an academic path, and when more constructive relations with law enforcement are struck. What do we need to understand in order to make these outcomes more likely for more members of afflicted communities? Would things have turned out differently for Puppet, Mookie, Huc, and Arturo if their family lives had had more structure and if their parents had provided more direction and guidance? How can we address the absence of parenting and early voids in the development of connections, so necessary in leading the child to engagements, involvements, and beliefs? First of all, we must not forget that families and other household members do not exist in a vacuum.[15] A long history of racism and poverty has had lingering effects on how family life is structured and organized, and whether it can effectively participate in society. Moreover, schooling for minority youth and relations with law enforcement in general affect family life, since poor people often receive short shrift from authorities in these institutions.

Schooling problems have especially plagued the lives and careers of blacks and Latinos in the United States. Both groups have a long and well-documented history of exclusion from or isolation within public schools, along with other forms of unfair and unequal scholastic treatment, such as the racism that affects testing and tracking learning programs.[16]

How people support their families and where people live is often a direct result of discrimination in jobs and housing. A concomitant effect of discrimination is separate and unequal schooling. In Los Angeles, the busing program initiated in the 1970s attempted to partially rectify the situation by sending inner-city children to more affluent neighborhoods with bigger and newer schools, more equipment, and well-trained, experienced teachers. But, as we know from the stories of Mookie and Arturo, this venture had its downside. In short, efforts to change and improve educational opportunities and learning programs for under-served youth still have a long way to go before we rid ourselves of the deeply rooted inequities of the past.

As for law enforcement and the overall criminal justice system, the Rodney King beating and the Ramparts Station scandals tell it all. The youngsters in this book have all had brushes with the law, and their over-all attitude toward police remains hostile. This makes perfectly good sense, since they have been lawbreakers. However, an attitude of distrust and fear of police is shared by many law-abiding, poor ethnic minority residents. This makes for poor police-community relations, full of recriminations and antagonisms rather than open and constructive com-munication. Imagined and fabricated incidents on both sides often over-take and dominate the dialogue to further harden attitudes. Among gang members, the consensus is that police are always hassling them, and hardly anything positive transpires between gangs and police. Are there ways to change this? Can police entertain and develop youth programs to reach preteen children before they become gang members and it's too late? How about the community in general?

Perhaps we should consider whether the gang problem and the dynamics leading up to it are so rooted and intractable that there is no way we can seriously rectify them. The response to this proposition will have implications for the changes taking place among urban youth throughout the world.[17] A natural outcome of a free-market economic system based on competition, such as ours and those that are spreading widely into other areas of the world, is economic inequality—winners and losers. The greater the economic gap between winners and losers, the more structurally embedded the marginalization of large segments of the population becomes, usually along racial and cultural lines. Are we incapable of redistribution strategies and the development of safety nets for the unfortunate, uncompetitive, untalented, or, simply, for the "out-siders"?[18] When income gaps occur, do we point a finger at those with the lowest income and charge them with being socially irresponsible, or do we recognize the social culpability of those owning the corporations who close businesses and plants and move them abroad, ignoring the economic hardships they create at home?

If it is true that pronounced inequality has to accompany this eco-nomic system, where privilege and ethnocentrism prevail in deciding who wins or loses, then we must also acknowledge that certain outcomes should be expected. For example, marginalization of all stripes will interfere with the social processes that lead to conformity. Families and children cannot conform if they have no access to the dominant culture and lack a mode of identifying with it.[19] If, in addition, their ethnic subculture becomes reshaped in their lives through errant acculturation—that is, if they are led to subscribe not to the dominant values and norms of U.S. society but instead to deviant, antisocial standards—they will be even more hamstrung in their adaptation and adjustment to the city. Children from fragmented family and neighborhood backgrounds will be forced to substitute another social and cultural process to guide them through an unconventional life.[20] When this occurs, resulting in gangs, law-abiding citizens of society hope that suppression works. But there are limitations, clearly, to this strategy. Thus, we must consider alternative (indeed, supplemental) strategies that are directed at other focal points and have different dynamics. We no longer have any choice in the matter. Safety nets and ways of formulating redistribution schemes must be fashioned in innovative, creative ways.

Let us consider a strategy that parents utilize on a daily basis, an approach that could be instructive for policymakers interested in combating gangs. In raising a child it is usual to balance the use of rewards with that of punishments; carrots and sticks, in combination and as needed, is how we raise our children to conform. Providing love, affection, and emotional support is a common form of reward, and withholding the same is viewed as punishment. As we have seen in the life histories, this basis for establishing connections was often nonexistent or unevenly practiced. What tended to dominate the early lives of our young gang members was punishment or pain of one sort or another. No one, least of all other members of the community or representatives of society, was there to fill the void early on and to consistently give balance to how they were treated. Much later in their lives, society stepped in, but only with more of the same—punishment. Most parents would cringe at this unbalanced approach to persuading a child to conform. Do low-income children not deserve a chance to be raised in a balanced way?

For a variety of reasons, our solution to the gang problem and the youth that join gangs has simply been suppression and a markedly uneven application of law enforcement.[21] The persistence of this strategy is epitomized in the recent California juvenile crime bill Proposition 21, which passed and is now a law.[22] Everything about a youth's early life is ignored, cavalierly tossed aside as insignificant and outside the purview of meaningful solutions to the problem. Little consideration is given to the macrohistorical experiences and macrostructural backgrounds that triggered and set in motion the social control disruptions. Though some government and political leaders of late have begun to reconsider the importance of having strategies that begin earlier in the lives of youth from gang-infested areas, the allocation of resources and level of investment in prevention and intervention are pale in comparison to those earmarked for suppression efforts. The will to bring about constructive change is still largely absent. Because of the backlash against the Great Society, and all the rest of what the 1960s represents, such prevention and intervention social programs and approaches for years were considered, at best, as liberal pork-barrel politics.[23] Barely hidden below the surface of this politically charged assessment is a moral judgment. Accordingly, it was "values" that mattered, and therefore social programs were ineffective in remedying the problems of population segments many considered lacking in values.

We are not two nations, we are one; we are not two separate societies, an inner city and everything outside it. What is needed today to address gang problems (and other social problems as well) is a balance of prevention, intervention, and law enforcement,[24] the carrots and sticks that enable parents to help their children conform. We must begin to think of the children of our society, particularly the less fortunate, as ours to care for at an early age. Detractors will claim that this strategy is unworkable, impractical, and if implemented, another expensive form of welfare. Failing to realize that the present criminal justice apparatus is also a form of welfare, criminal justice welfare, these naysayers forget that hundreds of billions of dollars are spent every year to warehouse hundreds of thousands of largely poor, ethnic minority peoples[25] and to pay hospitalization and rehabilitation costs of gang-related violence (over $1 billion annually in Los Angeles alone).[26] Sadly, the usual approach to youth crime continues despite studies that show that the tactics of early intervention and prevention cost far less, yield greater benefits, and far surpass in savings those of the current strategy.[27]

In California the prison population has spiraled out of control. The costs for this narrow punishment strategy are exorbitant. For every new prison bed that is budgeted, there will be less money available for higher education. Each prison bed means eliminating support for four community college students, or two California State University students, or one University of California student. In 1995, the California state budget for 150,000 prisoners stood at $4 billion, the same amount budgeted for the more than 700,000 children educated by the Los Angeles Unified School District. Since then, with a rising state economy, the LAUSD budget has doubled to more than $8 billion,[28] but prison costs have also increased sharply. A recent report underscored the same disparity for New York City, which now spends $8,000 a year for each child in its public schools but $93,000 a year for each child in the new juvenile detention center in the South Bronx.[29]

The unilateral suppression strategy is a failure, for the numbers of gangs, gang members, gang crimes and homicides, prisons, and prisoners have risen dramatically, and overall street influences have only increased.[30] The brief (since 1995) "precipitous" drop in crime, including homicides, that authorities frequently and fondly cited in the late 1990s appears to be headed back upward.[31] The decrease in crime was undoubtedly the by-product of a strong economy (now softening), but the cyclical nature of low and high crime rates continues to escape adherents of the belief that only suppression constitutes a successful anti-gang, anticrime strategy.

Few parents think that sticks alone can help them raise their child; neither should we expect that just getting tougher on crime, as with the "three strikes" policy, can make a major difference.[32] Nor should we start off with sticks and then throw in carrots later; most experts hold that extremes and inconsistencies create great problems in child rearing outcomes.[33] Recent research also shows that in the use of sticks by the legal system, a different kind of inconsistency is present: Black and brown children receive tougher treatment than white children "from arrest through plea bargaining to sentencing."[34] Can we afford *not* to adopt a more balanced approach with all of our children of all racial and cultural groups?

Law enforcement, of course, will always have to be a part of the maintenance of social control. Such extraordinary force is necessary at times to stem harmful or destructive nonconformist behavior. But law enforcement's approach to street gangs should not be permanently one-dimensional. In the last twenty years or more, law enforcement has had virtually unparalleled public support in addressing the gang problem. Only recently, and sheepishly, have some law enforcement leaders begun to question their policy of relying solely on suppression. One high-ranking official in the Los Angeles County Sheriff's Department admitted at a Gang Investigators Association conference that officials didn't know what would work. The same person decades earlier had been instrumental in starting the specialized gang detail OSS (Operation Safe Streets; now Safe Streets Bureau) to "nip the gang problem in the bud." At a press conference in the late 1980s, Chief Darryl Gates of the LAPD and Sheriff Sherman Block acknowledged that law enforcement alone could not stem the gang problem because the problem had social roots. That is where attention should be directed, they stated, acknowledging it would seem belatedly that it is the roots, not the buds, that should have been the focus of gang eradication efforts. The nature of the public debate forces experts and observers to stake out either a "tough" or a "soft" position on this problem, when what is actually needed is support for a strategy that balances prevention, intervention, and law enforcement. Why not take this broader, reflective approach and be smart on crime?

In a more holistic approach, prevention, intervention, and law enforcement strategies can follow a logical, developmental path. Prevention must begin in the early childhood years and continue up to age 8 or 9. Communities and agencies must take a proactive approach in addressing the primary problems of the general population in low-income areas, as well as factor in secondary prevention for specific at-risk youths and any related issues. Intervention actions must be aimed at the crucial pre-teen years, from about age 9 to 12 or 13, and should involve treatment and work with youths who are peripherally but not yet deeply connected to the streets. Dissuading youth early on from the attitudes and behavior that clearly lead to delinquent and criminal paths opens the possibility of a return to more prosocial activities. Finally, suppression is the strategy that we must rely on to stop the spread of delinquency and criminal behavior during the ages from 13 to 20 years for those who, despite our best prevention and intervention efforts, have nevertheless joined in gang activities. Here the criminal justice system applies a punitive and corrective approach to control destructive and violent behavior that often goes beyond members of the street populations. In tandem, and as needed, prevention, intervention, and law enforcement strategies can be utilized throughout the life of the individual.

Of late, with a nationwide drop in the still-high incidence of crime and gang activities, the position of public officials, especially law enforcement leaders, has changed slightly. Aggressive policing is still emphasized, but soft suppression is beginning to make actual inroads, perhaps a step toward a more balanced law enforcement approach. As a case in point, community-oriented policing strategies are currently being integrated into large-city police forces.[35] The aim of this outreach effort is to initiate and nurture closer relations and liaisons with community residents. The strategy is based on the belief that combating crime is a problem-solving enterprise that requires community participation in identifying and implementing solutions. As a slogan popular with advocates of these strategies has it, what we need is to be smart on crime prevention, not just tough on crime.

The Los Angeles County Sheriff's Department, now under the leadership of a new sheriff, Lee Baca, an early advocate of community policing, has undertaken a large-scale effort to disseminate practical and detailed community-policing programs and activities throughout the Southern California region. In addition, the department has also developed an intervention effort, referred to as VIDA (Vital Intervention through Directional Alternatives). In this program, courts redirect first-time, primarily young male offenders, about 13 to 17 years old, to the VIDA program, instead of meting out the usual punishments and detention obligations. The program consists of sixteen weeks under the supervision and personal direction of off-duty sheriff's deputies. It also includes weekly drills and exercises, tutoring and counseling, meetings and counseling sessions with parents, and preliminary overtures to other caretakers such as teachers and probation officers in order to enlist their cooperation and achieve coordination of efforts.

Another tack, one that encounters some community resistance because of its history of misuse against minorities, is enforcement of a 10:00 P.M. curfew. Youngsters caught loitering late at night would be apprehended and taken to the police station. The curfew violators' parents would be phoned and asked to pick up their children. At the station, the parents would be mildly reprimanded and asked if they would agree to attend a family and parenting counseling clinic instead of posting bail for their children. In this instance, soft suppression is integrated with other strategies.

Prevention, intervention, and law enforcement can often be interwoven. It requires, though, that various agencies and sectors agree to cooperate with each other in addressing the gang problem in their communities. A few years ago, a Los Angeles city council initiative undertook this integrated approach to the city's youth violence problem. First, key city council members put together a panel of public officials, experts, and community activists to host a series of public hearings and deliberations in different neighborhoods. After gathering information from the hearings, the city's Community Development Department fashioned a program titled L.A. Bridges, which involves linkages and partnerships among educators, parents, and law enforcement. The bridges metaphor emerged from the public hearings as a way to underscore the need for a cooperative and coordinated structure to combat gangs and violence. Most participants understood that this complex problem required a multileveled strategy and early prevention and intervention efforts. The program that was finally formulated is based in twenty-five local middle schools spread throughout the city, mostly in locations where gangs and violence are a major problem. It is too soon yet to tell how (or whether) L.A. Bridges is making a difference, considering that city politics has occasionally interfered with it.[36] However, it does approximate the approach that I am advocating here. I expect this strategy to have good outcomes, as have comparable programs throughout the nation.[37]

Private efforts can also lead to new strategies to combat street gangs and the problems of urban street youth. The Boys and Girls Clubs of America, since the era of "pavement children," have fashioned prevention and intervention programs to help such youth. More recently, a new initiative—the Inner-City Games—has attempted to address the social, recreational, and educational needs of low-income children throughout the United States. With humble beginnings in the Hollenback neighborhood of East Los Angeles, this program, headed by Danny Hernandez, attracted the attention of movie icon Arnold Schwarzenegger; soon after, Mr. Schwarzenegger helped launch a nationwide drive to replicate and expand similar youth programs. With the support and assistance of a broad network of individual donors, the Inner-City Games is now operating in close to twenty major cities.

A public policy shift toward the family, similar to the changes under way in policing, should be formulated and cultivated for low-income populations.[38] Programs to address the strains and problems of modern families are now numerous, especially so in inner-city communities where poverty and sheer survival mark daily living arrangements. Some programs are only sketchily thought out; others are quite successful innovations.

Marginalization generally erodes families and personal lives in low-income areas, but even in the poorest populations where some are especially chewed up, others remain strong and intact, even thrive. It bears repeating that only a small percentage of Chicano youth in most neighborhoods actually joins local gangs, anywhere from 4 to 14 percent. The other ethnic group gangs also have but a small portion of their youth population in gangs (the Vietnamese especially are known for having a lot of schoolboys and schoolgirls). Why aren't all the youths in these poverty-stricken and disrupted neighborhoods in gangs? What makes the difference?

Observers have noted a contrast between the poor and the working poor,[39] the difference being between giving up in despair and continuing to struggle, still hoping to make ends meet. While there is disagreement among researchers about the importance of economic issues in explaining gangs and gang behavior,[40] it is clear from my research that gangs and gang members are indeed primarily generated in low-income ethnic minority areas. The investigation focusing on family life and dynamics in a housing project in East Los Angeles that I conducted between 1992 and 1995 found further that gang members tended to come from the poorest of the poor and that the poorest poor had many more emotional and personal problems.[41] In fact, when household heads, mostly females, were asked what assistance or help they wished for, the poorest opted for personal and family counseling and assistance in tending their children. The slightly better-off family heads selected job training, English as a Second Language classes, and citizenship classes. Even in the same community, where reliance on welfare, housing assistance, and food stamps characterized almost all of the residents, there was internal variation. What this means for family support programs and assistance is that when resources are targeted for low-income areas, a special focus should be placed on the families and individuals most in need, who will warrant most of the time and attention.

Schooling and educational issues in the context of social control dysfunctions are of even higher import.[42] School is where most of a child's day is spent, under the guidance and purview of public employees. Next to parents, schools are society's best opportunity to ensure the conformity needed to maintain societal equilibrium, for connections, engagements, involvements, and beliefs are modeled and taught in schools by teachers, playmates, and other influences.

Massive changes must be introduced in urban schools in general. The first priority is to provide resources and expenditures to make up for the severe disadvantages faced by students in poor neighborhoods (and, therefore, those faced by their teachers also). Beyond that, we must hire thoroughly trained and prepared teachers, ensure that they are adequately paid, develop teacher training programs that explicitly address inner-city populations, reexamine the learning curriculum and formulate innovative strategies to revise and revamp it, initiate outreach efforts to forge stronger links to parents and communities, solicit and cultivate leadership and supervision styles and approaches that are change-oriented, recruit leaders who take risks and are willing to experiment, and apply pressure on government bodies, local to national, to generate and contribute resources and research expertise to transform urban inner-city schools and communities.[43]

Specifically, for the most marginalized, low-income children, many of whom are street-socialized, we should begin to formulate a national strategy to guide and monitor them throughout their public school experience.[44] Key to this objective is ensuring that each child learns to read. One report states that to make this happen there must be "committed principals, experienced teachers, involved parents and a campus pre-school."[45] For example, in an experimental program in Los Angeles known as Ten Schools (referring to the schools selected from low-income ethnic minority communities as a comparison group), students have shown marked improvements in reading and math skills when additional staffing and resources were made available.[46] Previously, I have argued for a continuation of the Head Start learning program by instituting a GetSmart phase in elementary school and a StaySmart one for middle school, and a student of mine has suggested even more continuity by adding BeSmart for high school, a policy recommendation labeled follow-through by other researchers.[47] The basic goal in this sequence of developmental phases is to maintain a continuous hold on the child, to help minimize the chances of anyone falling through the cracks. In this way, the small percentage of children in any low-income neighborhood who might become gang members will receive extra attention and monitoring. Coordination with parents and the overall community, as envisioned in the L.A. Bridges program, for example, is essential in this approach.[48]

There are many different strategies that can be utilized to regain control in the classroom and educate and better guide youth that might be street-socialized and also become gang members. In addition to the strategies discussed above, there are others that directly deal with the gang subculture itself, some aimed at co-opting or subverting gang values and norms. For example, the group psychology of the gang is a formidable force that teachers (as well as parents and police) have encountered and judged a hindrance to learning. Students from a gang are bonded in ways that encourage hostile and negative behavior, teacher admonishments to the contrary. Ironically, many remedial learning programs in elementary and middle school that target gang children place them and similarly street-raised youth together in the same learning groups; this grouping is often practiced to an even greater extent later on by means of alternative and continuation high schools. Such placements actually bond gang members further; in some cases, they bring potential gang members together for the first time. Thus the opportunity to learn what is taught on the streets is duplicated and reaffirmed in the school setting. Teachers and parents from various neighborhoods need to meet regularly and brainstorm on ways to counter gang subcultural values and norms.[49]

Because the seeds of the solutions to the gang problem are found in its root causes, there is always an opportunity to salvage many of the children who have been marginalized and left to the streets, despite the powerful historical and structural forces that have undermined the social control institutions of family, school, and law enforcement. The cross-cultural assessment of gangs presented here accounts for differences in time, place, and peoples but also reveals striking similarities, enough to generate universal pubic policy ideas and concerted actions designed to make a difference. With such policies and programs, we can assist and shape the future of families that until now have lost out, restructure and improve schools and schooling routines that have obviously fallen short, and develop partnerships to include peoples and communities in new criminal justice programs that encourage youth to respect society and its laws because respect is tendered to them.

Gangs will be with us for a long time and will continue to cause disruptions for society unless we do something about them now. Shoring up and strengthening social control institutions should be our first priority.

Families are first on the list of institutions, but the most difficult to address and assist because family life is mostly a private matter. Schools and the criminal justice apparatus are in the public trust, and thus they are more available to assistance and their shortcomings are easier to rectify. Let us at least start there as we figure out how to formulate a balanced strategy that makes the family the linchpin in a coordinated and cooperative effort among all parties.

Notes

Foreword

1. Furstenberg et al. 1999.
2. Whyte 1949: xviii.
3. Coleman 1961: 11.
4. Moore 1978; Vigil 1988.
5. Willis 1977.
6. Fine actually deals only with sex and violence, ignoring experimentation with drugs and alcohol, which, in my opinion, are just as important and just as much in the province of the peer group. Cf. Moore 1991.
7. High school football may seem to be a comparable venue of socialization to hypermasculinity, but the delinquencies of such pampered males are very different from those of street youth. Cf. Schwendinger and Schwendinger 1985.
8. Cf. Moore 2001; Miller 2001.

Chapter One

1. Haskins 1974: 31.
2. Moore 1998; Maxson, Klein, and Cunningham 1993; Curry and Decker 1998; Huff 1996; Yablonsky 1997; Canada 1995.
3. Researchers and writers who recorded compelling portraits of immigrant Polish, German, Irish, and Italian youths include Ashbury 1927, Thrasher 1927, and Yablonsky 1997.
4. Oliver, Johnson, and Farrell 1993; *Los Angeles Times*, May 12, 1992; Wilson 1987; Johnson and Oliver 1991, 1992; Hagedorn 1988.
5. Escobar 1998.
6. Klein 1995a; Decker and Van Winkle 1996; Boyle 1995; see Klein 1995a, 1971, and Bursik and Grasmick 1993 for definitions of gangs.
7. OJJDP 1996.
8. Klein 1995b.

9. Curry 1995; Campbell 1990.
10. Giordano 1978.
11. OJJDP 1996.
12. Decker and Van Winkle 1994; Padilla 1993; 13. Canada 1995; Currie 1993.
13. Katz 1991.
14. Scheer 1995, 2000; MacTalk 1999; Jacobs 1977.
15. Bogardus 1926; Moore 1978; Vigil 1988.
16. Montemayor 2000.
17. Melville 1994.
18. McAdoo 1993.
19. Campbell 1990.
20. Vigil 1988; Vigil and Yun 1998.
21. Moore and Hagedorn 2001; Moore 1991.
22. Quicker 1983; Chesney-Lind and Sheldon 1992.
23. Hernandez 1998.
24. African Americans approximate this dynamic in their rural South to urban North and West migration (Frazier 1966), and thus the U.S. system of formal education, while not new to them, has been kept out of their reach.
25. Orfield 1988; Suzuki and Valencia 1997; Valencia 1991; Moreno 1999; Clark 1983; Kozol 1992; Oakes 1985.
26. Buriel 1984.
27. Vigil 1993a.
28. Moore, Vigil, and Levy 1995.
29. Vigil 1999.
30. Fields 1991; Presidential Advisory Commission 1999.
31. Kawachi 1997.
32. Campbell 1990.
33. Lauderback et al. 1992.
34. See Willis 1977 for a discussion of the similar development of an oppositional culture by the British laboring class.
35. Wilson 1987; Moore and Vigil 1993; Farley 1987.
36. Vigil 2002.
37. Jackson and Rudman 1993; Zatz 1987.
38. Spergel and Curry 1998; Klein 1995b.
39. Vigil 1996; Hazlehurst and Hazlehurst 1998.
40. Hazlehurst and Hazlehurst 1998; Hecht 1998.
41. Szanton Blanc 1995.
42. Vigil 1998.
43. Vigil 2002.
44. Alonso 1999.
45. Waters 1999.
46. Katz 1988.
47. Vigil 1988.

Chapter Two

1. Cartwright, Thompson, and Schwartz 1975.
2. Over the years there have been many theories that incorporate these elements meaningfully. See, for example, Vigil 1988a and Covey, Menard, and Franzese 1992.
3. Haviland 1988: 289; Ember and Ember 1990; Haviland 1988.
4. Edgerton 1978; Haviland 1988.
5. Wiatrowski, Griswold, and Roberts 1981.
6. Covey, Menard, and Franzese 1992: 173; see also Vigil 1988a.
7. See Vigil 1988a; Thrasher [1927] 1963; Shaw and McKay 1942; Cloward and Ohlin 1960; Moore 1978, 1991; Hagedorn 1988; Spergel and Curry 1998; Klein 1995; Decker and Van Winkle 1996.
8. Freud 1923.
9. Edgerton 1978.
10. Campbell 1991.
11. Decker and Van Winkle 1996.
12. Erikson 1956; Vigil 1988b.
13. Poe-Yamagata and Butts 1996.
14. Campbell 1991.
15. Dietrich 1998.
16. Merton 1949; Cloward and Ohlin 1960.
17. Cohen 1955.
18. Foley and Ward 1992.
19. Vigil 1999.

Chapter Three

1. Moore 1978.
2. Bogardus 1934.
3. Waters 1999.
4. Samora 1971; Cornelius, Chavez, and Castro 1982; Chavez 1998.
5. Chavez 1998.
6. Most gang members were male youths, but females have always been a part of these developments, initially simply as loosely affiliated groups. In many instances, the girls' groups were transformed into gang associates that actively participated in gang activities, while occasionally they fashioned gangs of their own.
7. Moore, Vigil, and Garcia 1983: 183.
8. Research includes Moore 1978, 1991; Horowitz 1983; Vigil 1988; and Klein 1995.
9. Autobiographical accounts include Rodriguez 1993 and Hernandez 1998.
10. Some shifts in approach did occur in the late 1940s and early 1950s after the Zoot Suit riots and during the War on Poverty in the late 1960s (see chapters 5 and 11).
11. Griswold del Castillo 1980.
12. Camarillo 1979.

13. Vigil 2002.
14. Ranker 1958.
15. Moore 1978: 56.
16. Gustafson 1940: 112.
17. Connell and Lopez 1996.
18. Romo 1983; Bogardus 1934.
19. Gomez-Quinones 1994.
20. Kienle 1912: 32.
21. Vigil 1988.
22. Vigil 1995.
23. Hayes-Bautista et al. 1993.
24. Vigil 1988.
25. Gonzalez 1990.
26. Kozol 1992; Mirande 1985.
27. Bogardus 1934; Hill [1928] 1968.
28. U.S. Commission on Civil Rights 1970.
29. Valencia 1994.
30. Vigil 1988, 1997, 1999.
31. Morales 1972; Mandel 1982; Gonzales 1981; U.S. Commission on Civil Rights 1970.
32. Mirande 1985.
33. McWilliams 1968; Mazon 1984.
34. Vigil 1987, 1988, 1990.
35. Katz 1988.
36. Vigil 1997.
37. Villela and Gastelum 1980.
38. Howell 1999.
39. See Vigil 1988 for a fuller description and analysis of these attributes.
40. Moore 1978.
41. Erikson 1956.
42. Vigil 1996.
43. Vigil 1988.
44. Mendoza-Denton 1996.
45. Vigil 1997.

Chapter Five

1. Menchaca 2001.
2. DuBois 1913.
3. De Graaf 1970: 329.
4. Garcia 1985.
5. "Neither unemployment nor poverty are common themes in the literature and observations of the black community prior to the Great Depression" (De Graaf 1970: 340), but that is not to say that, as a prospering ethnic group (DuBois 1913), African Americans in Los Angeles were spared economic discrimination and other obstacles and barriers. (De Graaf 1970).

6. Brown 1965. As we shall see, this immigration pattern, in which the first wave of migrants are better educated, trained, and financed than those who follow, is quite common among other groups as well.

7. Collins 1980; Gadwa 1999.

8. Collins 1980.

9. Davis 1992.

10. De Graaf 1970; Gadwa 1999.

11. The new national law was aimed at limiting immigration of white ethnics to the East Coast and Japanese to the West Coast.

12. Collins 1980: 10.

13. De Graaf 1970; Adler 1977; Collins 1980.

14. Adler 1977.

15. Tolbert 1980: 35.

16. De Graaf 1970.

17. Collins 1980; Gadwa 1999.

18. Lapp 1987.

19. Gadwa 1999.

20. McWilliams 1969; Bunch 1990; Adler 1977.

21. Apparently, black quasi gangs such as the Boozies, Goodlows, Blogettes, and the Driver Brothers began to appear prior to World War II.

22. Moore et al. 1983; Davis 1992.

23. Davis 1992.

24. Collins 1980.

25. *Ibid.*

26. Bunch 1990; Collins 1980.

27. Collins 1980.

28. Davis 1992; Collins 1980; Adler 1977.

29. Smith 1978.

30. Collins 1980.

31. Wilson 1987; Anderson 1990.

32. Smith 1978.

33. Bunch 1990; Collins 1980.

34. Bullock 1969: 35.

35. Collins 1980: 79.

36. Adler 1977: 325.

37. Bunch 1990.

38. *Ibid*: 124.

39. Bullock 1969: 22.

40. Davis 1992.

41. Alonso 1999: 71.

42. *Ibid*: 97.

43. *Ibid*.

44. *Ibid*: 134.

45. Shakur 1993.

46. Davis 1992: 300.

47. Wilson 1987.

48. Coleman 1966.

49. Davis 1992.

50. The Black Panther and Symbionese Liberation Front shoot-outs took place in 1971 and 1974 respectively. The latter was a media event of high magnitude because it was associated with the Patty Hearst kidnapping. In 1979 Eula Love, an older mother who threatened police with a knife, was shot dead in front of her children.

51. Weinstein 1999.

52. Texeira 2000.

53. With most gangs peer pressure is from a multiple-aged group, since the ages of gang members may range from 15 to 25.

54. Davis 1992: 307.

Chapter Seven

1. Liu 1979.

2. Haines 1989.

3. Hawthorne 1982; Marsh 1980.

4. Kelly 1977.

5. Gold 1989: 416.

6. Stern 1981.

7. Liu 1979.

8. Strand and Jones 1985; Kibria 1993.

9. Tran 1998.

10. Cooper 1990.

11. Grant 1979.

12. Evans 1995.

13. Grant 1979; Liu 1979.

14. Phan 1998.

15. Nguyen and Henkin 1982.

16. Stern 1981.

17. Bach and Bach 1980.

18. Efron 1990.

19. Efron 1990; Zhou and Bankston 1998.

20. Larson 1988.

21. Rutledge 1992.

22. Phan 1998.

23. Gold and Kibria 1989.

24. Arax 1987; ORR 1987.

25. Rutledge 1992: 123.

26. Gold 1989.

27. Long and Ricard 1996.

28. Vigil and Yun 1990; Rutledge 1992.

29. Kibria 1993.

30. Zhou and Bankston 1998.

31. Vigil, Yun, and Long 1993; Vigil and Yun 1990.

32. Rutledge 1992.

33. Smith and Tarello 1995.
34. *Ibid.*
35. Sanders 1994; Hunt, Joe, and Waldorf 1997.
36. Berkman 1984.
37. Song 1992.
38. Vigil and Yun 1990.
39. *Ibid.*
40. *Ibid.*
41. *Ibid.*
42. *Ibid.*
43. Mishan 1993.
44. Hunt, Joe, and Waldorf 1997.
45. Zhou and Bankston 1998.
46. Vigil and Yun 1990.
47. *Ibid.*
48. For many Vietnamese in the Los Angeles area, gangs and crime are their top concern (Emmons and Reyes 1989).

Chapter Nine

1. Chinchilla, Hamilton, and Loucky 1993.
2. Lopez, Popkin, and Telles 1996; Ortiz 1999.
3. Connell and Lopez 1999.
4. Ward 1987: 33.
5. Ward 1987: 57; Suarez-Orozco 1989: 53.
6. Suarez-Orozco 1989: 52; Ferris 1987: 2; Oyola 1996: 2.
7. Ward 1987: 65, 293; Suarez-Orozco 1989: 53; Oyola 1996: 2.
8. Darling, Aug. 9, 1999.
9. Olivo 1999.
10. Chinchilla and Hamilton 1996; Ward 1987.
11. Lopez, Popkin, and Telles 1996.
12. Amnesty International 1990: 108.
13. Chinchilla and Hamilton 1997: 72; Suarez-Orozco 1989: 55; Amnesty International 1990: 1, 21.
14. However, wealthy Salvadorans were routinely given visas to live in Miami.
15. Quoted in Chinchilla and Hamilton 1997: 8.
16. Chinchilla and Hamilton 1996: 53; Jamail and Loucky 1987: 5; Suarez-Orozco 1989: 126; Ward 1987: x, 2; Americas Watch 1991: 108; see also Cohon 1981 and Castro 1984. In these circumstances, many organizations have mounted efforts to help alleviate the problems facing the Salvadoran population of the city, especially those related to food, English-language training, and legal counseling. There are also facilities for community function referrals and for such services as immunization, tuberculosis testing, and pregnancy testing. Counseling for individuals and families is available through health education classes (e.g., alcohol abuse and tobacco awareness classes), adult classes in ESL, and other adult education classes. Job search skills training is provided with public funds from the Community Devel-

opment Department (CDD) in an effort to help counter youth gang participation and violence.

The Church of Our Lady Queen of Angels at La Placita (located near the civic center, about four miles from Pico-Union) has offered facilities for functions within the Central American community. La Placita is known as a sanctuary for refugee families from El Salvador and Guatemala, a place where in the 1980s one could turn for help. Similarly, the Central American Refugee Center (CARECEN) and El Rescate (The Rescue) are community organizations with immigrant staff that provide a wide range of services, including food, English-language training, and legal counseling, which many Salvadorans are afraid to seek from outside organizations (Chinchilla and Hamilton 1996: 70–71).

The Berendo-Hoover Healthy Start Family Center is in limited operation. It offers off-site referrals for such services as immunization, tuberculosis testing, and pregnancy testing. Limited on-site and off-site counseling for individuals and families is available. Health education classes (e.g., for alcohol abuse and tobacco awareness) are available at the center, as are adult classes in ESL and other adult education classes (along with childcare for those enrolled in the classes).

17. Ward 1987: 128–129, 134–136; Amnesty International 1990: 1; Russell 1984: 107; see also Becklund 1984, 1985 and Applegate 1986.

18. Chinchilla and Hamilton 1996.

19. Chinchilla, Hamilton, and Loucky 1993.

20. Ward 1987: 196; Suarez-Orozco 1989: 90; Chinchilla and Hamilton 1996: 53–54.

21. Chinchilla, Hamilton, and Loucky 1993.

22. Local Salvadorans' concern for their homeland is evident in the energy they exert in hometown associations. Indeed, such associations are the most common type of Salvadoran community organizations, offering recent immigrants an opportunity for cultural solidarity. Their efforts are frequently focused on civic projects being carried out in their communities of origin, such as building clinics, providing disaster relief, and maintaining communication between emigres and their home communities. Funds for these projects in El Salvador are raised by organizing events such as annual festivals dedicated to the patron saints of the respective communities. The significant involvement of the Salvadoran consulate and El Rescate in the promotion and support of community hometown associations creates a unique political dynamic within the Salvadoran community.

23. Jamail and Loucky 1987: 4–5.

24. Beyette 1984.

25. Darling, Aug. 9, 1999.

26. Classes in job search skills, such as how to complete applications, are conducted by volunteers from Atlantic Richfield Company. The program is actively seeking funds to expand its services and offer a variety of additional services. L.A. Bridges is an organization created with public funds from the Community Development Department (CDD) in an effort to help counter youth gang participation and violence. In the Pico-Union area, L.A. Bridges has been administered by a program already in existence, Berendo-Hoover Healthy Start. Central to this program are the Berendo Family Center and its collaborative partners, such as Para Los Niños,

ARCO-Adopt a School, Clínica Para Las Américas, Americorp, University of Southern California Mobile Dental Clinic, the L.A. County Department of Health Services, and other private and public agencies and organizations. The goals of the L.A. Bridges program are to improve youths' well-being by providing access to preventive and continuing health care; to enhance students' and families' awareness of violence prevention strategies, thereby reducing the overall incidence of community and individual violence; and to enhance families' overall functioning, knowledge, and empowerment. Parallel efforts include the Berendo Family Center's group sessions, designed to help parents deal with their children's problems, and youth counseling programs such as Star and Para Los Niños.

Another organization that has proved useful in ameliorating Salvadoran youth problems is the Youth Fair Chance program. It is a program whose purpose is to improve the life opportunities of youth in high-poverty areas by providing a comprehensive array of youth services. The Youth Empowerment Project also provides a variety of services for youths, including computer and career training, and has emerged as a defender of some gang members against injunctions (Becerra, August 2, 1998). Youth Fair Chance is designed to focus resources on targeted high-poverty neighborhoods such as Pico-Union. This is done by encouraging comprehensive strategies that link education, employment, social services, and juvenile justice, as well as recreation programs, to youths' daily activities (Maldonado 1997: 7). This effort targets street youth. When such children have been made wards of the court, they must follow a strict dress code and participate in five hours of classes and three hours of workshops daily. One Mara Salvatrucha gang member, nicknamed Psycho, evidently benefited from this program—he has gone on to acquire his own auto repair business (Maldonado 1997).

In 1995 another organization, the Salvadoran American Leadership and Educational Fund (SALEF 1999), was founded. Its mission is "to promote the civic participation and representation of the Salvadoran and other Latino communities in Los Angeles as well as to advocate for [their] economic, educational, and political advancement and growth." In one year, with the help of supporters from corporate and philanthropic organizations, SALEF was able to triple the number of scholarships available to Central American and Latino youth. SALEF also helped to increase the number of registered voters among the Central American immigrants in Los Angeles from 4 percent in 1996–1997 to 6 percent in 1998–1999, according to the SALEF Annual Awards and Scholarship Banquet program.

27. Oyola 1996: 9.

28. O'Connor 1998.

29. Lopez and Connell 2000.

30. Helford and Reich 2001.

31. Connell and Lopez 1996.

32. Rodriguez and DeCesare 1995.

33. Connell and Lopez 1996, 1999.

34. Connell and Lopez 1999; Newton 1999; Newton and O'Neill 1999.

35. Connell and Lopez 1996, 1999.

36. Becerra, Aug. 5, 1998.

37. Krikorian 1998.

38. Davis 1992: 287.
39. Newton 1998; Newton and O'Neill 1999.
40. Davis 1992: 287.
41. Alex Sanchez 1999.
42. Wilkinson 1994.
43. Rose-Avila 1998.
44. McDonald 1994.
45. Wilkinson 1994.
46. DeCesare 1999; Homies Unidos 1998; Gage 1998; Sanchez 1995.
47. Rose-Avila 1998.
48. Hong 1999: 2.
49. Chinchilla and Hamilton 1996: 55.

Chapter Eleven

1. Hobfoll 1998.
2. Weinstein 1999.
3. DeCesare 1999; Darling 1999.
4. Waters 1999; Romo and Falbo 1996.
5. Berry and Blassingame 1982.
6. Nazario 1993.
7. McClanahan and Sandefur 1994; Mitchell 1992.
8. Moore and Vigil 1987.
9. Puppet's childhood brings to mind *Always Running*, the excellent 1993 autobiographical account of the life of Luis Rodriguez.
10. Saluter and Lugaila 1996.
11. Thornberry 1994.
12. NCES 1998.
13. California Youth Authority 1999.
14. Fine and Mechling 1993.
15. Stack 1974; Williams 1990.
16. Moreno 1999; Coleman 1990; Vigil 1997.
17. Blanc 1995.
18. Friedman 1999.
19. Vigil 1997.
20. Austin and Willard 1998.
21. Meddis and Edmonds 1994.
22. Hubler 2000; ACLU 1999.
23. Frammolino 1999.
24. Goldstein and Huff 1993; Coolbaugh and Hansel 2000.
25. Blumstein, Cohen, and Miller 1980; Petersilia 1992; Mauer 1992; MacTalk 1999.
26. Hutson, Anglin, and Pratts 1994; Hutson et al. 1995; Monmaney 1995; Stokke 1999.
27. Greenwood 1996; Rubin 1999.
28. Ritsch 2001.

29. Huffington 2001.

30. Klein 1995; Wilson 2000.

31. Martin 2000.

32. Elkannman 1996.

33. Loeber and Stouthamer-Loeber 1986.

34. Texeira 2000; see also Krikorian 1996.

35. Lamb 1997.

36. Johnson 2000; Daunt 2000.

37. Catalano, Loeber, and McKinney 1998.

38. Thornberry et al. 1999; Sampson and Laub 1994.

39. Velez-Ibañez 1993.

40. Spergel and Curry 1998.

41. See preface, this volume; see also Vigil 1995.

42. Katz 1995.

43. Goldstein and Kodluboy 1998.

44. Schroeder 1998; Vigil 1999.

45. Sahagun 1999: 2.

46. Merl 1992.

47. Vigil 1993; Dadgostar 1999; Orfield and Kaufman 1992.

48. Come 1995.

49. Heath and McLaughlin 1993; Vigil 1993; Vigil 1999; Vigil 1988b; Vigil 1999, Phillips 1999.

References

Foreword

Coleman, James. 1961. *The Adolescent Society*. New York: Free Press of Glencoe.

Connell, R. W. 1987. *Gender and Power*. Stanford, Calif.: Stanford University Press.

Fine, Gary Alan. 1987. *With the Boys*. Chicago: University of Chicago Press.

Furstenberg, Frank F., Jr., Thomas D. Cook, Jackquelynne Eccles, Glen H. Elder, Jr., and Arnold Sameroff. 1999. *Managing to Make It*. Chicago: University of Chicago Press.

Miller, Jody. 2001. *One of the Guys: Girls, Gangs, and Gender*. New York: Oxford University Press.

Moore, Joan W. 1978. *Homeboys*. Philadelphia: Temple University Press.

_____. 1991. *Going Down to the Barrio*. Philadelphia: Temple University Press.

_____. 2001. *Female Gangs: A Focus on Research*. Washington, D.C.: Office of Juvenile Justice and Delinquency Prevention, Office of Justice Programs, U.S. Department of Justice.

Schwendinger, H., and J. Schwendinger. 1985. *Adolescent Subcultures and Delinquency*. New York: Praeger.

Vigil, James Diego. 1988. *Barrio Gangs*. Austin: University of Texas Press.

_____. 1997. *Personas Mexicanas*. Fort Worth, Tex.: Harcourt-Brace.

Whyte, William Foote. 1949. *Street Corner Society*. Chicago: University of Chicago Press.

Willis, Paul. 1977. *Learning to Labor: How Working Class Kids Get Working Class Jobs*. New York: Columbia University Press.

Chapter 1

Alonso, A. 1999. "Territoriality among African-American Street Gangs in Los Angeles." Master's thesis, Department of Geography, University of Southern California.

Ashbury, H. 1927. *The Gangs of New York*. Garden City, N.Y.: Garden City Publishing.

Bogardus, E. 1926. *The City Boy and His Problems*. Los Angeles: House of Ralston, Rotary Club of Los Angeles.

Boyle, Gregory J. September 29, 1995. "Victimizers Call Us to Compassion, Too." *Los Angeles Times*, B4.

Buriel, R. 1984. "Integration with Traditional Mexican American Culture and Sociocultural Adjustment." In *Chicano Psychology*, 2d ed., edited by J. L. Martinez and R. Mendoza, 253–271. New York: Academic Press.

Bursik, R. J., Jr., and H. G. Grasmick. 1993. *Neighborhoods and Crime*. New York: Lexington.

———. 1995a. "Defining Gangs and Gang Behavior." In *The Modern Gang Reader*, edited by M. W. Klein, C. L. Maxson, and J. Miller, 8–13. Los Angeles: Roxbury Publishing.

———. 1995b. "The Effect of Neighborhood Dynamics on Gang Behavior." In *The Modern Gang Reader*, edited by M. W. Klein, C. L. Maxson, and J. Miller, 114–124. Los Angeles: Roxbury Publishing.

Campbell, Anne. 1990. "Female Participation in Gangs." In *Gangs in America*, edited by C. Ronald Huff, 163–182. Thousand Oaks, Calif.: Sage Publications.

———. 1991. *The Girls in the Gang*, 2d ed. Cambridge, Mass.: Blackwell.

Canada, G. 1995. *FistSticksKnivesGuns*. Boston: Beacon.

Chesney-Lind, Meda, and Randall G. Sheldon. 1992. *Girls: Delinquency and Juvenile Justice*. Pacific Grove, Calif.: Brooks/Cole Publishing.

Chesney-Lind, Meda, Randall G. Sheldon, and Karen A. Joe. 1996. "Girls, Delinquency, and Gang Membership." In *Gangs in America*, 2d ed., edited by C. Ronald Huff, 185–204. Thousand Oaks, Calif.: Sage Publications.

Clark, Reginald. 1983. *Family Life and School Achievement: Why Poor Black Children Succeed or Fail*. Chicago: University of Chicago Press.

Currie, Elliot. 1993. *Reckoning: Drugs, the Cities, and the American Future*. New York: Hill and Wang.

Curry, G. D. November 1995. "Responding to Female Gang Involvement." Paper presented at the American Society of Criminology annual meeting.

Curry, G. D., and S. H. Decker. 1998. *Confronting Gangs: Crime and Community*. Los Angeles, Calif.: Roxbury Publishing.

Cutler, William. 2000. *Parents and Schools: The 150–Year Struggle for Control in American Education*. Chicago: University of Chicago Press.

Decker, Scott, and B. Van Winkle. 1994. "Slinging Dope: The Role of Gangs and Gang Members in Drug Sales." *Justice Quarterly* 11 (4): 583–604.

———. 1996. *Life in the Gang: Family, Friends, and Violence*. New York: Cambridge University Press.

Escobar, E. 1998. *Race, Police, and the Making of a Political Identity: Police-Chicano Relations in Los Angeles, 1900–1945*. Berkeley: University of California Press.

Farley, J. E. 1987. "Disproportionate Black and Hispanic Unemployment in U.S. Metropolitan Areas." *American Journal of Economics and Sociology* 46 (2): 129–150.

Fields, C. June 1991. "Hispanic Pipeline." *Change Magazine*, 30–36.

Frazier, E. F. 1966. *The Negro Family in the United States*. Rev. ed., abr. Chicago: University of Chicago Press.

Giordano, Peggy C. 1978. "Girls, Guys and Gangs: The Changing Social Context of Female Delinquency." *Journal of Criminal Law and Criminology* 69 (1): 126–132.

Hagedorn, J. M., with Perry Macon. 1988. *People and Folks: Gangs, Crime and the Underclass in a Rust-belt City*. Chicago: Lake View Press.

Haskins, J. 1974. *Street Gangs: Yesterday and Today*. New York: Hastings House.

Hazlehurst, K., and C. Hazlehurst, eds. 1998. *Gangs and Youth Subcultures: International Explorations.* New Brunswick, N.J.: Transaction Publishers.

Hecht, T. 1998. *At Home in the Street: Street Children of Northeast Brazil.* New York: Cambridge University Press.

Hernandez, Arturo. 1998. *Peace in the Streets: Breaking the Cycle of Gang Violence.* Washington, D.C.: Child Welfare League of America.

Huff, C. R., ed. 1996. *Gangs in America.* 2d ed. Thousand Oaks, Calif.: Sage Publications.

Jackson, P., and C. Rudman. 1993. "Moral Panics and the Response to Gangs in California." In *Gangs: The Origins and Impact of Contemporary Youth Gangs in the United States,* edited by S. Cummings and D. J. Monti, 257–276. Albany: State University of New York Press.

Jacobs, J. 1977. *Statesville: The Penitentiary in Mass Society.* Chicago: University of Chicago Press.

Johnson, J., and M. Oliver. 1991. "Economic Restructuring and Black Male Joblessness in U.S. Metropolitan Areas." *Urban Geography* 12 (6): 542–562.

——. 1992. "Structural Changes in the U.S. Economy and Black Male Joblessness: A Reassessment." In *Urban Labor Markets and Job Opportunity,* edited by G. Peterson and W. Vroman, 113–147. Washington, D.C.: Urban Institute Press.

Katz, Jack. 1988. *Seductions of Crime: Moral and Sensual Attractions in Doing Evil.* New York: Blackwell.

Katz, Jesse. December 8, 1991. "Gang Killings in L.A. County Top a Record 700." *Los Angeles Times,* A1, 23.

Kawachi, J. A. 1997. "A Holistic Approach toward Dropout Prevention Policies for Minority Youth in the United States." Paper submitted to the Honors 196 seminar "Urban Poverty and Public Policy," University of California, Los Angeles.

Klein, M. 1971. *Street Gangs and Street Workers.* Englewood Cliffs, N.J.: Prentice-Hall.

——. 1995a. *The American Street Gang.* New York: Oxford University Press.

——. September 19, 1995b. "Deference to Gangs Makes Them Kings of the Roost." *Los Angeles Times,* B3.

Kozol, Jonathan. 1992. *Savage Inequalities: Children in America's Schools.* New York: HarperPerennial.

Lauderback, David, Joy Hanson, and Dan Waldorf. 1992. "'Sisters Are Doin' It for Themselves': A Black Female Gang in San Francisco." *Gang Journal* 1: 57–72.

Los Angeles Times. May 12, 1992. *Understanding the Riots: Los Angeles Before and After the Rodney King Case.* Insert, Sunday edition.

MacTalk [newsletter]. September 1999. "Prison Guards—A Major Force in California." *MacTalk* 8 (9): 3.

Maxson, C. L. 1998. *Gang Members on the Move.* Bulletin. Washington, D.C.: Office of Juvenile Justice and Delinquency Prevention, U.S. Department of Justice.

Maxson, C. L., M. W. Klein, and L. C. Cunningham. 1993. *Street Gangs and Drug Sales.* Report to the National Institute of Justice. Washington, D.C.: National Institute of Justice, Office of Justice Programs, U.S. Department of Justice.

Maxson, C. L., K. J. Woods, and M. W. Klein. 1996. "Street Gang Migration: How Big a Threat." *National Institute of Justice* 230: 26–31.

McAdoo, Harriet Pipes. 1993. *Family Ethnicity.* Thousand Oaks, Calif.: Sage Publications.

Melville, M. 1994. "Hispanic Ethnicity, Race and Class." In *Handbook of Hispanic Cultures in the United States: Anthropology*, edited by T. Weaver, 85–106. Houston: Arte Público Press.

Montemayor, Raymond. 2000. *Adolescent Diversity in Ethnic, Economic, and Cultural Contexts*. Thousand Oaks, Calif.: Sage Publications.

Moore, J. W. 1978. *Homeboys*. Philadelphia: Temple University Press.

———. 1991. *Going Down to the Barrio: Homeboys and Homegirls in Change*. Philadelphia: Temple University Press.

———. 1998. "Understanding Youth Street Gangs: Economic Restructuring and the Urban Underclass." In *Cross-Cultural Perspectives on Youth and Violence*, edited by M. Watts, 17–35. Stamford, Conn.: JAI Press.

Moore, J. W., and J. Hagedorn. 2001. *Female Gangs: A Focus on Research*. Washington, D.C.: Office of Juvenile Justice and Delinquency Prevention, U.S. Department of Justice.

Moore, J. W., and J. D. Vigil. 1993. "Barrios in Transition." In *In the Barrios: Latinos and the Underclass Debate*, edited by J. Moore and R. Pinderhughes, 27–49. New York: Russell Sage Foundation.

Moore, J. W., J. D. Vigil, and J. Levy. 1995. "Huisas of the Street: Chicana Gang Members." *Latino Studies* 6 (1): 27–48.

Moreno, J. F., ed. 1999. *The Elusive Quest for Equality*. Cambridge: Harvard Educational Review, Harvard University Press.

NIJ (National Institute of Justice). 1994. *Gender and Gangs*. Prepared by Gang Crime and Law Enforcement Recordkeeping. Washington, D.C.: U.S. Department of Justice.

Oakes, J. 1985. *Keeping Track: How Schools Structure Inequality*. New Haven, Conn.: Yale University Press.

OJJDP (Office of Juvenile Justice and Delinquency Prevention). June 1996. *Female Offenders in the Juvenile Justice System: Statistic Summary*. Washington, D.C.: U.S. Department of Justice.

———. 1999. *1997 National Youth Gang Survey*. Washington, D.C.: National Youth Gang Center, U.S. Department of Justice.

Oliver, M. L., J. H. Johnson, and W. C. Farrell. 1993. "Anatomy of a Rebellion: A Political-Economic Analysis." In *Reading Rodney King/Reading Urban Uprising*, edited by R. G. Gooding-Williams, 117–141. New York: Routledge.

Orfield, G. 1988. "Exclusion of the Majority: Shrinking College Access and Public Policy in Metropolitan Los Angeles." *Urban Review* 20: 147–163.

Padilla, F. 1993. *The Gang as an American Enterprise*. New Brunswick, N.J.: Rutgers University Press.

Presidential Advisory Commission on Educational Excellence for Hispanic Americans. 1999. *Our Nation on the Fault Line: Hispanic American Education*. Prepared by Richard A. Figueroa and Sonia Hernandez. Washington, D.C.: The Commission.

Quicker, John C. 1983. *Homegirls: Characterizing Chicana Gangs*. San Pedro, Calif.: International Universities Press.

Scheer, R. August 27, 1995. "New National Monument: The Jailhouse." *Los Angeles Times*, B3.

———. March 7, 2000. "We Locked 'Em Up, Threw Away the Key." *Los Angeles Times*, B7.

Spergel, I. A., and G. D. Curry. 1998. "The National Youth Gang Survey: A Research and Development Process." In *The Modern Gang Reader*, edited by M. W. Klein, C. L. Maxson, and J. Miller, 254–265. Los Angeles: Roxbury Publishing.

Suzuki, Lisa, and Richard Valencia. 1997. "Race, Ethnicity and Measured Intelligence: Educational Implication." *American Psychologist* 52 (10): 42–56.

Szanton Blanc, C., with contributors. 1995. *Urban Children in Distress: Global Predicaments and Innovative Strategies*. Florence, Italy: UNICEF.

Thrasher, F. 1927. *The Gang*. Chicago: University of Chicago Press.

Valencia, R. 1991. *Chicano School Failure and Success: Research and Policy Agendas for the 1990s*. London: Falmer Press.

Vigil, J. D. 1988. *Barrio Gangs: Street Life and Identity in Southern California*. Austin: University of Texas Press.

——. 1993. "The Established Gang." In *Gangs: The Orgins and the Impact of Contemporary Youth Gangs in the United States*, edited by S. Cummings and D. Monti, 95–112. Albany: State University of New York Press.

——. 1996. "Understanding Life in an East Los Angeles Public Housing Project: A Focus on Gang and Non-Gang Families." Working paper, Center for the Study of Urban Poverty, University of California, Los Angeles.

——. 1998. *From Indians to Chicanos: The Dynamics of Mexican American Culture*, 2nd ed. Prospect Heights, Ill.: Waveland Press.

——. 1999. "Streets and Schools: How Educators Can Help Chicano Marginalized Gang Youth." *Harvard Educational Review* 69 (3): 270–288.

——. 2002. "Community Dynamics and the Rise of Street Gangs." In *Latinos! Remaking America*, edited by M. Suarez-Orozco. Berkeley: University of California Press; Cambridge, Mass.: Harvard University Press.

Vigil, J. D., and S. C. Yun. 1998. "Vietnamese Youth Gangs in the Context of Multiple Marginality and the Los Angeles Youth Gang Phenomenon." In *Gangs and Youth Subcultures: International Explorations*, edited by K. Hazlehurst and C. Hazlehurst, 117–139. New Brunswick, N.J.: Transaction Publishers.

Waters, T. 1999. *Crime and Immigrant Youth*. Thousand Oaks, Calif.: Sage Publications.

Willis, P. E. 1977. *Learning to Labour*. Farnborough, England: Saxon House.

Wilson, W. J. 1987. *The Truly Disadvantaged*. Chicago: University of Chicago Press.

Yablonsky, Lewis. 1997. *Gangsters: Fifty Years of Madness, Drugs, and Death on the Streets of America*. New York: New York University Press.

Zatz, M. S. 1987. "Chicano Youth Gangs and Crime: The Creation of a Moral Panic." *Contemporary Crises* 11: 129–158.

Chapter 2

Bureau of Justice Statistics. 1999a. *Local Police Departments, 1997*. Washington, D.C.: U.S. Department of Justice.

——. 1999b. *Sheriffs' Departments, 1997*. Washington, D.C.: U.S. Department of Justice.

Buriel, R. 1984. "Integration with Traditional Mexican American Culture and Sociocultural Adjustment." In *Chicano Psychology*, edited by J. L. Martinez and R. Mendoza, 257–271. New York: Academic Press.

Campbell, Anne. 1991. *The Girls in the Gang*, 2d ed. Cambridge, Mass.: Blackwell.

Cartwright, Desmond S., Barbara Thompson, and Hershey Schwartz, eds. 1975. *Gang Delinquency*. Monterey, Calif.: Brooks/Cole Publishing.

Cloward, R. A., and L. E. Ohlin. 1960. *Delinquency and Opportunity: A Theory of Delinquent Gangs*. New York: Free Press.

Cohen, A. K. 1955. *Delinquent Boys: The Culture of the Gang*. Glencoe, Ill.: Free Press.

Connell, R., and R. J. Lopez. September 19, 1999. "Rampart Probe May Put Gang Injunction at Risk." *Los Angeles Times*, A1, 21–22.

Covey, H. C., S. Menard, and R. J. Franzese. 1992. *Juvenile Gangs*. Springfield, Ill.: Charles C. Thomas Publishers.

Decker, Scott, and B. Van Winkle. 1996. *Life in the Gang: Family, Friends, and Violence*. New York: Cambridge University Press.

Dietrich, L. 1998. *Chicana Adolescents: Bitches, 'Ho's, and Schoolgirls*. Westport, Conn.: Praeger.

Edgerton, R. B. 1978. *Deviant Behavior and Cultural Theory*. Addison-Wesley Module in Anthropology, no.37. Reading, Mass.: Addison-Wesley Publishing.

Ember, C. R., and M. Ember. 1990. *Cultural Anthropology*. Englewood Cliffs, N.J.: Prentice-Hall.

Erikson, Erik H. 1956. "Ego Identity and the Psychosocial Moratorium." In *New Perspectives for Research on Juvenile Delinquency*, edited by Helen L. Witmer and Ruth Kotinsky, 1–23. U.S. Children's Bureau Publication, no. 356. Washington, D.C.: U.S. Government Printing Office.

Foley, J., and V. Ward. October 19, 1992. "A Grab Bag of Steps to Eliminate 'Recreation Apartheid.'" *Los Angeles Times*, B2.

Freeman, R. B. 1991. *Crime and the Employment of Disadvantaged Youths*. Cambridge, Mass.: National Bureau of Economic Research.

Freud, Sigmund. 1923. *Group Psychology and the Analysis of the Ego*. New York: W. W. Norton.

Hagedorn, J. M., with Perry Macon. 1988. *People and Folks: Gangs, Crime and the Underclass in a Rust-belt City*. Chicago: Lake View Press.

Haviland, W. A. 1988. *Cultural Anthropology*. New York: Holt, Rinehart and Winston.

Klein, M. W. 1995. *The American Street Gang*. New York: Oxford University Press.

McAdoo, Harriet Pipes. 1993. *Family Ethnicity*. Thousand Oaks, Calif.: Sage Publications.

Mead, M. [1928] 1961. *Coming of Age in Samoa*. 3d ed. New York: Morrow.

Meddis, S. V., and P. Edmonds. September 29, 1996. "Rehabilitation on a Small Scale." *USA Today*, A10–14.

Merton, R. 1949. *Social Theory and Social Structure*. Glencoe, Ill.: Free Press.

Moore, J. W. 1978. *Homeboys*. Philadelphia: Temple University Press.

———. 1991. *Going Down to the Barrio: Homeboys and Homegirls in Change*. Philadelphia: Temple University Press.

Orfield, G. 1988. "Exclusion of the Majority: Shrinking College Access and Public Policy in Metropolitan Los Angeles." *Urban Review* 20: 147–163.

Poe-Yamagata, Eileen, and Jeffrey A. Butts. 1996. *Female Offenders in the Juvenile Justice System: Statistics Summary*. Washington, D.C.: Office of Juvenile Justice and Delinquency Prevention, U.S. Department of Justice.

Redfield, R. 1941. *The Folk Culture of Yucatán*. Chicago: University of Chicago Press.

Rodriguez, L. 1991. *The Concrete River*. Willimantic, Conn.: Curbstone Press.

Shaw, C., and R. McKay. 1942. *Juvenile Delinquency and Urban Areas*. Chicago: University of Chicago Press.

Spergel, I. A., and G. D. Curry. 1998. "The National Youth Gang Survey: A Research and Development Process." In *The Modern Gang Reader*, edited by M. W. Klein, C. L. Maxson, and J. Miller, 254–265. Los Angeles: Roxbury Publishing.

Thrasher, F. [1927] 1963. *The Gang*. Chicago: University of Chicago Press.

Valencia, R., ed. 1991. *Chicano School Success and Failure: Research and Policy Agendas for the 1990s*. London: Falmer Press.

Vigil, J. D. 1988a. *Barrio Gangs: Street Life and Identity in Southern California*. Austin: University of Texas Press.

_____. 1988b. "Group Processes and Street Identity: Adolescent Chicano Gang Members." *Ethos* 16 (4): 421–445.

_____. 1990. "Cholos and Gangs: Culture Change and Street Youth in Los Angeles." In *Gangs in America: Diffusion, Diversity, and Public Policy*, edited by R. Huff, 116–128. Thousand Oaks, Calif.: Sage Publications, 1990.

_____. 1993a. "The Established Gang." In *Gangs: The Origins and Impact of Contemporary Youth Gangs in the United States*, edited by S. Cummings and D. Monti, 95–112. Albany: State University of New York Press.

_____. 1993b. "Gangs, Social Control, and Ethnicity: Ways to Redirect." In *Identity and Inner-City Youth: Beyond Ethnicity and Gender*, edited by S. B. Heath and M. W. McLaughlin, 94–119. New York: Teachers College Press.

_____. 1998. *From Indians to Chicanos: The Dynamics of Mexican American Culture*. Prospect Heights, Ill.: Waveland Press.

_____. 1999. "Streets and Schools: How Educators Can Help Chicano Marginalized Gang Youth." *Harvard Educational Review* 69 (3): 270–288.

_____. 2002. "Community Dynamics and the Rise of Street Gangs." In *Latinos! Remaking America*, edited by M. Suarez-Orozco. Berkeley: University of California Press; Cambridge, Mass.: Harvard University Press.

Vigil, J. D., and S. C. Yun. 1990. "The Vietnamese Youth Gangs in Southern California." In *Gangs in America: Diffusion, Diversity, and Public Policy*, edited by R. Huff, 146–162. Thousand Oaks, Calif.: Sage Publications.

_____. 1998. "Vietnamese Youth Gangs in the Context of Multiple Marginality and the Los Angeles Youth Gang Phenomenon." In *Gangs and Youth Subcultures: International Explorations*, edited by K. Hazlehurst and C. Hazlehurst, 117–139. New Brunswick, N.J.: Transaction Publishers.

Vigil, J. D., S. C. Yun, and J. M. Long. 1993. "Youth Gangs, Crime, and the Vietnamese in Orange County." In *The Ecology of Crimes and Drugs in the Inner City*, edited by Jeff Fagan, 1–56. New York: Social Science Research Council.

Wiatrowski, M. D., D. B. Griswold, and M. K. Roberts. 1981. "Social Control Theory and Delinquency." *American Sociological Review* 46: 525–541.

Chapter 3

ACLU (American Civil Liberties Union). May 1999. *ACLU Calls Juvenile Crime Bill a Cruel Hoax on America's Children and Families*. Press release. Los Angeles: ACLU.

Bloch, H. A., and A. Niederhoffer. 1958. *The Gang: A Study in Adolescent Behavior.* New York: Philosophical Library.

Bogardus, E. S. 1934. *The Mexican in the United States.* USC Social Science Series, no. 8. Los Angeles: University of Southern California Press.

Camarillo, A. 1979. *Chicanos in a Changing Society: From Mexican Pueblos to American Barrios in Santa Barbara and Southern California, 1848–1930.* Cambridge: Harvard University Press.

Chavez, L. R. 1998. *Shadowed Lives: Undocumented Immigrants in American Society.* 2d ed. Fort Worth: Harcourt Brace College Publishers.

Connell, R., and R. Lopez. November 17, 1996. "An Inside Look at the 18th St.'s Menace." *Los Angeles Times*, A1, 15–18.

Cornelius, W. A., L. R. Chavez, and J. G. Castro. 1982. *Mexican Immigrants and Southern California: A Summary of Current Knowledge.* Working Papers in U.S.-Mexican Studies, no. 36. La Jolla, Calif.: Center for U.S.-Mexican Studies, University of California, San Diego.

Dembo, R., A. Nola, and J. V. Harold. 1984. *A Framework for Understanding Nondelinquent and Delinquent Life-styles in the Inner City.* N.p.

Erikson, Erik H. 1956. "Ego Identity and the Psychosocial Moratorium." In *New Perspectives for Research on Juvenile Delinquency*, edited by Helen L. Witmer and Ruth Kotinsky, 1–23. U.S. Children's Bureau Publication, no. 356. Washington, D.C.: U.S. Government Printing Office.

Fox, R. G. 1977. *Urban Anthropology: Cities in Their Cultural Settings.* Englewood Cliffs, N.J.: Prentice-Hall.

Geertz, C. 1973. *The Interpretation of Culture.* New York: Basic Books.

Gettin, J., and D. Reyes. October 2, 1983. "The Newest Slums—Out in the Suburbs." *Los Angeles Times*, A1, 20.

Gomez-Quinones, J. 1994. *Mexican American Labor, 1790–1990.* Albuquerque: University of New Mexico Press.

Gonzales, A. 1981. "Mexicano/Chicano Gangs in Los Angeles: A Socio-historical Case Study." Ph.D. diss., School of Social Welfare, University of California, Berkeley.

Gonzales, G. 1990. Chicano Education in the Era of Segregation. Philadelphia: Balch Institute Press.

Griswold del Castillo, R. 1980. *The Los Angeles Barrio, 1850–1890.* Los Angeles: University of California Press.

Gustafson, C. V. 1940. "An Ecological Analysis of the Hollenbeck Area of Los Angeles." Master's thesis, Department of Sociology, University of Southern California.

Hayes-Bautista, D., E. Garcia, R. Brook, and S. Chen. 1993. *Chartbook on Racial and Ethnic Health Indicators in Los Angeles County.* Los Angeles: Center for the Study of Latino Health, University of California, Los Angeles.

Hernandez, A. 1998. *Peace in the Streets: Breaking The Cycle of Gang Violence.* Washington, D.C. Child Welfare League of America.

Hill, M. [1928] 1968. "An Americanized Program for the Ontario Schools." In *California Controversies*, edited by Leonard Pitt, 102–122. Reprint, Glenview, Ill.: Scott, Foresman.

Horowitz. R. 1983. *Honor and the American Dream: Culture and Identity in a Chicano Community.* New Brunswick, N.J.: Rutgers University Press.

Howell, J. C. April 1999. "Youth Gang Homicides: A Literature Review." *Crime and Delinquency* 45 (2): 208–211.

Katz, J. 1988. *Seductions of Crime*. New York: Basic Books.

Kienle, J. E. 1912. "Housing Conditions among the Mexican Population of Los Angeles." Master's thesis, Department of Sociology, University of Southern California.

Klein, Malcolm. 1995. *The American Street Gang*. New York: Oxford University Press.

Kozol, J. 1992. *Savage Inequalities: Children in America's Schools*. New York: HarperPerennial.

Mandel, J. 1982. *Police Use of Deadly Force in Hispanic Communities: Final Report*. Washington, D.C.: National Council of La Raza.

Mazon, M. 1984. *The Zoot-Suit Riots: The Psychology of Symbolic Annihilation*. Austin: University of Texas Press.

McWilliams, C. 1968. *North from Mexico: The Spanish-Speaking People of the United States*. New York: Greenwood Press.

Mendoza-Denton, Norma. 1996. *"Muy Macha": Gender and Ideology in Gang Girls' Discourse about Makeup*. Ethos 61: 47–63.

Mirande, A. 1985. *The Chicano Experience*. Notre Dame, Ind.: University of Notre Dame Press.

———. 1987. *Gringo Justice*. Notre Dame, Ind.: University of Notre Dame Press.

Moore, J. W. 1978. *Homeboys: Gangs, Drugs, and Prison in the Barrios of Los Angeles*. Philadelphia: Temple University Press.

———. 1991. *Going Down to the Barrio*. Philadelphia: Temple University Press.

Moore, J. W., J. D. Vigil, and R. Garcia. 1983. "Residence and Territoriality in Gangs." *Journal of Social Problems* 31 (2): 182–194.

Morales, A. 1972. *Ando sangrando* (I Am Bleeding). La Puente, Calif.: Perspectiva Publishers.

———. 1982. "The Mexican American Gang Member: Evaluation and Treatment." In *Mental Health and Hispanic Americans*, edited by R. Becerra, M. Karno, J. Escobar, 133–152. New York: Grune and Stratton.

O'Conner, A. M. June 3, 2000. "Suit Alleges Harassment of L.A. Gang Peace Group Homies Unidos. Members Say Officers in Scandal-Tainted Rampart Division Violated Rights." *Los Angeles Times*, A1, 9.

Oliver, M. L., J. H. Johnson, and W. C. Farrell. 1993. "Anatomy of a Rebellion: A Political-Economic Analysis." In *Reading Rodney King/Reading Urban Uprising*, edited by R. G. Gooding-Williams, 117–141. New York: Routledge.

Ranker, J. E., Jr. 1958. "A Study of Juvenile Gangs in the Hollenbeck Area of East Los Angeles." Master's thesis, Department of Sociology, University of Southern California.

Rodriguez, L. 1993. *Always Running: La Vida Loca, Gang Days in L.A.* Willimantic, Conn.: Curbstone Press.

Romo, R. 1983. *East Los Angeles: History of a Barrio, 1900–1930*. Austin: University of Texas Press.

Rubel, A. J. 1965. "The Mexican American *Palomilla*." *Anthropological Linguistics* 4: 92–97.

Samora, J. 1971. *Los Mojados: The Wetback Story*. Notre Dame, Ind.: University of Notre Dame Press.

U.S. Commission on Civil Rights. 1970. *Mexican Americans and the Administration of Justice in the Southwest*. Washington, D.C.: U.S. Government Printing Office.

_____. 1971. *Report I: Ethnic Isolation of Mexican Americans in the Public Schools of the Southwest*. Washington, D.C.: U.S. Government Printing Office.

Valencia, A. A. Winter 1994. "The Degree That Parents and Significant Others Influence Anglo American and Mexican American Students to Pursue and Complete University Studies." *Journal of Educational Issues of Language Minority Students* 14 (21): 301–317.

Vigil, J. D. 1979. "Adaptation Strategies and Cultural Life Styles of Mexican American Adolescents." *Hispanic Journal of Behavioral Sciences* (UCLA) 1 (4): 375–392.

_____. 1988. *Barrio Gangs: Street Life and Identity in Southern California*. Austin: University of Texas Press.

_____. 1990. "Culture Change and Street Youth." In *Gangs in America*, edited by C.R. Huff, 116–128. Thousand Oaks, Calif.: Sage Publications.

_____. 1995. *Understanding Life in an East Los Angeles Public Housing Project: A Focus on Gang and Non-Gang Families*. Occasional Working Paper Series. Los Angeles: Center for the Study of Urban Poverty, University of California, Los Angeles.

_____. 1996. "Street Baptism: Chicano Gang Initiation." *Human Organization* 55 (2): 149–153.

_____. 1997. *Personas Mexicanas*. Fort Worth, Tex.: Harcourt-Brace.

_____. 1999. "Streets and Schools: How Educators Can Help Chicano Marginalized Gang Youth." *Harvard Educational Review* 69 (3): 270–288.

_____. 2002. "Community Dynamics and the Rise of Street Gangs." In *Latinos! Remaking America*, edited by M. Suarez-Orozco. Berkeley: University of California Press; Cambridge, Mass.: Harvard University Press.

Villela, Samuel, and Silvia Gastelum. 1980. *Los "Cholos" de Culiacan*. Culiacan: Universidad Autonoma de Sinaloa.

Waters, T. 1999. *Crime and Immigrant Youth*. Thousand Oaks, Calif.: Sage Publications.

Wolck, W. 1973. "Attitudes toward Spanish and Quechua in Bilingual Peru." In *Language Attitudes,* edited by Roger Shuy and Ralph W. Fosold, 87–101. Washington, D.C.: Georgetown University Press.

Chapter 5

Adler, Patricia Rae. 1977. "Watts: From Suburb to Black Ghetto." Ph.D. diss., University of Southern California.

Albin, Ray R. December 1988. "The Perkins Case: The Ordeal of Three Slaves in Gold Rush California." *California History* 67 (4): 48-71.

Alonso, A. 1999. "Territoriality among African-American Street Gangs in Los Angeles." Master's thesis, Department of Geography, University of Southern California.

Anderson, E. Frederick. 1980. *The Development of Leadership and Organization Building in the Black Community of Los Angeles, from 1900 through World War II*. Saratoga, Calif.: Century Twenty One Publishing.

Anderson, Elijah. 1990. *Streetwise: Race, Class, and Change in an Urban Community*. Chicago: University of Chicago Press.

Asante, Molefi K., and Mark T. Mattson. 1992. *Historical and Cultural Atlas of African Americans*. New York: Macmillan.

Baker, Robert. June 26, 1988. "Homeboys: Cold Killers and Fearful Innocents." *Los Angeles Times*, A29.

Beasley, Delilah L. 1919. *The Negro Trail Blazers of California*. Los Angeles: n.p.

Bond, J. Max. 1936. "The Negro in Los Angeles." Ph.D. diss., University of Southern California.

Brooks, Joyce Marie DeLoach. 1979. "A Case Study: The Role of Black Groups in Achieving Educational Equity for Black Children in the Los Angeles Unified School District." Ph.D. diss., University of California, Los Angeles.

Broome, Homer E. 1977. *LAPS's Black History*. Stockton, Calif.: Stockton Trade Press.

Brown, Claude. 1965. *Manchild in the Promised Land*. New York: Simon and Schuster.

Bullock, Paul, ed. 1969. *Watts: The Aftermath: An Inside View of the Ghetto by the People of Watts*. New York: Grove Press.

Bunch, Lonnie G. 1990. "A Past Not Necessarily Prologue: The Afro-American in Los Angeles Since 1900." In *20th Century Los Angeles: Power, Promotion, and Social Conflict*, edited by Norman M. Klein and Martin J. Schiesl, 22–48. Claremont, Calif.: Regina Books.

Burch, Edward A. 1948. "Attitudes of Employers Engaged in Manufacturing in the Los Angeles Area Relative to the Employment of Negroes." Master's thesis, University of Southern California.

Carr, Harry. 1935. *Los Angeles: City of Dreams*. New York: D. Appleton-Century.

Case, Frederick E. 1972. *Black Capitalism: Problems in Development. A Case Study of Los Angeles*. New York: Praeger Publishers.

Cole, Jr., Olen. Winter 1991. "Black Youth in the National Youth Administration in California, 1935–1943." *Southern California Quarterly* 73 (4): 61–80.

Coleman, James. 1966. *Equality of Educational Opportunity*. Washington, D.C.: U.S. Government Printing Office.

Collins, Keith E. 1980. *Black Los Angeles: The Maturing of the Ghetto, 1940–1950*. Saratoga, Calif.: Century Twenty One Publishing.

Crimi, James E. 1941. "The Social Status of the Negro in Pasadena, California." Master's thesis, University of Southern California.

Daniels, Roger. 1972. *Racism in California*. New York: Macmillan.

Davidson, Devin A. 1992. "Black to Latino Neighborhood Succession and the Quality of Life in Los Angeles County." Master's thesis, University of California, Los Angeles.

Davis, Mike. 1992. *City of Quartz: Excavating the Future in Los Angeles*. London: Verso.

De Graaf, Lawrence Brooks. 1962. "Negro Migration to Los Angeles, 1930 to 1950." Ph.D. diss., University of California, Los Angeles.

———. August 1970. "The City of Black Angels: Emergence of the Los Angeles Ghetto, 1890–1930." *Pacific Historical Review* 39 (3): 320–344.

———. May 1980. "Race, Sex, and Region: Black Women in the American West, 1850–1920." *Pacific Historical Review* 49 (2): 128–157.

Draper, Harold. 1946. *Jim-Crow in Los Angeles*. Los Angeles: Workers Party.

DuBois, W. E. B. August 1913. "Colored California." *Crisis* 6 (4).

Ervin, James M. 1931. "The Participation of the Negro in the Community Life of Los Angeles." Master's thesis, University of Southern California.

Fisher, James A. December 1965. *The California Negro, 1860: An Analysis of State Census Returns*. California History Series. San Francisco: San Francisco Negro Historical and Cultural Society.

———. December 1969. "The Struggle for Negro Testimony in California, 1851–1863." *Southern California Quarterly* 51 (4): 48–72.

———. 1971. "A History of the Political and Social Development of the Black Community in California, 1850–1950." Ph.D. diss., State University of New York at Stony Brook.

———. September 1971. "The Political Development of the Black Community in California, 1850–1950." *California Historical Quarterly* 50 (3).

Forbes, Jack D. [1968?]. *Afro-Americans in the Far West: A Handbook for Educators*. Berkeley, Calif.: Far West Laboratory for Educational Research and Development.

France, Edward Everett. 1962. "Some Aspects of the Migration of the Negro to the San Francisco Bay Area since 1940." Ph.D. diss., University of California. Berkeley.

Frye, Hardy. April 1968. *Negroes in California from 1841 to 1875*. California History Series. San Francisco: San Francisco Negro Historical and Cultural Society.

Gadwa, R. 1999. "The Social History of Leimert Park: The Civil Rights Movement to Little Africa." Senior thesis, under Professor Szelenyi, Sociology Department, University of California, Los Angeles.

Garcia, Mikel. 1985. "Adaptation Strategies of the Los Angeles Black Community, 1883–1919." Ph.D. diss., University of California, Irvine.

Garcia, Mikel, and Jerry Wright. Fall/Spring 1989. *Consciousness in Black Los Angeles, 1886–1915*. CAAS report. Los Angeles: Center for Afro-American Studies, University of California.

Goode, Kenneth G. 1974. *California's Black Pioneers: A Brief Historical Survey*. Santa Barbara, Calif.: McNally and Loftin.

Greer, Scott. 1952. "The Participation of Ethnic Minorities in the Labor Unions of Los Angeles County." Ph.D. diss., University of California, Los Angeles.

Hayden, Dolores. Fall 1989. "Biddy Mason's Los Angeles, 1856–1891." *California History* 68 (3).

Hobbs, Thadeaus. 1960. "The Dynamics of Negroes in Politics in the Los Angeles Metropolitan Area: 1945–1956." Master's thesis, University of Southern California.

Johnson, Milo P. 1945. "The Trade and Industrial Education of Negroes in the Los Angeles Area." Master's thesis, University of California, Los Angeles.

Kaiser, Evelyn. 1939. "The Unattached Negro Woman on Relief: A Study of Fifty Unattached Negro Women on Relief in the Compton District Office of the State Relief Administration of California, in Los Angeles." Master's thesis, University of Southern California.

Katz, William Loren. 1987. *The Black West*. 3d ed. Seattle, Wash.: Open Hand Publishing.

Lapp, Rudolph M. 1987. *Afro-Americans in California*. 2d ed. San Francisco: Boyd and Fraser Publishing.

Los Angeles Times. February 12, 1909. *The Emancipated*. Special issue.

Marmorstein, Gary. Winter 1988. "Central Avenue Jazz: Los Angeles Black Music of the Forties." *Southern California Quarterly* 70 (4).

Maslow-Armand, Laura. July 1987. "Desegregation, Social Mobility and Political Participation: Los Angeles, 1978–1982." *Revue francaise d'etudes americaines* 33.

McWilliams, C. 1968. *North from Mexico: The Spanish-Speaking People of the United States.* New York: Greenwood Press.

Melching, Richard. Summer 1974. *The Activities of the Ku Klux Klan in Anaheim, California, 1923–1925. Southern California Quarterly* 56 (2).

Menchaca, M. 2001. *Recovering History, Constructing Race.* Austin: University of Texas Press.

Moore, J. W., J. D. Vigil, and R. Garcia. 1983. "Residence and Territoriality in Gangs." *Journal of Social Problems* 31 (2): 182–194.

Oliver, M., and T. Shapiro. 1995. *Black Wealth, White Wealth.* New York: Routledge.

Rothstean, Mignon E. 1950. "A Study of the Growth of the Negro Population in Los Angeles and Available Housing Facilities between 1940 and 1946." Master's thesis, University of Southern California.

Salley, Robert Lee. 1963. "Activities of the Knights of the Ku Klux Klan in Southern California, 1921–1925." Master's thesis, University of Southern California.

Sandoval, Sally Jane. 1973. "Ghetto Growing Pains: The Impact of Negro Migration on the City of Los Angeles, 1940–1966." Master's thesis, California State University, Fullerton.

Savage, W. Sherman. 1976. *Blacks in the West.* Westport, Calif.: Greenwood Press.

Shakur, Sanyika. [a.k.a. Monster Kody Scott]. 1993. *Monster: The Autobiography of an L.A. Gang Member.* New York: Atlantic Monthly Press.

Smith, Alonzo Nelson. 1978. "Black Employment in the Los Angeles Area, 1938–1948." Ph.D. diss., University of California, Los Angeles.

Spickard, Paul R. July 1993. "Work and Hope: African American Women in Southern California during World War II." *Journal of the West* 32 (3) 77–93.

Stromquist, Nellie and J. D. Vigil. 1996. "School Violence in the United States." In *Prospects: International Journal of Education,* edited by J.C. Tedesco, 361–383. Paris: UNESCO.

Sweeting, Anthony. 1992. "The Dunbar Hotel and Central Avenue Renaissance, 1781–1950." Ph.D. diss., University of California, Los Angeles.

Texeira, E. May 22, 2000. "Justice Is Not Color-Blind, Studies Find." *Los Angeles Times,* B1, 8.

Thurman, A. Odell. 1973. *The Negro in California before 1890.* San Francisco: R and E Research Associates.

Tolbert, Emory J. 1980. *The UNIA and Black Los Angeles: Ideology and Community in the American Garvey Movement.* Los Angeles: Center for Afro-American Studies, University of California, Los Angeles.

Unrau, Harian D. 1971. "The Double V Movement in Los Angeles during the Second World War: A Study in Negro Protest." Master's thesis, California State University, Fullerton.

Weinstein, H. December 15, 1999. "Rampart Probe May Now Affect over 3,000 Cases." *Los Angeles Times,* A1, 23.

Wheeler, B. Gordon. *Black California: The History of African-Americans in the Golden State.* New York: Hippocrene Books, 1993.

Williams, Dorothy S. 1961. "Ecology of Negro Communities in Los Angeles County: 1940–1959." Ph.D. diss., University of Southern California.

Wilson, W. J. 1987. *The Truly Disadvantaged.* Chicago: University of Chicago Press.

Woolsey, Ronald C. Summer 1983. "A Southern Dilemma: Slavery Expansion and the California Statehood Issue in 1850—A Reconsideration." *Southern California Quarterly* 65 (2)5–32.

Chapter 7

Arax, M. December 15, 1987. "Lost in L.A." *Los Angeles Times Magazine*, 10–18, 42–48.

Bach, R. R., and J. B. Bach. 1980. "Employment patterns of Southeast Asian refugees." *Monthly Labor Review* 103: 31–38.

Berkman, L. September 30, 1984. "Banks Catering to Asians Facing a Culture Gap." *Los Angeles Times*, A1, 24.

Cloward, R. A., and L. E. Ohlin. 1960. *Delinquency and Opportunity: A Theory of Delinquent Gangs*. Glencoe, Ill.: Free Press.

Cooper, J. April 13, 1990. "Refugees Have Made It a Remarkable Fifteen Years." *Los Angeles Times*, A1, 19.

Efron, S. March 21, 1990. Officials Hit Same Sewing Shops Again. *Los Angeles Times*, B1, 4.

Emmons, S., and D. Reyes. February 5, 1989. "Gangs, Crime Top Fear of Vietnamese in Orange County." *Los Angeles Times*, A1, 24.

Evans, M. C. July 28, 1995. "For Many, Hearts Still in Vietnam." *Orange County Register*, 1, 22–23.

Freeman, J. M. 1989. *Hearts of Sorrow: Vietnamese-American Lives*. Stanford: Stanford University Press.

——. 1995. *Changing Identities: Vietnamese Americans, 1975–1995*. Boston: Allyn and Bacon.

Gold, S. J. 1989. "Differential Adjustment among New Immigrant Family Members." *Journal of Contemporary Ethnography* 17 (4): 408–434.

Gold, S. J., and N. Kibria. August 10, 1989. "Vietnamese Refugees and Mobility: Model Minority or New Underclass?" Paper presented at the American Sociological Association annual meeting, San Francisco.

Grant, B. 1979. *The Boat People*. Harmondsworth, England: Penguin Books.

Haines, D. W., ed. 1989. *Refugees as Immigrants: Cambodians, Laotians, and Vietnamese*. Totowa, N.J.: Rowman and Littlefield Publishing.

Hawthorne, L. 1982. *Refugee: The Vietnamese Experience*. Melbourne: Oxford University Press.

Hunt, G., K. Joe, and D. Waldorf. 1997. "Culture and Ethnic Identity among Southeast Asian Gang Members." *Free Inquiry: Gangs, Drugs, and Violence* 25 (1): 9–21.

Kelly, G. 1977. *From Vietnam to America: A Chronicle of the Vietnamese Immigration to the United States*. Boulder, Colo.: Westview Press.

Kibria, N. 1993. *Family Tightrope: The Changing Lives of Vietnamese Americans*. Princeton, N.J.: Princeton University Press.

Larson, D. October 23, 1988. "Honor Thy Parents." *Los Angeles Times Magazine*.

Liu, W. T. 1979. *Transition to Nowhere: Vietnamese Refugees in America*. Nashville, Tenn.: Charter House Publishers.

Long, P. Du Phuoc, and L. Ricard. 1996. *The Dream Shattered: Vietnamese Gangs in America*. Boston: Northeastern University Press.

Marsh, R. E. 1980. "Socioeconomic Status of Indochinese Refugees in the United States: Progress and Problems." *Social Security Bulletin* 43: 11–12.

Merton, R. 1949. *Society Theory and Social Structure*. Glencoe, Ill.: Free Press.

Mishan, A. 1993. "Vietnamese Gangs: Identity and Discourse in 'Little Saigon.'" Master's thesis, University of Southern California.

Nguyen, L. T., and A. B. Henkin. 1982. "Vietnamese Refugees in the United States: Adaptation and Transitional Status." *Journal of Ethnic Studies* 9 (4): 101–116.

ORR (Office of Refugee Resettlement). 1987. *Report to Congress*. Washington, D.C.: U.S. Government Printing Office.

Phan, H. T. August 16, 1998. "Escaping from Welfare: Vietnamese Refugees Face Cultural Obstacles in Search for Work." *Orange County Register*, A1, 12.

Rutledge, P. 1992. *The Vietamese Experience in America*. Bloomington: Indiana University Press.

Sanders, W. B. 1994. *Gangbangs and Drive-Bys*. New York: Aldine de Gruyter.

Smith, M. P., and B. Tarello. 1995. "Who Are the 'Good Guys'? The Social Construction of the Vietnamese 'Other.'" In *The Bubbling Caldron: Race, Ethnicity, and the Urban Crisis*, edited by M. A. Smith and J. R. Feagin. Minneapolis: University of Minnesota Press.

Song, J. L. 1992. "Attitudes of Chinese Immigrants and Vietnamese Refugees toward Law Enforcement in the United States. *Justice Quarterly* 9 (4): 703–719.

Stern, L. M. 1981. "Response to Vietnamese Refugeees: Surveys of Public Opinion." *Social Work* 26: 306–311.

Strand, P. J., and W. Jones. 1985. *Indochinese Refugees in America*. Durham, N.C.: Duke University Press.

Tran, T. August 24, 1998. "Projects to Revitalize Little Saigon Examined." *Los Angeles Times*, B1, 3.

Vigil, J. D., and S. C. Yun. 1990. "Vietnamese Youth Gangs in Southern California." In *Gangs in America*, edited by C. R. Huff, 146–162. Thousand Oaks, Calif.: Sage Publications.

———. 1996. "Southern California Gangs: Comparative Ethnicity and Social Control." In *Gangs in America*, 2d ed., edited by C. R. Huff, 139–156. Thousand Oaks, Calif.: Sage Publications.

Vigil, J. D., S. C. Yun, and J. M. Long. 1993. "Youth Gangs, Crime, and the Vietnamese in Orange County." In *The Ecology of Crimes and Drugs in the Inner City*, edited by Jeff Fagan, 1–56. New York: Social Science Research Council.

Chapter 9

Americas Watch. 1991. *El Salvador's Decade of Terror: Human Rights Since the Assassination of Archbishop Romero*. New Haven, Conn.: Yale University Press.

Amnesty International. March 1990. *Reasonable Fear: Human Rights and U.S. Refugee Policy*. New York: Amnesty International USA.

Applegate, Jane. May 29, 1986. "Salvadorans Ask Strip-Search Ban at U.S. Prison." *Los Angeles Times*.

Becerra, Hector. August 2, 1998. "City Attorney Seeks Injunction against Street Gang Members." *Los Angeles Times*, home ed., B3.

———. August 5, 1998. "Gang Members Barred from Meeting Publicly." *Los Angeles Times*, home ed., B3.

Becklund, Laurie. February 20, 1985. "Salvadoran Men Languish in INS Center in Desert." *Los Angeles Times*, A1, 3.

Bernard, W. S. 1976. "Immigrants and Refugees: Their Similarities, Differences, and Needs." *International Migration Review*, 14 (4): 267–268.

Beyette, Beverly. May 1, 1984. "Refugee Kids Haunted by the Horror of War." *Los Angeles Times*, A1, 11.

Castro, Tony. May 6, 1984. "A Bit of El Salvador and Pico & Union." *Los Angeles Herald Examiner*, A1, 14.

Chinchilla, Norma, and Nora Hamilton. 1996. "Negotiating Urban Space: Latina Workers in Domestic Work and Street Vending in Los Angeles." *Humboldt Journal of Social Relations* 22 (1): 25–35.

_____. 1997. "Ambiguous Identities: Central Americans in Southern California." Working Paper, Chicano/Latino Research Center 14, University of California, Santa Cruz.

Chinchilla, Norma, Nora Hamilton, and James Loucky. 1993. "Central Americans in Los Angeles: An Immigrant Community in Transition." In *In the Barrios: Latinos and the Underclass Debate*, edited by Joan Moore and Raquel Pinderhughes, 51–78. New York: Russell Sage Foundation.

City News Service. April 13, 1998. "Hollywood Gang."

Cohon, J. Donald, Jr. 1981. "Psychological Adaptation and Dysfunction among Refugees." *International Migration Review*, 15 (1/2): 255–275.

Connell, Rich, and Robert J. Lopez. November 17, 1996. "An Inside Look at 18th St.'s Menace." Part 1 of 3-part series. *Los Angeles Times*, Al, 32.

_____. September 19, 1999. "Rampart Probe May Put Gang Injunction at Risk." *Los Angeles Times*, A1, 21–22.

Darling, Juanita. June 27, 1995. "The War on Disposable People." *Los Angeles Times*, H1.

_____. August 9, 1999. "El Salvador's War Legacy: Teen Violence." *Los Angeles Times*, home ed., A1.

_____. November 21, 1999. "Mothers of the Banished." *Los Angeles Times Magazine*, 20.

Davis, Mike. 1992. *City of Quartz: Excavating the Future in Los Angeles*. London: Vintage.

"A Decade of Death." March 2000. Web site: <www.streetgangs.com>. Accessed March 2000.

DeCesare, Donna. July/August 1999. *Deporting America's Gang Culture. Mother Jones*, 44–51.

Ferris, Elizabeth G. 1987. *The Central American Refugees*. New York: Prager Publishers.

Gage, Julienne. March/April 1998. *Sojourners*, pp. 34–37.

Hanson, Captain Robert B. February 3, 2000. "Alex Sanchez." Editorial. *Los Angeles Times*, B8.

Hayden, Tom. January 26, 2000. "We Need Peace Makers Like Alex Sanchez." Commentary *Los Angeles Time*, home ed., B11.

Helford, D., and K. Reich. July 31, 2001. "3,000 Locked in School for 6 Hours after Gunfire." *Los Angeles Times*, A1, 13.

Hernandez, Sandra. February 13, 1998. "Reno Relents on Refugees: Deportation Hiatus to Mark Turning Point?" *L.A. Weekly*, 17.

Homies Unidos. 1998. *Solidaridad y violencia en las pandillas del gran San Salvador.* San Salvador: UCA Editores.

Hong, Peter Y. November 21, 1999. "San Salvador's Mayor Discusses L.A.'s Importance." *Los Angeles Times*, home ed., B1.

Jamail, Milton, and James Loucky. 1987. "Los Angeles: 'Tell Pedro So Juan Understands." *NACLA Report on the Americas* 21 (3): 4–5, 12.

Katz, Susan Roberta. Winter 1977. "Presumed Guilty: How Schools Criminalize Latin Youth." *Social Justice* 77: 66–87.

Krikorian, Michael. March 6, 1998. "City Seeks Injunction against 40 Hollywood Gang Members." *Los Angeles Times*, home ed., B3.

Leiken, Robert S. 1984. "The Salvadoran Left." In *Central America: Anatomy of Conflict*, edited by Robert Leiken, 111–130. New York: Pergamon Press.

LeMoyne, James. February 5, 1989. "The Guns of El Salvador." *New York Times Magazine*, 17.

Lopez, D., E. Popkin, and E. Telles. 1996. "Central Americans: At the Bottom, Struggling to Get Ahead." In *Ethnic Los Angeles*, edited by R. Waldinger and M. Bozorgmehr, 279–304. New York: Russell Sage Foundation.

Lopez, R. J., and R. Connell. June 7, 2000. "The Class of 89." Special report. *Los Angeles Times*, S1.

Los Angeles Times. June 5, 1997. "Welcome Drop in Dropouts." Editorial. B6.

Maldonado, R. 1997. "Giving Los Angeles Youth a Second Chance." Paper submitted to the Honors 7B seminar "Urban Poverty and Public Policy," University of California, Los Angeles.

Marosi, Richard. July 3, 1999. "Gang Membership Up, Crime Down." *Los Angeles Times*, Orange County ed., B1.

McDonald, Patrick. December 3, 1994. "Salvadorians Fear Deportation. *Los Angeles Times*.

Montgomery, Tommie Sue. 1984. "El Salvador: The Roots of Revolution." In *Central America: Crisis and Adaptation*, edited by Steve C. Ropp and James A. Morris, 67–118. Albuquerque: University of New Mexico Press.

Newsweek. October 11, 1999. "L.A.'s Dirty War on Gangs: A Trail of Corruption Leads to Some of the City's Roughest Cops," 72.

Newton, Jim. September 20, 1999. "LAPD Corruption Probe May Be Test for City Leaders." *Los Angeles Times*, A1, 12.

Newton, Jim, and Ann W. O'Neill. September 21, 1999. Captain under Fire as Rampart Probe Expands." *Los Angeles Times*, A1, 24.

O'Connor, Ann-Marie. March 19, 1998. "School is Top Issue for 2 Immigrant Groups." *Los Angeles Times*, metro ed., B1.

Olivo, Antonio. April 11, 1999. Salvadorans Stake Their Claim in Southland Political Game. *Los Angeles Times*, B3.

Ortiz, Al. November 23, 1999. Personal interview.

Oyola, Tamara. 1996. "An Ethnographic Study of Salvadoreños: Socioeconomic Factors That Influence Migrant Youth and Participation in Gangs." Paper submitted to Urban Anthropology course, University of California, Los Angeles.

Rivera, Geraldo. June 2000. Inside the L.A. Police Scandal." *Rivera Live*. TV news. Web site: <www.MSNBC.com>.

Rodriguez, Luis J, and Donna DeCesare. Spring 1995. "The Endless Game of Death: Central American Gang Members in California. *Grand Street*, p. 61.

Rose-Avila, Magdaleno. March 28, 1998. "Sí Se Puede (Yes, It Can Be Done)." *Los Angeles Times*, home ed., B7.

Russell, Philip L. 1984. *El Salvador in Crisis*. Austin, Tex.: Colorado River Press.

SALEF (Salvadoran American Leadership Educational Fund). 1999. Annual awards and scholarship banquet program.

Sanchez, Alex. December 17, 1999. Personal interview.

Sanchez, Gilbert D. November 24, 1999. Personal interview.

Sanchez, Ray. July 4, 1995. "Marked for Death: El Salvador's Tattooed Teens Face the 'Shadow.'" *Newsday*, A11.

Stanley, William Deane. 1987. "Economic Migrants or Refugees from Violence? A Time-Series Analysis of Salvadoran Migration to the United States." *Latin American Research Review* 22 (1): 132–154.

Suarez-Orozco, Marcelo. 1989. *Central American Refugees and U.S. High Schools: A Psychosocial Study of Motivation and Achievement*. Stanford, Calif.: Stanford University Press.

TRPI/NALEO (Tomas Rivera Policy Institute and National Association of Latino Elected and Appointed Officials) Educational Fund. 1997. *Diversifying the Los Angeles Area Latino Mosaic: Salvadoran and Guatemalan Leader's Assessments of Community Public Policy Needs*. Claremont: Tomas Rivera Policy Institute.

Vaquerano, Carlos. November 23, 1999. Personal interview.

Vargas, Zaragosa. 1996. "Historical Perspectives on Latina/o Workers in the U.S." *Humboldt Journal of Social Relations: An Interdisciplinary Approach to the Social Sciences* 22 (1): 11–23.

Ward, Thomas W. 1987. "The Price of Fear: Salvadoran Refugees in the City of the Angels." Ph.D. diss., University of California, Los Angeles.

Westphal, Sylvia P. January 26, 2000. "Hayden Seeking to Block Deportation." *Los Angeles Times*, home ed., B7.

Wilkinson, Tracy. June 16, 1994. "Gangs Find Fresh Turf in Salvador." *Los Angeles Times*, A1, 23.

_____. November 7, 1997. "Distance Puts a Strain on Salvadoran Family Ties." *Los Angeles Times*, A1, 16–17.

_____. September 19, 1999. "Latina Nannies Rear a Generation en Español." *Los Angeles Times*, A3.

Chapter 11

ACLU (American Civil Liberties Union). May 1999. *ACLU Calls Juvenile Crime Bill A Cruel Hoax on America's Children and Families*. Press release. Los Angeles: ACLU.

Anderson, E. 1990. *Streetwise: Race, Class and Change in an Urban Community*. University of Chicago Press.

Austin, J., and M. Willard. 1998. *Generations of Youth: Youth Cultures and History in Twentieth-Century America*. New York: New York University Press.

Berry, M., and J. W. Blassingame. 1982. *Long Memory: The Black Experience in America*. New York: Oxford University Press.

Blanc, C. S., with contributors. 1995. *Urban Children in Distress: Global Predicaments and Innovative Strategies*. Florence, Italy: UNICEF.

Blumstein, A., J. Cohen, and H. Miller. 1980. "Demographically Disaggregated Projections of Prison Populations." *Journal of Criminal Justice* 8: 1–25.

Bursik, R. J., and H. G. Grasmick. 1993. *Neighborhoods and Crime.* New York: Lexington.

California Youth Authority. 1999. *Summary Fact Sheet.* Sacramento, Calif.: California Youth Authority.

Catalano, R. F., R. Loeber, and K. C. McKinney. 1998. *School and Community Interventions to Prevent Serious and Violent Offending.* Washington, D.C.: Office of Juvenile Justice and Delinquency Prevention, U.S. Department of Justice.

Cohen, S. 1980. *Folk Devils and Moral Panics: The Creation of the Mods and Rockers.* New York: St. Martin's.

Coleman, J. 1990. *Equality and Achievement in Education.* Boulder, Colo.: Westview Press.

Come, B. 1995. "Family Literacy in Urban Schools: Meeting the Needs of At-Risk Children." *Reading Teacher* 48 (7): 566.

Coolbaugh, K., and C. J. Hansel. 2000. *The Comprehensive Stategy: Lessons Learned from the Pilot Sites.* Washington, D.C.: Office of Juvenile Justice and Delinquency Prevention, U.S. Department of Justice.

Dadgostar, H. 1999. "Imaginado Mañana: An Evaluation of Pico-Aliso Community Team Outreach." Paper submitted to the Honors 196B seminar "Urban Poverty and Public Policy," University of California, Los Angeles.

Darling, J. August 9, 1999. "El Salvador's War Legacy: Teen Violence." *Los Angeles Times,* A1, 10.

Daunt, T. April 27, 2000. "Council Votes to Fund Anti-Gang Program." *Los Angeles Times,* B3.

Davis, M. 1990. *City of Quartz: Excavating the Future in Los Angeles.* London: Verso.

DeCesare, D. July/August 1999. *Deporting America's Gang Culture. Mother Jones,* 44–51.

Elkannman, P. T. 1996. *The Tough on Crime Myth: Real Solutions to Cut Crime.* New York: Plenum Press.

Fine, G. A., and J. Mechling. 1993. "Child Saving and Children's Culture at Century's End." In *Identity and Inner-City Youth: Beyond Ethnicity and Gender*, edited by S. B. Heath and M. McLaughlin, 120–146. New York: Teachers College Press.

Frammolino, R. January 17, 1999. "Title 1's $18 Billion Fails to Close Gap." *Los Angeles Times,* A1, 22.

Friedman, T. L. 1999. *The Lexus and the Olive Tree.* New York: Farrar, Straus and Giroux.

Goldstein, A. P., and C. R. Huff, eds. 1993. *The Gang Intervention Handbook.* Champaign, Ill.: Research Press.

Goldstein, A. P., and D. W. Kodluboy. 1998. *Gangs in Schools: Signs, Symbols, and Solutions.* Champaign, Ill.: Research Press.

Greenwood, P. W. 1992. "Reforming California's Approach to Delinquent and High Risk Youth." In *Urban America: Policy Choices for Los Angeles and the Nation*, edited by J. B. Steinberg, D. W. Lyon, and M. E. Vaiana, 111–138. Santa Monica, Calif.: Rand.

———. 1996. *Diverting Children from a Life of Crime: Measuring Costs and Benefits.* Santa Monica, Calif: Rand.

Heath, S. B., and M. W. McLaughlin, eds. 1993. *Identity and Inner-City Youth: Beyond Ethnicity and Gender.* New York: Teachers College Press.

Hernandez, A. 1998. *Peace in the Streets: Breaking the Cycle of Gang Violence.* Washington, D.C: Child Welfare League of America.

Hobfoll, S. E. 1998. *Stress, Culture, and Community: The Psychology and Philosophy of Stress.* New York: Plenum Press.

Hubler, S. March 30, 2000. "Turning Troubled Children into Public Enemies No. 1." *Los Angeles Times*, B1.

Huffington, A. July 29, 2001. "Activists Turn the Tide Against More Jail for Juveniles." *Los Angeles Times*, M5.

Hutson, H. R., D. Anglin, and M. J. Pratts. 1994. "Adolescents and Children Injured or Killed in Drive-by Shootings in Los Angeles." *The New England Journal of Medicine* 330(5): 324–327.

Hutson, H. R., D. Anglin, D. N. Kyriacou, J. Hart, and K. Spears. 1995. "The Epidemic of Gang-Related Homicide in Los Angeles County from 1979 through 1994." *The Journal of the American Medical Association* 274(13): 1031–1036.

Jackson, P., and C. Rudman. 1993. "Moral Panics and the Response to Gangs in California." In *Gangs: The Origins and Impact of Contemporary Youth Gangs in the United States*, edited by S. Cummings and D. J. Monti, 257–276. Albany: State University of New York Press.

Jackson, R. K., and W. McBride. 1985. *Understanding Street Gangs.* Costa Mesa, Calif.: Custom Publishing.

Jessor, R., ed. 1998. *New Perspectives on Adolescent Risk Behavior.* New York: Cambridge University Press.

Johnson, J. April 21–27, 2000. "Bridges Backers Concerned about Cuts." *Los Angeles Times*, Our Times supplement.

Katz, M. B. 1995. "Urban Schools." In *Improving Poor People: The Welfare State, The "Underclass," and Urban Schools as History.* Princeton: Princeton University Press.

Klein, M. W. 1971. *Street Gangs and Street Workers.* Englewood Cliffs, N. J.: Prentice Hall.

———. 1995. *The American Street Gang.* New York: Oxford University Press.

Krikorian, G. February 13, 1996. "Study Questions Justice System's Racial Fairness." *Los Angeles Times*, A1, 17–18.

Lamb, D. April 8, 1997. "New Approach Cripples Boston's Gang Network." *Los Angeles Times*, A1, 16.

Loeber, R., and M. Stouthamer-Loeber. 1986. "Family Factors as Correlates and Predictors of Juvenile Conduct Problems and Delinquency." In *Crime and Justice*, vol. 7, edited by M. Tonry and N. Morris, 29–150. Chicago: University of Chicago Press.

Los Angeles Times. May 12, 1992. *Understanding the Riots: Los Angeles Before and After the Rodney King Case.* Insert, Sunday edition.

MacTalk [newsletter]. September 1999. "Prison Guards—A Major Force in California." *MacTalk* 8 (9): 3.

Mauer, M. 1992. "Americans behind Bars." *Criminal Justice* 6: 12–18, 38–39.

McClanahan, S., and G. Sandefur. 1994. *Growing Up with a Single Parent: What Hurts, What Helps.* Cambridge: Harvard University Press.

Meddis, S. V., and P. Edmonds. September 29, 1994. "Rehabilitation on a Small Scale." *USA Today*, A10–14.

Merl, J. June 15, 1992. "Troubled Schools Able to Help Pupils Realize Dreams." *Los Angeles Times*, B1, 3.

Mitchell, J. L. November 13, 1992. "Gangs in Affluent Black Turf." *Los Angeles Times*, A1, 26–27.

Monmaney, T. October 5, 1995. "Medical Researchers Call Gang Killings 'Epidemic' in County." *Los Angeles Times*, B1.

Moore, J. W., and R. Pinderhughes-Rivera, eds. 1993. *In the Barrios: Latinos and the Underclass Debate*. New York: Russell Sage Foundation.

Moore, J. W., and J. D. Vigil. 1987. "Chicano Gangs: Group Norms and Individual Factors Related to Adult Criminality." *Aztlan* 18 (2): 27–44.

Morales, A. 1982. "The Mexican American Gang Member: Evaluation and Treatment." In *Mental Health and Hispanic Americans*, edited by R. Becerra, M. Karno, and J. I. Escobar, 133–152. New York: Grune and Stratton.

Moreno, J. F., ed. 1999. *The Elusive Quest for Equality*. Cambridge: Harvard Educational Review, Harvard University Press.

NCES (National Center for Educational Statistics). 1998. *The Condition of Education: 1998 Educational Climate and Diversity of Educational Institutions*. Washington, D.C.: National Center for Educational Statistics. Web site: <www.nces.ed.gov/uces/pubs98/c98sece.html>. Accessed April 2000.

Nazario, S. December 11, 1993. "Grim Picture Painted for State's Black Men." *Los Angeles Times*, A1, 25.

OJJDP (Office of Juvenile Justice and Delinquency Prevention). September 1993. *Strengthening America's Families: Promising Parenting Strategies for Delinquency Prevention*. Booklet. Washington, D.C.: U.S. Department of Justice.

Oliver, M. L., J. H. Johnson, and W. C. Farrell. 1993. "Anatomy of a Rebellion: A Political-Economic Analysis." In *Reading Rodney King/Reading Urban Uprising*, edited by R. G. Gooding-Williams, 117–141. New York: Routledge.

Orfield, G., and A. Kaufman. October 1, 1992. "Follow-through to Avert Failure after Kindergarten." *Los Angeles Times*, B5.

Pertersilia, J. 1992. "Crime and Punishment in California: Full Cells, Empty Pockets, and Questionable Benefits." In *Urban America: Policy Choices for Los Angeles and the Nation*, edited by J. B. Steiner, D. W. Lyon, and M. E. Vaiana, 175–206. Santa Monica, Calif.: Rand.

Phillips, Susan A. 1999. *Wallbangin': Graffiti and Gangs in L.A.* Chicago: University of Chicago Press.

Ritsch, M. April 27, 2001. "$5.2 Billion School Budget Plan Detailed." *Los Angeles Times*, B2.

Rodriguez, L. 1993. *Always Running: La Vida Loca, Gang Days in L.A.* Willimantic, Conn.: Curbstone Press.

Romo, H., and T. Falbo. 1996. *Keeping Latino Youth in School*. Austin, Tex.: Hogg Foundation for Mental Health.

Rubin, E. L., ed. 1999. *Minimizing Harm: A New Crime Policy for America*. Boulder, Colo.: Westview Press.

Sahagun, L. January 24, 1999. "Unraveling a Riddle." *Los Angeles Times*, B2.

Saluter, A., and T. Lugaila. 1996. *Marital Status and Living Arrangements*. Washington, D.C.: U.S. Census Bureau.

Sampson, R. J., and J. H. Laub. 1994. "Urban Poverty and the Family Context of Delinquency: A New Look at Structure and Process in a Classic Study." *Child Development* 65: 523–540.

Schroeder, K. 1998. "Minorities in Public Schools: Social Context of Education." *Education Digest* 62 (6): 4.

Spergel, I. A., and G. D. Curry. 1998. "The National Youth Gang Survey: A Research and Development Process." In *The Modern Gang Reader*, edited by M. W. Klein, C. L. Maxson, and J. Miller, 254–265. Los Angeles: Roxbury Publishing.

Stack, C. 1974. All Our Kin: Strategies for Survival in a Black Community. New York: Harper Torchbooks.

Stokke, D. October 12, 1999. "Physicians Should Be Part of Solution to Gang Violence." University of Southern California. Photocopy.

Texeira, E. May 22, 2000. "Justice Is Not Color-Blind, Studies Find." *Los Angeles Times*, B1, 8.

Thornberry, T. P. 1994. *Violent Families and Youth Violence*. Washington, D.C.: National Criminal Justice Reference Service. Web site: <www.ncjrs.org/txtfiles/fs-9421.txt>. Accessed April 2000.

Thornberry, T. P., C. A. Smith, C. Rivera, D. Huizinga, and M. Sthouhamer-Loeber. 1999. *Family Disruption and Delinquency*. Washington, D.C.: Office of Juvenile Justice and Delinquency Prevention, U.S. Department of Justice.

Velez-Ibañez., C. 1993. U.S. "Mexicans in the Borderlands: Being Poor without the Underclass." In *In the Barrios: Latinos and the Underclass Debate*, edited by J. W. Moore and R. Pinderhughes-Rivera, 195–220. New York: Russell Sage Foundation.

Vigil, J. D. 1988a. *Barrio Gangs: Street Life and Identity in Southern California*. Austin: University of Texas Press.

———. 1988b. "Group Processes and Street Identity: Adolescent Chicano Gang Members." *Ethnos* 16 (4): 421–445.

———. 1993. "Gangs, Social Control, and Ethnicity: Ways to Redirect Street Youth." In *Identity and Inner-City Youth: Beyond Ethnicity and Gender*, edited by S. B. Heath and M. W. McLaughlin, 94–119. New York: Teachers College.

———. 1995. "Understanding Life in an East Los Angeles Public Housing Project: A Focus on Gang and Non-Gang Families." Working paper, Center for the Study of Urban Poverty, University of California, Los Angeles.

———. 1997. *Personas Mexicanas*. Fort Worth, Tex.: Harcourt-Brace.

———. 1999. "Streets and Schools: How Educators Can Help Chicano Marginalized Gang Youth." *Harvard Educational Review* 69 (3): 270–288.

Waters, T. 1999. *Crime and Immigrant Youth*. Thousand Oaks, Calif.: Sage Publications.

Weinstein, H. December 15, 1999. "Rampart Probe May Now Affect over 3,000 Cases." *Los Angeles Times*, A1, 23.

Williams, N. 1990. *The Mexican American Family*. New York: General Hall.

Wilson, J. J. May 2000. *Children as Victims*. Juvenile Justice Bulletin. Washington, D.C.: Office of Juvenile Justice and Delinquency Prevention, Office of Justice Programs, U.S. Department of Justice.

Woo, E. October 23, 1996. "Prison Spending Hurts Schools and Black Students, Report Says." *Los Angeles Times*, A1, 26.

Index

unemployment, 68, 73, 82
urbanization process, 32, 100, 103

Vietnamese gangs. *See* gangs: Viet-
namese
Vietnam War, 99, 106
Vital Intervention through Directional
Alternatives (VIDA), 171

War on Poverty, 74, 75, 82
Watts, 69, 70, 71, 73, 75, 76, 78
White Fence, 33, 45

white flight, 4, 70
Whyte, William F., x
Wilkins, Ron. *See* Sons of Watts
Willis, Paul, xi
Wilson, W. J., 4, 77
World War I and II, 161

YMCA, 70
Yun, Steve C., 7

Zoot Suit Riots, 42, 68, 78. *See also*
racial violence